The Roman Auxiliary Fort at Buciumi (Roman Dacia, Romania)

Coins in archaeological context

Cristian Găzdac
Emanoil Pripon

BAR International Series 2381
2012

Published in 2016 by
BAR Publishing, Oxford

BAR International Series 2381

The Roman Auxiliary Fort at Buciumi (Roman Dacia, Romania)

ISBN 978 1 4073 0971 2

© The authors individually and the Publisher 2012

The authors' moral rights under the 1988 UK Copyright,
Designs and Patents Act are hereby expressly asserted.

All rights reserved. No part of this work may be copied, reproduced, stored,
sold, distributed, scanned, saved in any form of digital format or transmitted
in any form digitally, without the written permission of the Publisher.

BAR Publishing is the trading name of British Archaeological Reports (Oxford) Ltd.
British Archaeological Reports was first incorporated in 1974 to publish the BAR
Series, International and British. In 1992 Hadrian Books Ltd became part of the BAR
group. This volume was originally published by Archaeopress in conjunction with
British Archaeological Reports (Oxford) Ltd / Hadrian Books Ltd, the Series principal
publisher, in 2012. This present volume is published by BAR Publishing, 2016.

Printed in England

PUBLISHING

BAR titles are available from:

	BAR Publishing
	122 Banbury Rd, Oxford, OX2 7BP, UK
EMAIL	info@barpublishing.com
PHONE	+44 (0)1865 310431
FAX	+44 (0)1865 316916
	www.barpublishing.com

Contents

Foreword (Professor Nicolae Gudea) iii

Acknowledgments v

BUCIUMI – the site and its history 1

Comments on numismatics 14

Catalogues

    Coin finds from archaeological excavations 30

    The Silviu Papiriu-Pop collection 86

Plates 88

Abbreviations and bibliography 94

List of Maps

Map 1. The Roman Empire pointing out the location of the province of Dacia and the fort of Buciumi
Map 2. Map of Roman Dacia pointing out the location of Buciumi
Map 3. The strategic keystone location of the auxiliary fort from Buciumi on the NW limes of Roman Dacia
Map 4. The location of the auxiliary fort on the topographic map of Buciumi locality
Map 5. BUCIUMI, the virtual location of the auxiliary fort on nowadays landscape

List of Figures

Fig. I. The auxiliary fort from Buciumi - the archaeological researched areas
Fig. II. The 1st phase (earthen) of the auxiliary fort from Buciumi, AD 106 - beginning of Hadrian's reign
Fig. III. The auxiliary fort from Buciumi by the 1st quarter of the 3rd century AD
Fig. IV. The auxiliary fort from Buciumi, 1st quarter of the 3rd century AD - AD 260/270
Fig. V. The *principia* of the auxiliary fort from Buciumi up to the 3rd century AD

List of Tables

Tab. 1. The coin finds from the auxiliary fort from Buciumi
Tab. 2-6. The coin finds by edifices

List of Graphs

Fig. 1. The auxiliary fort of Buciumi: no. of coins
Fig. 2. The auxiliary fort of Buciumi: finds/years of reign
Fig. 3. The auxiliary fort of Buciumi: finds/period
Fig. 4a. Barrack 1 - % no. of coins
Fig. 4b. Barrack 1 - % finds/period
Fig. 5a. Barrack 2 - % no. of coins
Fig. 5b. Barrack 2 - % finds/period
Fig. 6a. Barrack 3 - % no. of coins
Fig. 6b. Barrack 3 - % finds/period
Fig. 7a. Barrack 5 - % no. of coins
Fig. 7b. Barrack 5 - % finds/period
Fig. 8a. *Praetorium* - % no. of coins
Fig. 8b. *Praetorium* - % finds/period
Fig. 9. Graph of the coin finds by phases for the auxiliary fort of Buciumi
Fig. 10. Graph of the single coin finds by phases and periods for the auxiliary fort from Buciumi
Fig. 11. Graph of the percentage of the coefficient/period by phases for the auxiliary fort from Buciumi

Foreword

The research into the Roman provinces has moved from pure archaeological excavations within towns, forts, villages, farms, etc. – followed, in most of the cases, by excavation reports, more or less preliminary ones, and more seldom by monographs – to the investigaiton of the daily life of Roman civilians and soldiers and to economic aspects of life, that actually have influenced the entire Roman society. This type of research is the only way to help us deduce the level of romanization of a Roman province outside Italy.

The present book is focused on the coin finds from a Roman auxiliary fort situated in the province of Dacia (AD 106-108), more precisely, of Dacia Porolissensis (AD 119-275) which was located on the border of the village of Buciumi (Sălaj County). Located on the western border of Dacia Porolissensis, the fort was systematically researched between 1963 and 1976 and, owing to the published monograph, it is one of the best-known of its kind from Romania. The archaeological research was followed by reports and later by a monograph on a Roman site from Romania – the first archaeological monograph from Romania published in a western manner. Furthermore, extensive studies focused on reconstructions of parts (the gateways, corner towers, the headquarters, etc.) or the whole fort that followed the book.

Out of 477 coins, 462 derive from the excavations of this auxiliary fort. The remainder of fifteen coins come from a local collection. They were found on the territory of the fort as well. This study is of high importance because the coins allow, when well-studied, the dating of the archaeological contexts within the fort starting from the 1st phase of construction (the precinct with earthen *vallum*), up to the last phase of existence, and, especially, the various stages of use of various features within the fort: the precinct (gateways, corner and intermediary towers), the headquarters (*principia*), the commander's house (*praetorium*), the inner baths and other buildings.

The recent catalogues of coins were compared with the ones compiled at the time of initial analysis of the numismatic material (1972). This allowed the authors of this book a more accurate identification of coins, while their skills and knowledge helped in identifying the specific characteristics that were unknown before: countermarks and counterfeits. All these aspects led to a more accurate dating of construction phases or repairing works within the fort.

I am one of the last survivors of the team of archaeologists (M. Macrea, E. Chirilă, V. Lucăcel, C. Pop, N. Gudea, N. Branga) who excavated the fort of Buciumi, which at that time (1963-1976) became the best-known fort from Romania. At the same time, as one of the authors of the fort monograph published in1972 and as the author of the micro-monograph from 1997, I can affirm that the present book is very important for gathering all the coins found at the fort; for the manner and style of publication; for using the most recent instruments to identify the coins; for the complex analysis and re-interpretation of the numismatic spectrum of this fort.

The importance of this achievement will require a re-analysis of the old dating of various elements of the fort (fortification, *principia*, *praetorium*, barracks etc.) as well as other categories of artefacts.

The path followed by Cristian Găzdac, the founder of the series of Roman numismatic monographs from Romania, and the main author of the volumes published so far, contributes to the establishment of a solid basis for an economic history of Dacia, and, implicitly, to better understanding of this province. The foundation of this series is a great success of numismatics at Cluj-Napoca and Romania and it reprensents opening towards Europe through the most advanced level of research in the field of numismatics.

Professor Nicolae Gudea

Acknowledgments

We would like to thank Professor Christopher Howgego (Oxford – United Kingdom), Drs. Andrew Burnett, Richard Abdy (London - United Kingdom) for their useful advices.

We are grateful to our colleague and friend Dr. Felix Marcu (Cluj-Napoca – Romania) for his help in providing us with topographic photo.

We would like to thank Professor Nicolae Gudea (Cluj-Napoca – Romania) for his useful information on various aspects regarding the excavations at the auxiliary fort of Buciumi as well as for his valuable comments on the earlier version of this book.

We are indebted to the GERDA HENKEL FOUNDATION for its generous support to achieve the technical support of this volume.

The auxiliary fort and its history

Like in the case of the numismatic monograph of *Arcobadara* (Ilişua)[1] the approach in familiarizing the reader with the history and architecture of the auxiliary fort will massively use the information provided by N. Gudea and F. Marcu in their works on the auxiliary fort from Buciumi[2].

The auxiliary fort from Buciumi was part of the NW sector of the Roman frontier in the province of Dacia (maps 1, 2, 3). It was located on a terrace placed at the junction point between Lupului and Mihăiesei creeks. The fort controlled two main passes: those on Rag and Poicu creeks. The second one connected the fort with the one from Bologa. Placed between the fort of Bologa (in the south) and those from Romita and Porolissum (in the north) the fort from Buciumi has access ways also to the forts on the Agrij Creek, Românași, Romita, Porolissum and Tihău (map 3).

The location of this auxiliary fort has been mainly chosen based on three important elements (map 3): a) the excellent possibility to control a large sector of the forwarded lines of watchtowers on the Meseș Mountains; b) the possibility to simultaneously control two passes – the one on the Ragu Valley and the one on the Poicului Valley, the last one led to the fort from Bologa; c) the good connection with the forts on the Agrij Valley: Românași – Romita – Porolissum – Tihău.[3]

The fort has been already mentioned in the 16th century by the Transylvanian historian Stephanus Zamosius (István Szamosközi).[4]

Building phases

Following the systematic archaeological research the fort present two main phases of construction: the earthen phase, 125 x 160 m, 2 hectares, and the stone one, 134 x 167 m, 2.237 hectares. Therefore, the sizes of the fort were similar throughout its entire period of use. The fort is orientated NW-SE (maps 4, 5) and could, at least theoretically, garrison 1,000 soldiers.[5]

According to N. Gudea the earthen phase has two sub-phases: 1a and 1b.

In phase 1a there were two defensive ditches of the type *fossa punica* with palisade. The troop garrisoned here was *cohors I Augusta Ituraeorum*. At some point, either the entire unit or detachments of *cohors I Brittonum* could have been also garrisoned here in this phase as it has been suggested by some archaeological material.

The phase is re-dated between AD 106 and the beginning of Hadrian's reign.[6]

Phase 1b indicates that the fort had the same sizes. This phase consists in the change of barracks positions. The display of them was following the scheme: simple barrack – double barrack – simple barrack.

The troop garrisoned in this phase at Buciumi was *cohors II Augusta Nervia Brittonum Pacensis*. Other units or detachments that may have accompanied this troop were *cohors I Flavia Ulpia Hispanorrum milliaria* (in circa AD 115) and *cohors I Hispanorum*.

On the basis of archaeological material the dating of phase 1b was established as the period of AD 114/115 – beginning of the 3rd century AD[7] but the numismatic evidence correlated with archaeological context suggests a chronological sequence between the beginning of Hadrian's reign and the 1st quarter of the 3rd century AD.[8]

In phase 2 – the stone phase – the fort have the same orientation like in phase 1b. The peripheral wall replaced the wooden palisade. The defensive ditch was placed 5 m from the wall. It has a 13 m maximal width, and 3 m depth. The peripheral wall was made of lime blocks and it has a thickness of 1.30 m with a 1.50 m wide foundation and 0.70-0.80 m depth. Also in this phase were identified the berm and the *via sagularis*.

The troop garrisoned in this phase in the auxiliary fort from Buciumi was *cohors II Nervia Brittonum Pacensis pia fidelis milliaria Antoniniana*.

Regarding the dating of this phase the scholars agreed that it is a difficult task. While the construction date for the commander's house in stone was established to be the mid-2nd century AD, no reliable data came out for the peripheral wall. The beginning of the 3rd century AD was forwarded as a hypothetic data[9] while the numismatic spectrum within the historical background of Roman Dacia suggests 1st quarter of the 3rd century AD – AD 260/270.[10]

---

[1] GĂZDAC/GAIU 2011, 1-4.
[2] GUDEA 1997; MARCU 2009 36-53.
[3] GUDEA 1997, 8.
[4] GUDEA 1997, 12.
[5] MARCU 2009, 36.
[6] See chapter 'Comments on Numismatics'.
[7] GUDEA 1997, 28-40.
[8] See chapter 'Comments on Numismatics'.
[9] GUDEA 1997, 40-55.
[10] See chapter 'Comments on Numismatics'.

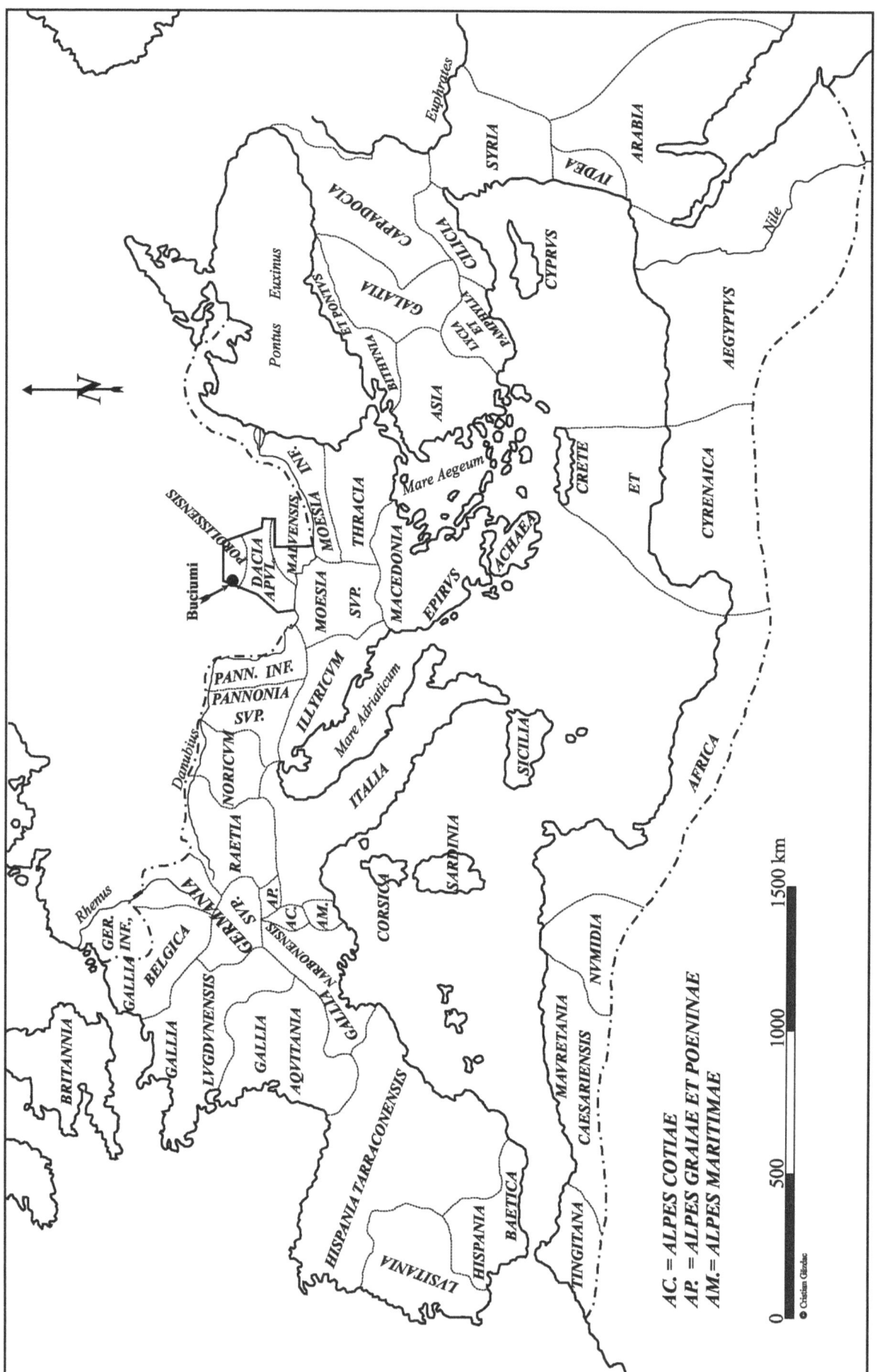

Map 1. The Roman Empire pointing out the location of the province of Dacia and the fort of Buciumi (based on Găzdac/Gudea 2006)

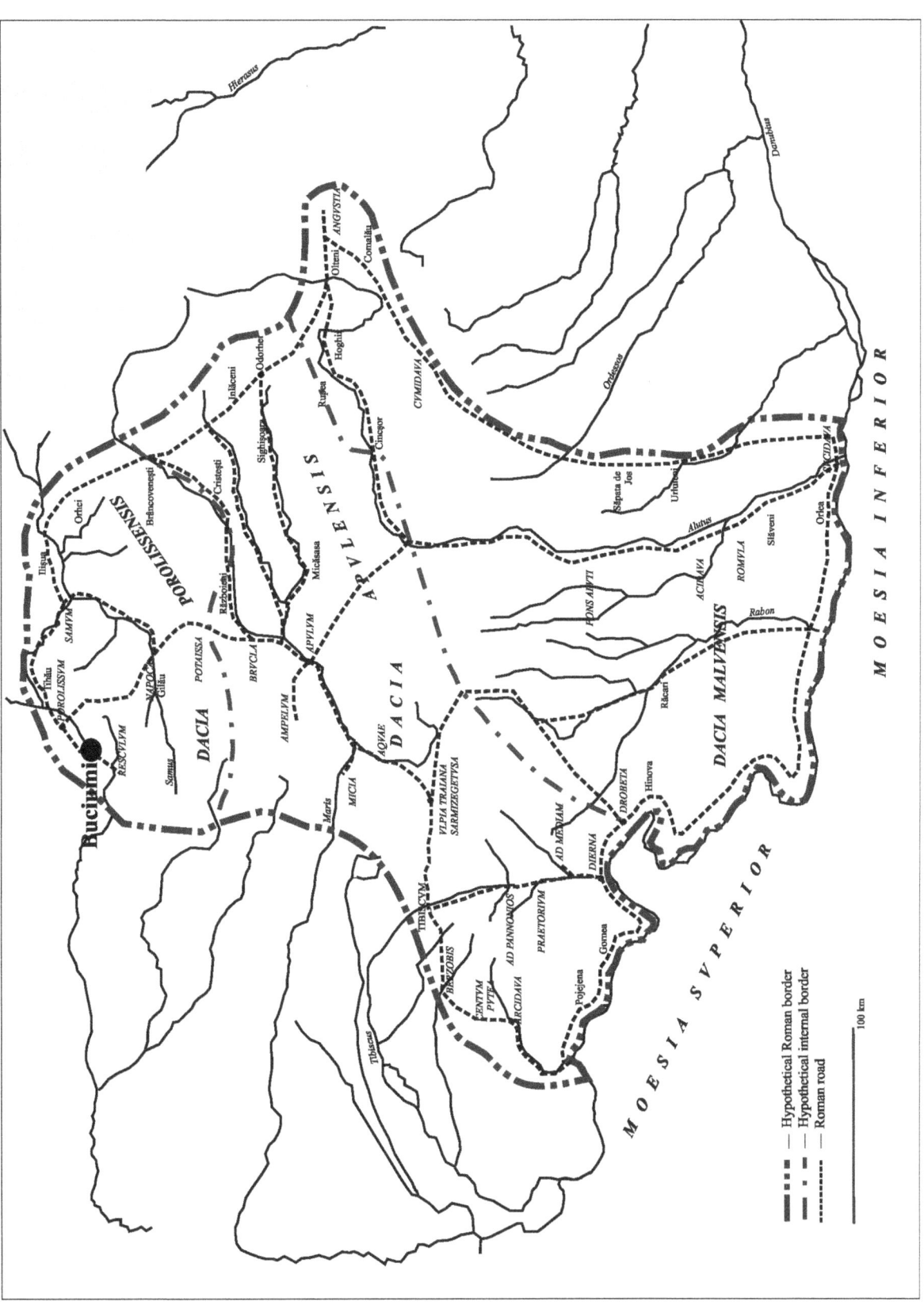

Map 2. Map of Roman Dacia pointing out the location of Buciumi

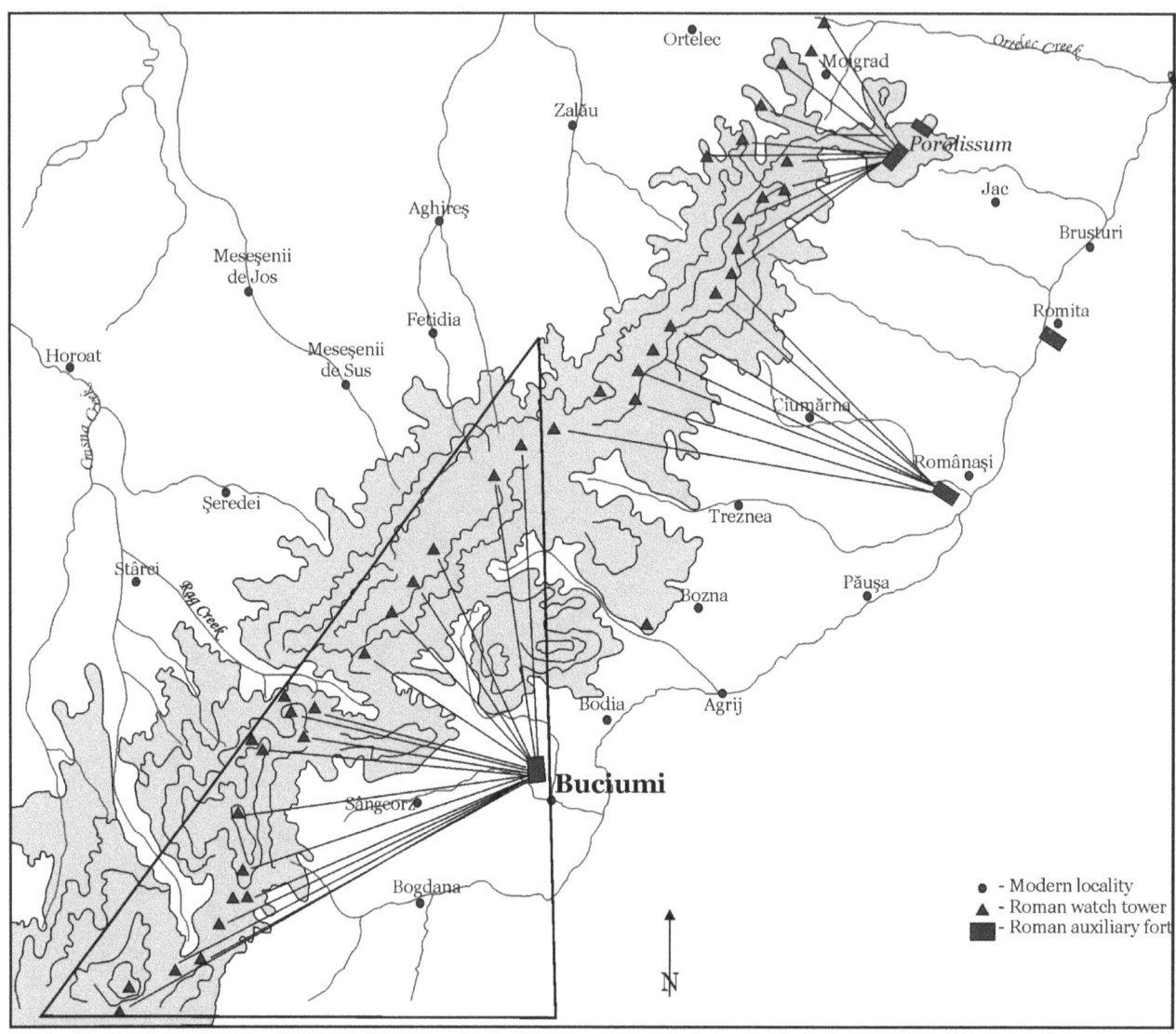

MAP 3. THE STRATEGIC KEYSTONE LOCATION OF THE AUXILIARY FORT FROM BUCIUMI ON THE NW LIMES OF ROMAN DACIA
(AFTER GUDEA 1997, 89, FIG. 6)

Following systematic excavations within the fort new buildings and repairing works were noticed for the period after AD 220 (!) (see below).[11]

The fort from Buciumi was amongst the most researched discovered and excavated forts from Romania. The systematic excavations began in 1963 under the supervision of Eugen Chirilă. The central buildings, those conventionally named 1, 2, 4, 5 from *praetentura* and the building C1 were entirely unveiled. Two others buildings from *praetentura* underwent testing excavations (fig. I).

The towers (figs. I, III-IV)[12]

Except for the towers from *porta praetoria*, those from the other gates show a semi-circular projection. The gateways for each gate are double, circa 8 m, only at *porta decumana* is a simple one.

The roads (figs. I-IV)[13]

The roads *via principalis* and *via praetoria* are 7.20 m and 6.30 m wide. The *via principalis* split the fort in two parts: *praetentura* – 1/3 of total area of the fort, and *latus* and *praetentura* – 2/3. The paths between buildings within the *praetentura* are 1.50-2 m wide while the one running around the *principia* is 6 m wide.

Within the *raetentura* the only path that could have been identified was running alongside between two buildings and was 4 m wide. The *via quintana* was not identified in the two main sections from *raetentura*.

---

[11] GUDEA 1997, 61.
[12] MARCU 2009, 36.
[13] MARCU 2009, 37.

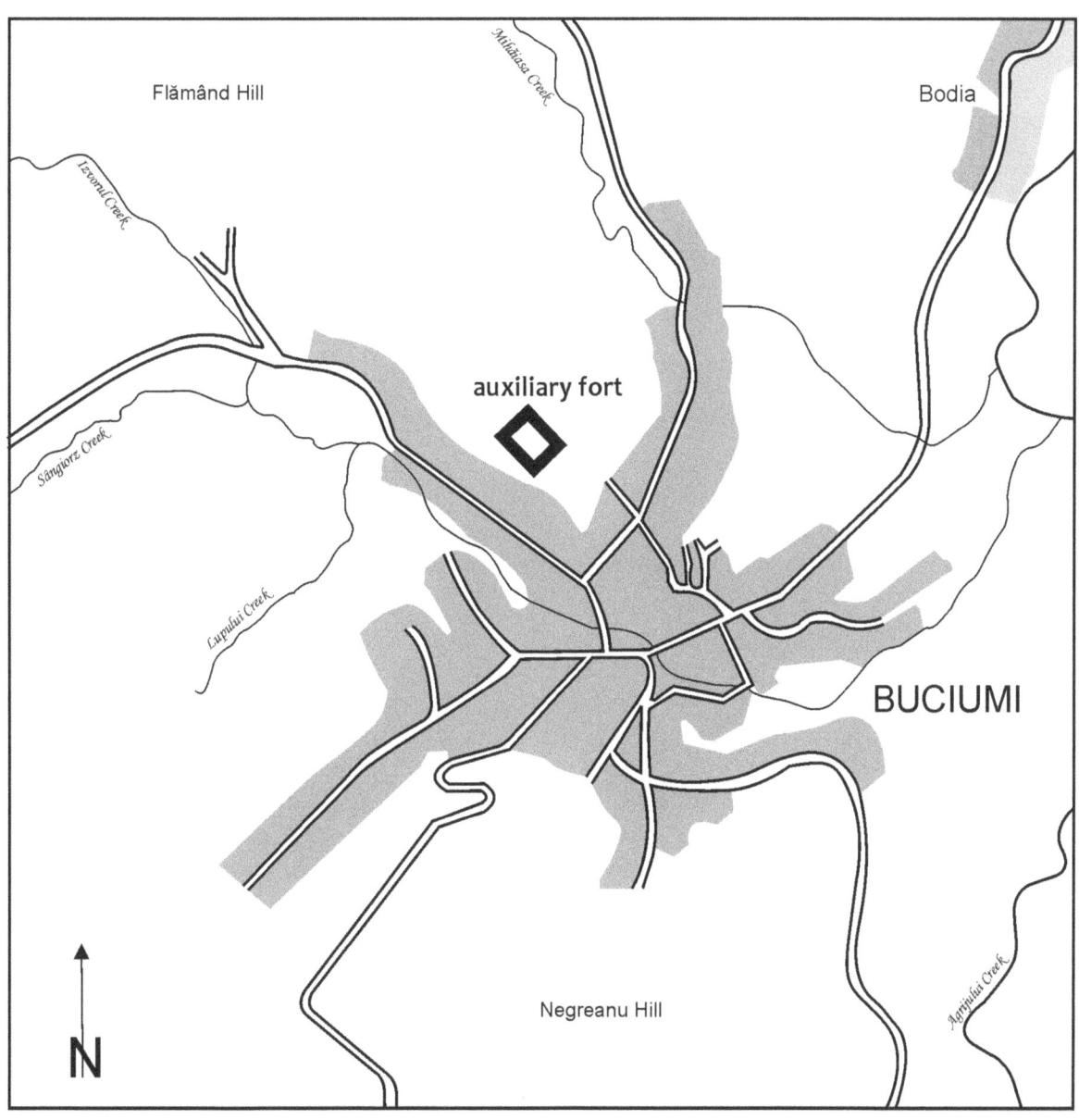

MAP 4. THE LOCATION OF THE AUXILIARY FORT ON THE TOPOGRAPHIC MAP OF BUCIUMI LOCALITY
(BASED ON GUDEA 1997, 90, FIG. 7)

At the junction point of *via principalis* and *via praetoria* towards *porta praetoria* two grit stone pedestals were noticed. One was located on the corner of barrack 1 (1 x 1 x 0.25) and the corner of barrack 4 (1.3 x 1.3 x 0.25). Their functionality is still uncertain.

The *principia* (figs. I-V)[14]

The first phase of this building is unknown as only few pillars' pits were identified. It has been considered to be built sometime in the mid-2nd century.

It measures 26 x 32 m and an area of 832 m². The building represents 3.7% of the overall area of the fort which is a normal value for the forts of auxiliary infantry units.

The building it is located on the longitudinal axis and symmetrical to the sides of fort. The construction material consists of stones mixed with bricks and walls of 0.80 m thickness.

The inner courtyard measures 251.10 m² (15.50 x 16.20 m), meaning 30% of the total area occupied by the *principia*. The pavement was made of large slabs but they do not run until the rooms' walls, which suggests the presence of a portico of 2-3 m long. This portico surrounded the courtyard on three sides, entrance included. In the SW corner of the courtyard a well was found – a normal feature for most of the headquarters buildings. On the wing sides the courtyard is flanked, on each side by two rooms (3.60 x 7 m and 3.60 x 8 m –the ones the west side; .3.3 x 7.6 m and 3.3 x 8 m – the ones on the east side). Although it was

[14] MARCU 2009, 38-40.

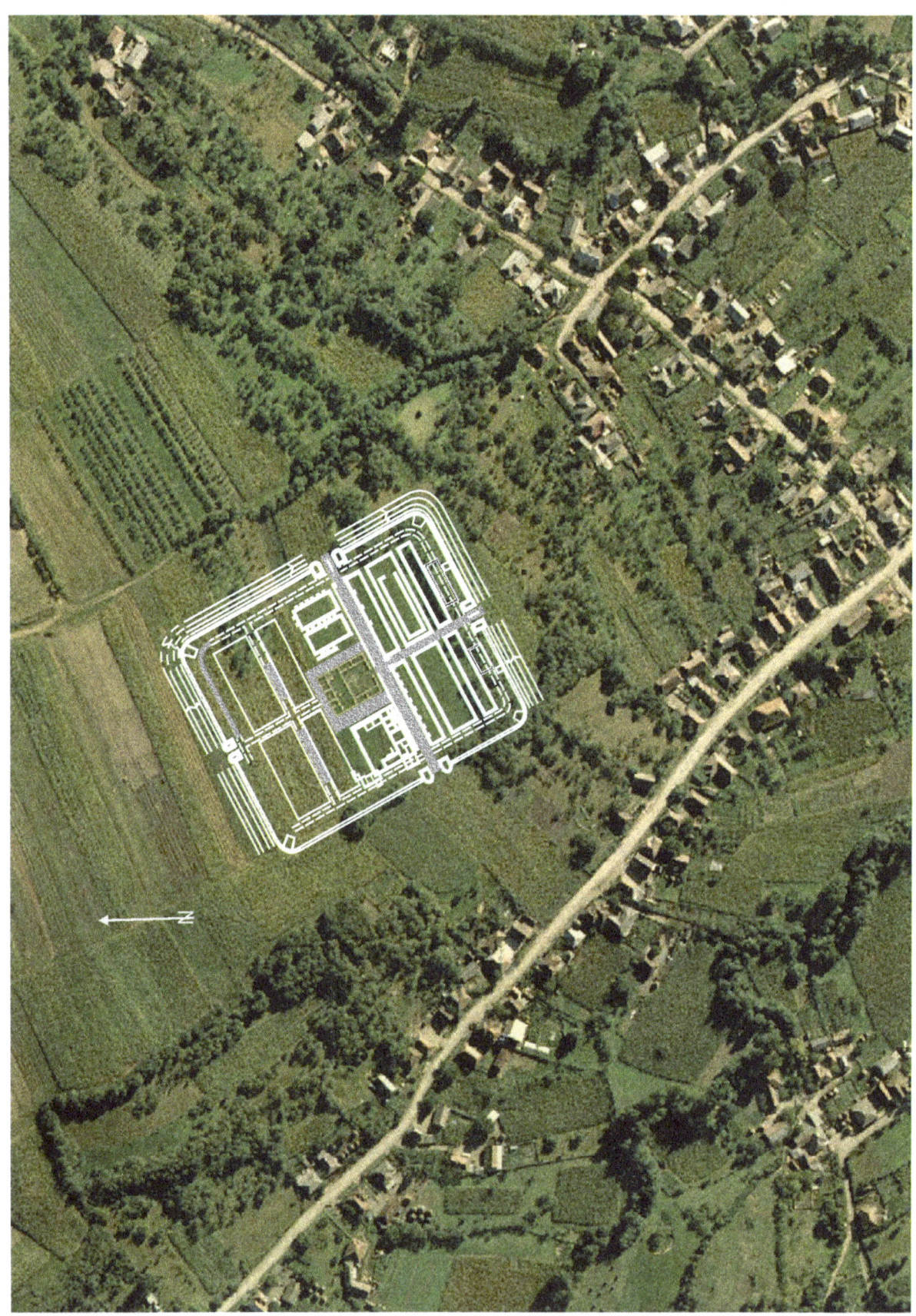

Map 5. BUCIUMI, the virtual location of the auxiliary fort on nowadays landscape.

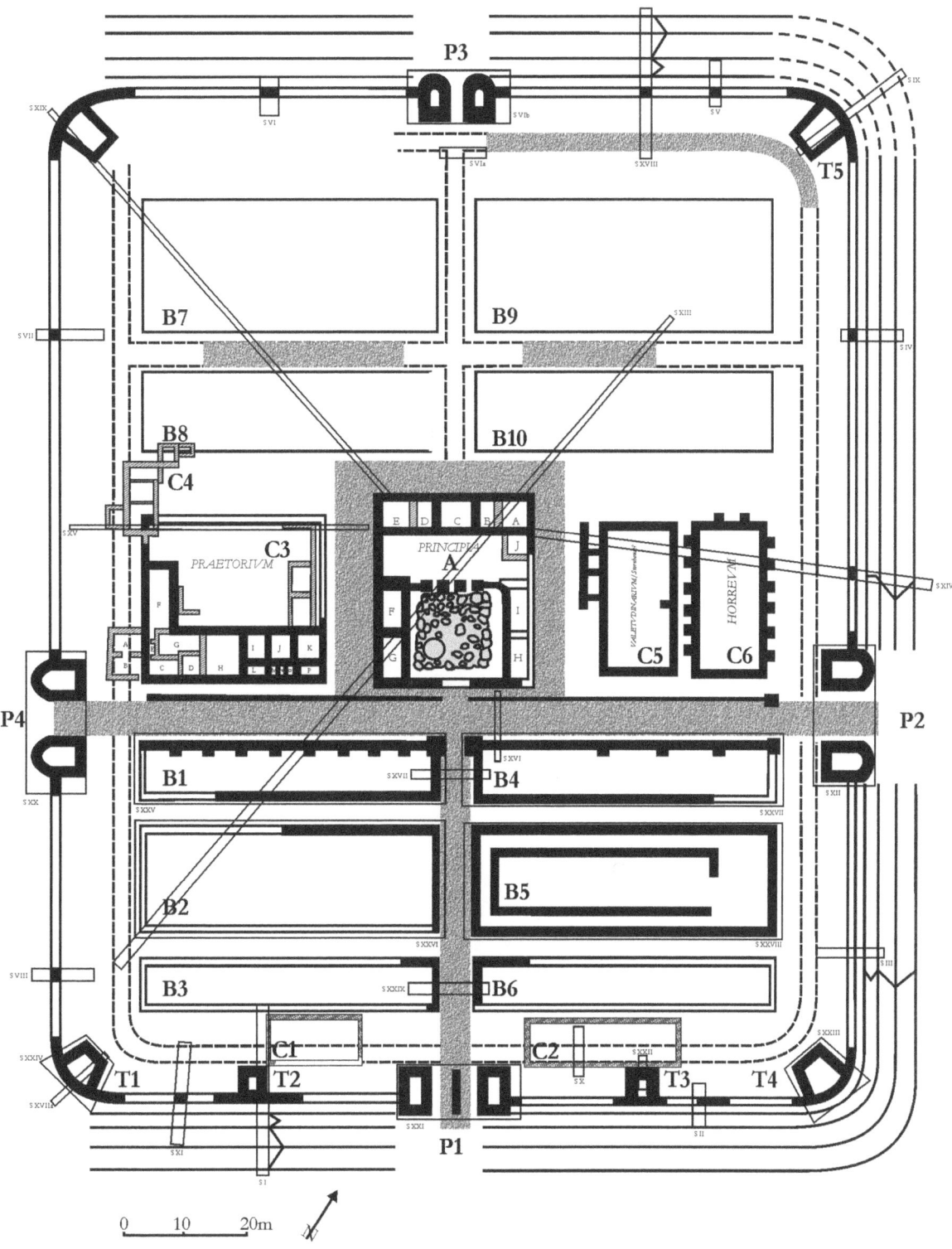

Fig. 1. The auxiliary fort from Buciumi - the archaeological researched areas
(based on Gudea 1997, 91, fig. 8)

supposed that these were the *armamentaria* there are still some debates about their real destination.

A wall, the *stylobat*, of 1 m wide was also discovered. Following the finding of a two column bases it was established an *intercolumnium* of 2.80 m.

The *basilica* has 24 x 8.25 m, 198 m². Two pedestals (1.20 x 1.20 m) were found inside. More fragments from inscriptions and an altar dedicated to Caracalla were found near them.

The *tribunalium* was unveiled in the NE corner of *basilica* sharing a wall with room A. Its sizes are 3.85 x 3.20 m and walls of 60 cm thickness poorly made of stone and bricks.

At some point all four rooms in the rear of the building had heating system. The poor made intermediary wall in the two large rooms (4.80 x 8.75 m) may have served for some military *collegia*.

One *aedes* of 4.80 x 5.70 m is located on the building axis without an apsis or any external projection. A pedestal (0.95 x 0.95 m) of stones and bricks that served as a base for either a statue or a trophy was found in the central part.

The *praetorium* (figs. I, III-IV)[15]

The commander's house (31 x 28 m) was discovered on the *latus dextrum*. It has a standard plan of a Mediterranean house, with a series of rooms displayed around a central courtyard. Its area of 868 m² represents 3.89% of the overall area of the fort.

The entrance was facing *via principalis*. Only the rooms alongside this road were excavated. One of the rooms (H) is larger than the others (6 x 8 m). Its functionality is assumed to be that of an entrance-court, an access way to the inner courtyard. The pavement in this space is made of pebble stones. At a certain moment this pavement was covered with *suspensura* which meant a change in functionality of this room. East of this entrance there are eight compartments grouped on two rows. Five of them are towards *via principalis*. Those at the ends (L, P) are larger (3 x 3.25 m, 3 x 3 m). The other three are each 1 x 1m. Their functionality is unknown. The other three rooms, facing the inner courtyard are each 4 x 4 m and they were all provided with a heating system. These rooms were destined to serve as kitchen. The heating system was introduced in a later phase.

West of entrance are four rooms grouped two by two (E, G, C, D) with similar sizes. The largest is room G (6 x 4 m) and the smallest is E (2.5 x 2.5 m). They seem to have been used a passage from the rooms on south side towards the west side. Except for these compartments all the other rooms were heated through a channel and *suspensurae*.

On the west side was a room of large sizes 10 x 4.75 m, also heated, which is considered to be a stable. In a later phase its destination was changed but the new one is unknown.

The sizes of the inner courtyard are unknown as only two sides were excavated. The only fragment of a wall in "L" shape is explained as an enlargement of room F when the portico was dismantled on this side. Later, in the 3rd century AD other compartments were added in the rear side and a small annex (C4) near the south corner. This annex that blocked *via sagularis* was split in two rooms (4.5 x 3.5 m, 4 x 2.75 m) which were, both, heated. They could serve as *latrinae*.

The *horrea* (figs. I, III-IV)[16]

Two buildings of rectangular shape and thick stone walls in the *latus sinistrum* were considered as *horrea*. They could have been preceded by other two built in wood.

The first *horreum* (C 5) located 13.70 m from *principia* has 25.30 x 12.80 m, 324 m², and the walls are 75 cm thick. Two compartments were noticed on the west side, near the NW corner (3.30 x 2.30 m; 3.95 x 2.30 m).

The absence of buttresses, the presence of those compartments, the low thickness value of walls for a *horreum*, and the fact that two *horrea* of such sizes would have been far more than enough for an auxiliary unit, may suggest that this building was something else than a *horreum*, more likely either a storeroom or even a hospital.

The other building considered as a *horreum* (C 6) is 26 x 13 m and an area of 338 m². Based on the shape (including the presence of buttresses) and thickness of the wall (75 cm) this *horreum* was a double one with a median longitudinal wall. The buttresses' interval is 2.80-3 m on the long side and 3.80 m on the short one. Their projection measures 0.65 m. The entrance was on the south side facing *via principalis*. Inside were found rows of pillars' pits of 25-30 cm diameter placed at 2, 4, 10 m from the western wall. The pillars were holding the wooden floor.

The barracks (figs. I-IV)[17]

In the *praetentura*, on each side of the *via praetoria*, three barracks were unveiled.

The barracks of the first phase of the fort were identified in *praetentura*: two in *praetentura dextra* and two in *praetentura sinistra*. There is a double barrack on each side of the *via praetoria*.

Barrack B 1 (50 x 9 m, area of 450 m²) – phase 1a – is displayed *per scamma* in *praetentura dextra* alongside *via principalis* with the officer room (8 x 8.50 m, area 68 m²) orientated towards *via sagularis*. As the structures were

---
[15] MARCU 2009, 40-42.
[16] MARCU 2009, 42-44.
[17] MARCU 2009, 44-51.

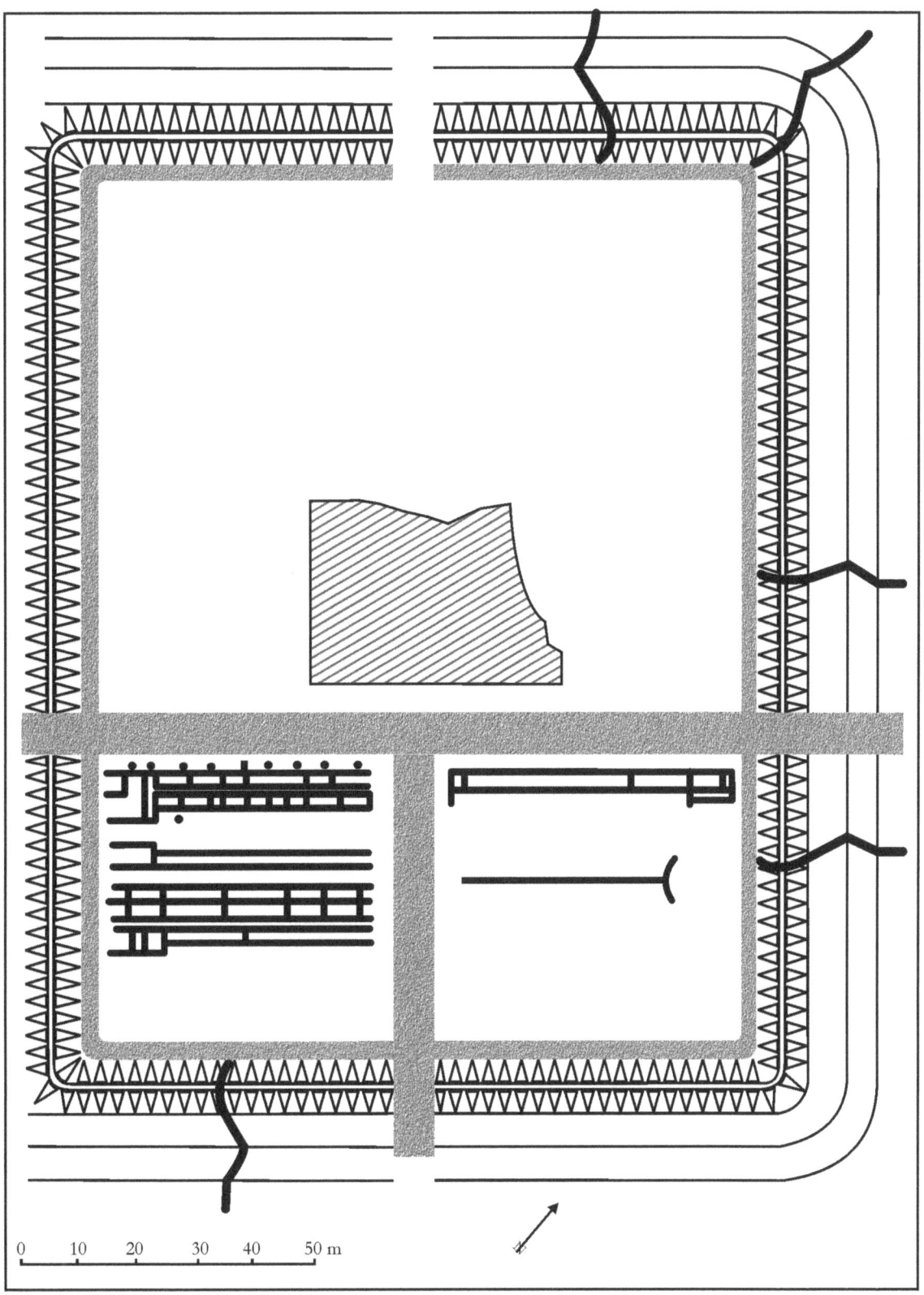

Fig. II. The 1st phase (earthen) of the auxiliary fort from Buciumi, AD 106 - beginning of Hadrian's reign (based on Gudea 1997, 93, fig. 10)

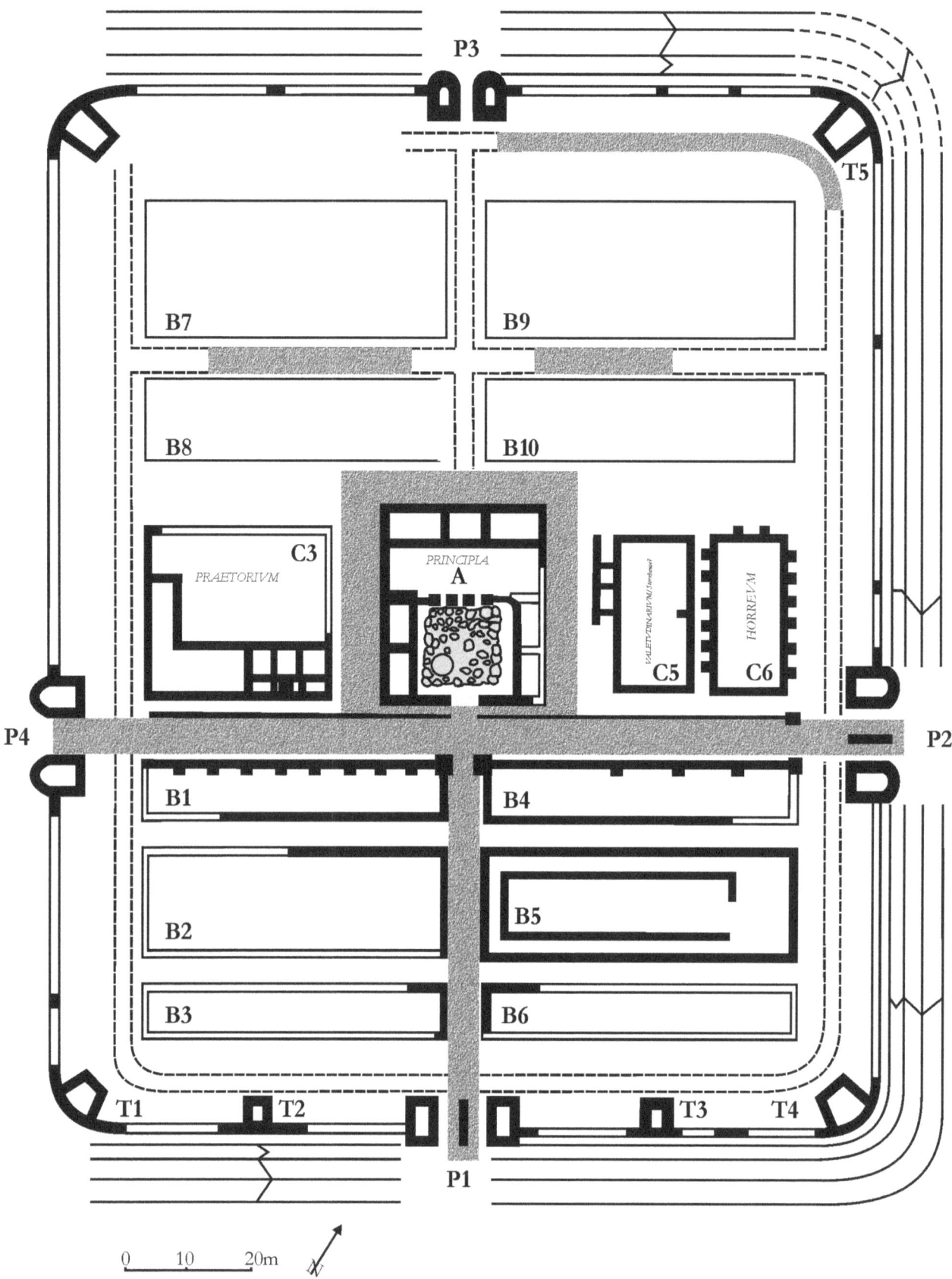

Fig. III. The auxiliary fort from Buciumi by the 1st quarter of the 3rd century AD
(based on Gudea 1997, 98, fig. 15)

very hard to identified 11 *contubernia* with *papilio* and *arma* (3.5 x 3.5 m).

In phase 1b the barrack plan underwent some changes. Only one row of rooms with veranda was identified. The officer room was extended, while at the end towards *via praetoria* a compartment was built on the entire wide side of the building – type A in the barrack typology of Davison. The reason was probably the incoming of the new unit in this auxiliary fort.

In phase 2 the wooden building was surrounded with a *stylobat*.

Barrack B 2 (50 x 19 m, area of 950 m²) also displayed *per scamma* in the vicinity of B1. The barracks placed back to back do not have a similar plan. The one facing B1 is represented by three longitudinal rows with some compartments. The second barrack consists of two longitudinal areas with an intermediary corridor. Unlike the barrack B1 in this case the corridor runs also in front of the officer room. The compartments of *papiliones* are identical with those on the rear side of the adjacent barrack. The *contubernia* is 40 m in length for each of the barracks.

In phase 1 b the double barrack has buildings of similar plan: one row of rooms like barrack B1.

In the last phase of habitation the barrack was surrounded with a *stylobat* of 60 cm wide.

The barracks in the *praetentura dextra*, in the first phase, belong to the type F of Davison's typology – two halves of barracks back to back with a corridor running on the entire longitudinal side.

The roof was made of tiles.

Barrack (?) B 4 is located in *praetentura sinistra* alongside *via principalis* and was entirely unveiled in 1970. It has a rectangular shape (49.25 x 9.40 m). In first phase the walls were made of adobe of 30-40 cm thick. The building is divided on the long side by a median wall. Other transversal walls were also noticed. In a later phase also this building was surrounded with a *stylobat*. The plan, sizes and the location of this building suggest the possibility that this building was used either as a stable or a storeroom.

A *fabrica* (?) (figs. I-IV)[18]

The building B 5 is located in the central part of the *praetentura sinistra*. Its sizes are – including the *stylobat* – 50 x 19 m, thus area of 950 m². The inner central room is 13 x 10.90 m. Four hearths were identified within this area that led to the supposition that this building may have been used as a *fabrica*.

Other buildings[19]

Over the NW corner of the *praetorium* and part of building B8 from *raetentura* a building (12.50 x 4 m) with three compartments was erected during the 3rd century AD (figs. I-IV). On the SE side it has a small apsis made of bricks. All compartments have heating system. It could have been a small bath connected to the commander's house.

Two buildings – C 1 (15 x 8 m, 120 m²) and C 2 (28 x 7.50 m, 210 m²) – were built up over the *via sagularis* and, partially, the *agger* (figs. I-IV). Despite the rich material layer the functionality of these two buildings is still unknown.

The troops

Although the first troop to be garrisoned in the auxiliary fort from Buciumi it has been considered the *cohors I Augusta Ituraerorum*[20] its presence it is still under debates.[21]

Owing to the large area and some findings (an inscribed bronze applique) also the *cohors I Ulpia Brittonum* could have been garrisoned at Buciumi.

Also the *cohors II Augusta Nervia Pacensis Brittonum milliaria peditata* was transferred at Buciumi sometime at the end of Hadrian's reign. It will remained at Buciumi until the Roman withdrwal from Dacia and received the epithet *Antoniniana*[22]

The baths

No systematic research has been carried out on the bath complex. Only one testing excavation took place in 1966 at the spot known as 'Fântânița Benții' (Bența's Well). This spot is located 150-200 m east from SE side of the fort. A number of walls from a large building together with fragments from water tubes were discovered.

In the 19th century C. Torma mentioned a rectangular building with a water pipeline made of bricks.[23]

The civilian settlement adjacent to the auxiliary fort of Buciumi

The territory of the civilian settlement was never systematically researched. On the basis of archaeological material brought to the light by chance – mainly agricultural works – it has been considered that the *vicus militaris* was located to the NE and SE of the auxiliary fort. Some testing excavations magnetically resistivity prospections indicate the presence of a main road coming

---

[18] MARCU 2009, 51.

[19] MARCU 2009, 51-52.
[20] BUCIUMI 1972, 117-118; GUDEA 1997, 25.
[21] MARCU 2009, 52.
[22] GUDEA 1997, 52; MARCU 2009, 53.
[23] GUDEA 1997, 63-64.

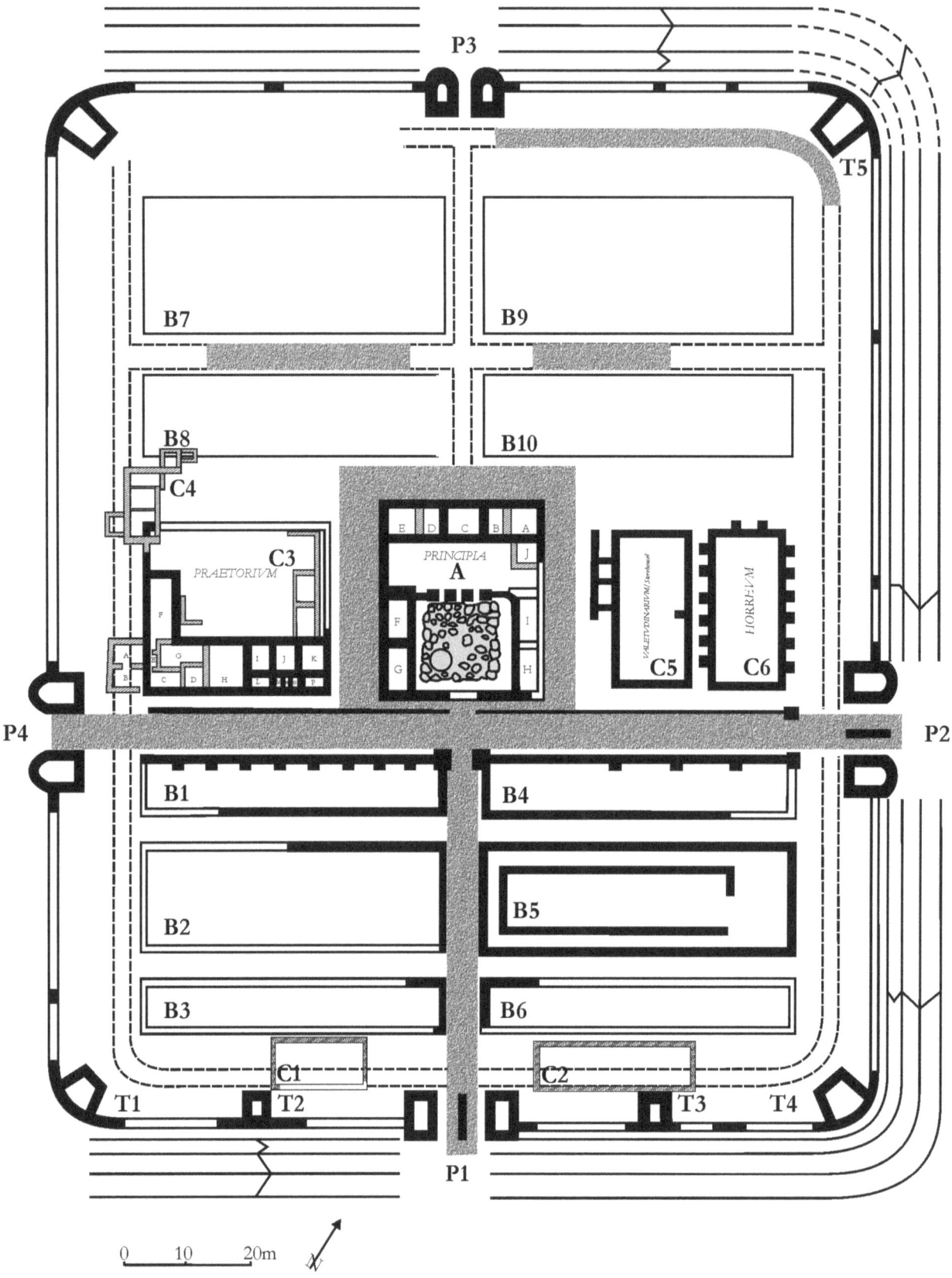

Fig. IV. The auxiliary fort from Buciumi, 1st quarter of the 3rd century AD - AD 260/270 (based on Gudea 1997, 106, fig. 23)

out from *porta sinistra* and some adjacent streets through the civilian settlements.[24]

The graveyard

The only information on the possible place for the auxiliary fort cemetery comes from the antiquarian S. Papiriu-Pop. Following the ploughing of agricultural parcel by tractors he noticed spots of firing, close to each other, shards, bones and ashes.

A funerary inscription – today lost – it is known to have been discovered at Buciumi. The tombstone mentions a soldier of the *cohors II Nervia Brittonum* and that those who placed the inscription were his wife and son.[25]

---

[24] GUDEA 1997, 62.

[25] GUDEA 1997, 64-65.

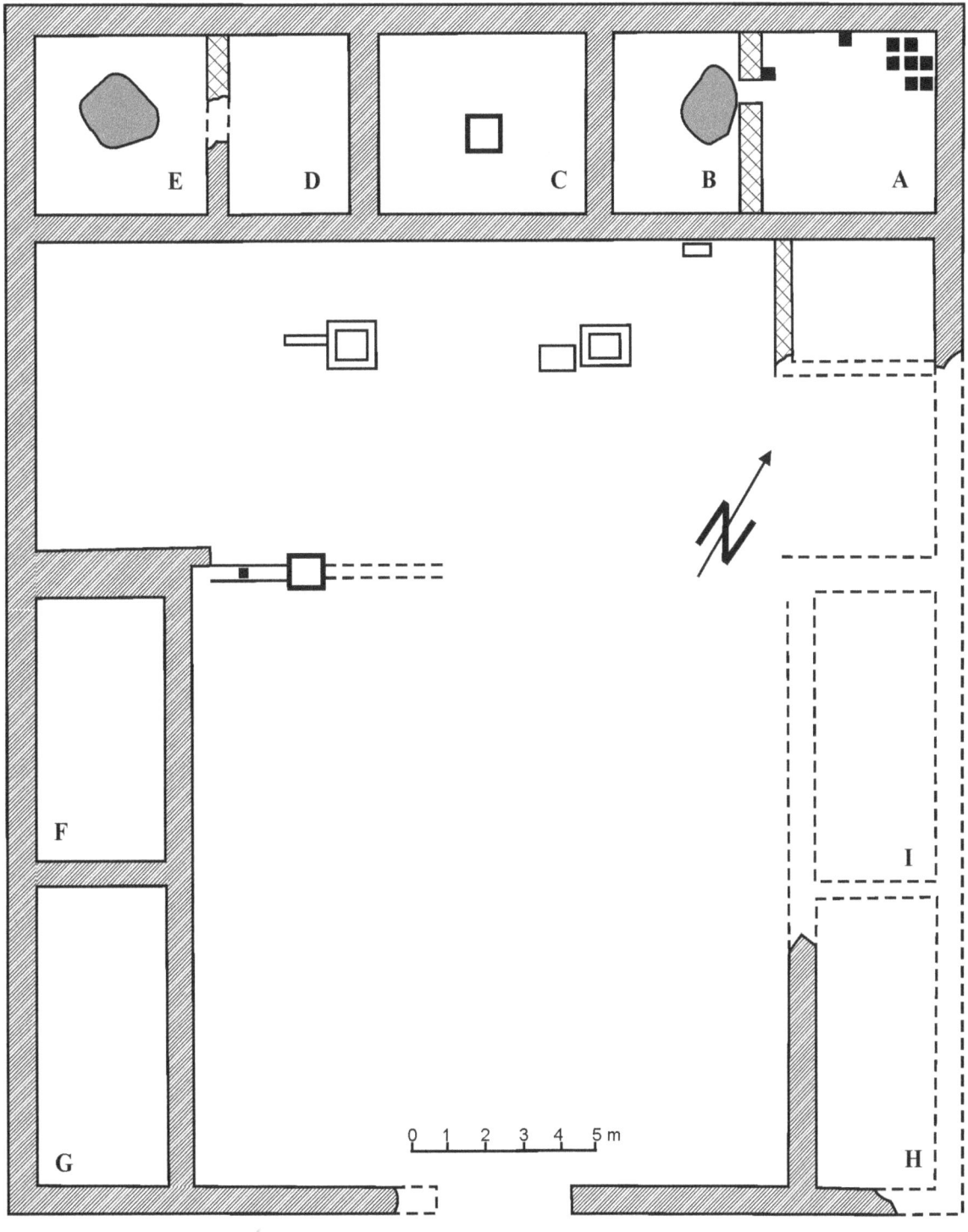

FIG. V. THE *PRINCIPIA* OF THE AUXILIARY FORT FROM BUCIUMI UP TO THE 3RD CENTURY AD
(AFTER GUDEA 1997, 101, FIG. 18)

Comments on Numismatics

Introduction

The numismatic evidence presented in this book comes from the archaeological campaigns carried out at the auxiliary fort of Buciumi, County of Sălaj, Romania. The archaeological investigations took place from 1963 to 1976[26], with a cleaning and testing excavations in 1997[27].

Some old records, from the 19th century, mention coins coming from Buciumi but there is neither a precise findspot – 'the surroundings of the fort' – nor any information on the number, metal or denomination of these pieces.[28]

The total number of coin finds is 477. Apart from 462 pieces coming from the excavations, 15 coins joined catalogue as part of the Silviu Papiriu-Pop collection, which were also found on the territory of this auxiliary fort.

The archaeological context was established for each coin that comes from site find discoveries. The result goes with the most intense areas archeologically researched up to the present – the ones of the auxiliary fort (inside and outside of the fort: watchtowers, gateways, towers, *principia*, *praetorium*, barracks, etc.).

The quantity and the quality of the numismatic evidence provided by this long time researched fort in Roman Dacia may allow us some observations on the numismatic spectrum with its general and specific patterns.

1. The coin finds

Unlike the other numismatic monographs dedicated to Roman sites from Dacia[29] in the case of the site of Buciumi, at the moment the numismatic evidence is provided only by the auxiliary fort.

Therefore, the patterns of coin finds from this fort may not have a comparable item from the adjacent civilian settlement (*vicus militaris*) – unexplored, yet – but, still can be compared with a general pattern of the Roman province of Dacia.

In order to have an image as accurate as possible on the development of the auxiliary fort of Buciumi through coin circulation the coins were also divided by chronological sequences based on important monetary policy or political changes with impact on the province of Roman Dacia.[30]

The chronological sequences are:

I. Augustus-Nero (27 BC-AD 68)
II. Vespasian-Domitian (AD 69-96)
III. Nerva-Trajan (AD 96-117)
IV. Hadrian (AD 117-138)
V. Antoninus Pius (AD 138-161)
VI. Marcus Aurelius (AD 161-180)
VII. Commodus (AD 180-192)
VIII. Septimius Severus-Caracalla (AD 193-218)
IX. Elagabalus-Maximinus I Thrax (AD 218-238)
X. Gordian III (AD 238-244)
XI. Phillip I (AD 244-249)
XII. Trebonianus Gallus (AD 251-253)

The graphic representations of the coin finds from this fort (figs. 1-3) indicate a strong similarity with other sites from Roman Dacia (e.g. *Ulpia Traiana Sarmizegetusa, Apulum, Porolissum, Arcobadara, Samum,* Gilău). The number of coins issued before the conquest of Dacia (AD 101-102, 105-106) is low a consequence of the long period of circulation of these pieces. The high values for the coins of Trajan is also a 'normal' feature for the sites in Dacia, as beside a strong coin injection in the new province and military payments, also the strong construction activities in this period – high dynamic of human presence – have led to the increase of loss of coinage.

The gradual decrease of the coefficients of coin finds after the reign of Trajan also goes with the general pattern of Dacia. The slowing down of construction activity at this fort in the next years, especially after the reign of Antoninus Pius (AD 138-161), is pointed out, by the gradual decrease of the coin finds issued in the period of AD 117-192 (figs. 1-3).

The very low index for the reigns of Marcus Aurelius and Commodus is also a common characteristic for Dacia and for Middle and Lower Danube provinces[31] and could be the effect of a low coin production[32].

The strong raise of the index, mainly for the reign of Septimius Severus, is another common aspect in Dacia following a large influx of a coinage that it was supposed to pass as a genuine silver denarius but it proved to have

---
[26] GUDEA 1997, 13-15.
[27] BUCIUMI 2000, 345-346.
[28] GOSS 1876, 320.
[29] *Ulpia Traiana Sarmizegetusa* (GĂZDAC/COCIŞ 2004), *Apulum* (GĂZDAC/SUCIU/ALFÖLDY-GĂZDAC 2009), *Porolissum* (GĂZDAC/GUDEA 2006), *Samum*, Gilău (GĂZDAC/ISAC 2007), *Arcobadara* (GĂZDAC/GAIU 2011).
[30] For a detailed explanation of establishing such chronological sequences see GĂZDAC 2010, 35-37.
[31] GĂZDAC 2010, 114-115.
[32] HARL 1996, 126-128.

The Roman Auxiliary Fort at Buciumi (Roman Dacia, Romania): Coins in archaeological context

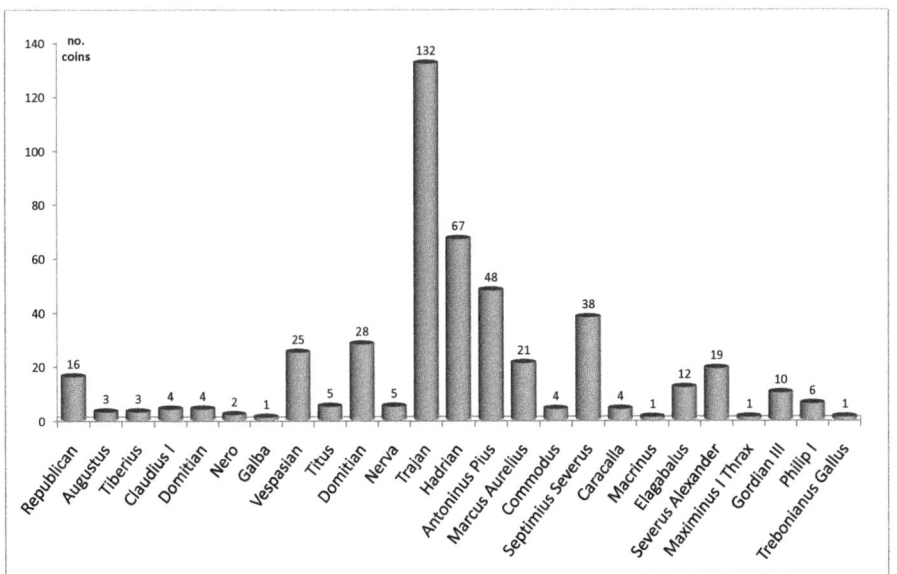

Fig. 1. The auxiliary fort of Buciumi: no. of coins

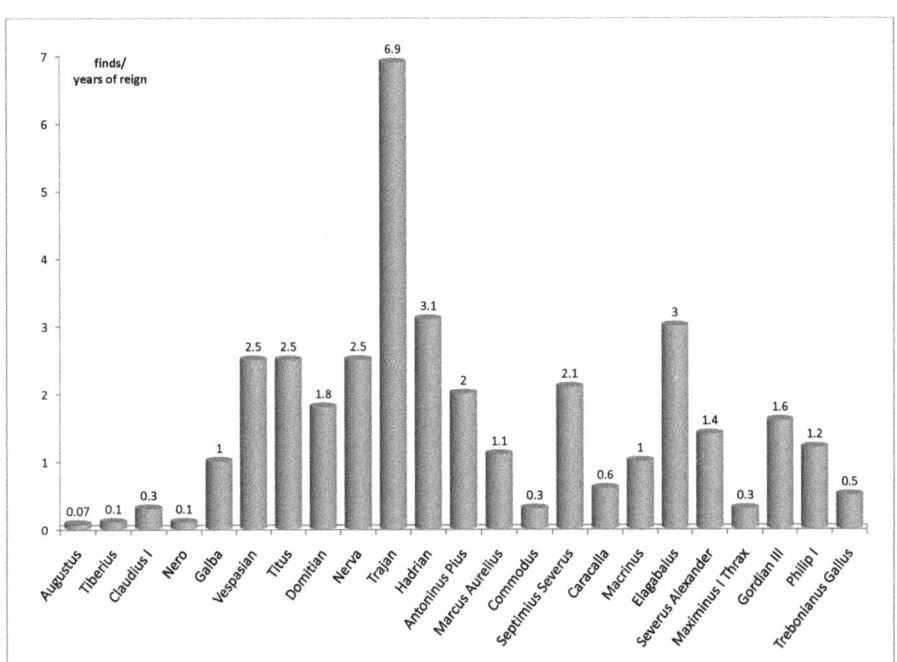

Fig. 2. The auxiliary fort of Buciumi: finds/years of reign

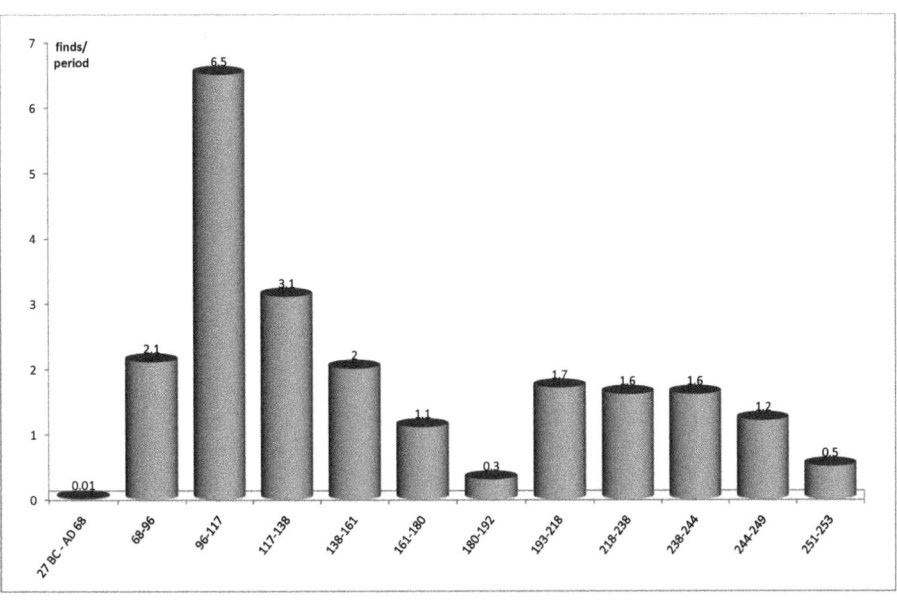

Fig. 3. The auxiliary fort of Buciumi: finds/period

ISSUER	Au		D		Ant		Plated/Copy		S		Dp	
	No	%	No	%	No	%	No	%	No	%	No	%
Republican			15	93.7								
Augustus												
Tiberius												
Claudius I											1	25
Julio-Claudian dynasty												
Nero												
Galba							1	100				
Vespasian	1	4	11	44			2	8	1	4		
Titus			4	80								
Domitian			2	7.1			4	14.2	2	7.1	1	3.5
Nerva			1	20								
Trajan			14	10.6			9	6.8	14	10.6	23	17.4
Hadrian			5	7.4			2	2.9	8	11.9	3	4.4
Antoninus Pius			11	22.9			6	12.5	10	20.8	5	10.4
M. Aurelius			3	14.2			5	23.8	6	28.5	4	19
Commodus			1	25			1	25	2	50		
Septimius Severus			12	31.5			26	68.4				
Caracalla			2	50			2	50				
Macrinus							1	100				
Elagabalus			10	83.3			2	16.6				
Severus Alexander			12	63.1			5	26.3	2	10.5		
Maximinus Thrax							1	100				
Gordian III					3	30	5	50	2	20		
Philip I					2	33.3	2	33.3	2	33.3		
Trebonianus Gallus					1	100						
Pseudo-autonoumous												
Unidentified							2	12.5	1	6.2		
TOTAL	1	0.2	103	21.5	6	1.2	76	15.9	50	10.4	37	7.7

TABLE 1. THE COIN FINDS FROM THE AUXILIARY FORT FROM BUCIUMI

been strongly counterfeited. The large number of plated silver coins with imperial portraits of the period AD 193-211 is largely supported by the presence of plated silver coins 68.4% of the coins (tab. 1). This aspect indicates that the counterfeited coinage was not a result of clandestine workshops – this does not totally exclude the presence of such workshops – but part of an imperial monetary policy[33].

Similar to other sites from Dacia the period after AD 218 shows a low value, especially the index of coins/period which gradually decreases towards the end of chronological segment when coins were found on the territory of this fort (figs. 1-3) – the last coin comes from Trebonianus Gallus (AD 251-253) (catalogue; tab. 1; figs 1-11).

A particular feature for the auxiliary fort of Buciumi is represented by the index value for the period of AD 244-249, the reign of Philip I (tab. 1; figs. 1-3). The similar index for the province of Dacia, and the other sites, well-documented and published, shows a strong increased. For both situations the explanation is the same: the massive/low presence of the coins of '*PROVINCIA DACIA*' type (catalogue nos. 439-440)[34]. At the moment this is the only fort from Dacia[35] where this coinage was found in such a low number (2).

---

[33] KING 1996, 262-263; GĂZDAC 2009, 1495-1496.

[34] GĂZDAC/ALFÖLDY-GĂZDAC 2008, 135-171; GĂZDAC 2010, 200-201.
[35] Taking into account only the well documented and published sites from Dacia: *Ulpia Traiana Sarmizegetusa, Apulum, Potaissa, Porolissum, Arcobadara, Samum*, Gilău (see bibliography).

As		Semis		Quadrans		Cast		Prov. Issues		Unident. Denom.		Total	finds/ years of reign	finds/ period
No	%	No	%	No	%	No	%	No	%	No	%			
								1	6.2			16	-	-
2	66.6							1	33.3			3	0.07	
3	100											3	0.1	
3	75											4	0.3	0.01
4	100											4	-	
2	100											2	0.1	
												1	1	
10	40											25	2.5	2.1
1	20											5	2.5	
14	50					3	10.7	2	7.1			28	1.8	
4	80											5	2.5	6.5
64	48.4	1	0.7	2	1.5	3	2.2	2	1.5			132	6.9	
45	67.1					2	2.9	2	2.9			67	3.1	3.1
14	29.1							2	4.1			48	2	2
1	4.7							2	9.5			21	1.1	1
												4	0.3	0.3
												38	2.1	
												4	0.6	1.7
												1	1	
												12	3	
												19	1.4	1.6
												1	0.3	
												10	1.6	1.6
												6	1.2	1.2
												1	0.5	0.5
								1	100			1	-	-
1	6.2									12	75	16	-	-
168	35.2	1	0.2	2	0.4	8	1.6	13	2.7	12	3	477		

Gold

One *aureus* of Vespasianus was found in the auxiliary fort from Buciumi (catalogue nr. 39; pl. I, 12)

Silver

Regarding the silver denominations, the coin finds from the auxiliary of Buciumi follow the same pattern known also for other sites from Dacia as the result of the imperial monetary policy.[36]

The *denarius* is the best represented (89.5 % of the total silver coins) amongst the silver denominations (tab. 1).

The *denarii* are present in the majority of the chronological sequences starting with the Republic up to the reign of Gordian III with the 'normal' gap for the Julio-Claudian dynasty.

This denomination also follows the general patterns of percentage fluctuations due to the presence/absence of other denominations, mainly bronze. For earlier sequences - the Republic, the Vespasian-Titus period the denarius holds a high percentage a consequence of an imperial monetary policy, as can be seen also at other Roman sites from *Dacia*.[37] The apparently small values of the *denarii* issued for Trajan and Hadrian, when the coefficient finds/year strongly increased for these reigns, may be explain

---

[36] This phenomenon has also been noticed for other important sites from Roman Dacia such as: *Ulpia Traiana Sarmizegetusa* (GĂZDAC/COCIŞ 2004, 121), *Apulum* (GĂZDAC/SUCIU/ALFÖLDY-GĂZDAC 2009, 234), *Porolissum* (GĂZDAC/GUDEA 2006, 166).

[37] *Ulpia Traiana Sarmizegetusa* (GĂZDAC/COCIŞ 2004, 121), *Apulum* (GĂZDAC/SUCIU/ALFÖLDY-GĂZDAC 2009, 233), *Porolissum* (GĂZDAC/GUDEA 2006, 164).

by looking at the number of bronze denominations for the same issuers. Those very small values, when compared to the rest of the issuers up to Commodus, of coins struck under Trajan and Hadrian represents a specific monetary pattern that illustrates the intense monetary circulation and evolution not only at Buciumi but also at the scale of the entire province of *Dacia*[38].

The *antoninianus* is present for the reigns of Gordian III, Philip I and Trebonianus Gallus but in very low numbers (tab. 1), another general pattern for the province of Dacia.[39]

As we are discussing the coin finds from an auxiliary Roman fort from Dacia we face another general pattern met at the military sites *Dacia*[40], but also for the western part of the Empire[41]: the plated *denarius*. For the case of silver coins of bearing the portraits of Septimius Severus the quantity of plated *denarii* goes double above the quantity of genuine *denarii* (tab. 1). This percentage of plated coins decreased for the next reigns when the *denarius* was still strongly represented – Elagabalus, Severus Alexander. As it has been already demonstrated the large number of plated *denarii* bearing the portraits of Septimius Severus and the following emperors is part of the imperial monetary policy regarding the army coin supply[42].

Still, a specific feature regarding the plated silver coins can be noticed in the case of this fort. There is a high percentage of plated silver coins for pieces bearing earlier emperors then Septimius Severus (Domitian, Trajan, Antoninus Pius, Marcus Aurelius) (tab. 1).

Bronze

If one would have already red the 6th volume of the numismatic series dedicated to the Roman sites from Romania – *Arcobadara* (Ilişua) – could easily note the similar pattern of bronze coin finds from that auxiliary fort and the one from Buciumi

We reproduce here – with slight changes – the text regarding the bronze coin finds from *Arcobadara*, as it perfectly fits with the spectrum from Buciumi. "Like in the case of the silver single coin finds the bronze denominations found at [Buciumi] reflect closely the imperial monetary policy. As in the cases of other similar sites from *Dacia* – *Ulpia Traiana Sarmizegetusa*[43], *Apulum*[44], *Porolissum*[45] [and *Arcobadara*][46] - for the coins issued in the period of AD 98-180 the most retrieved bronze denomination is the *as* - 'was not a coin that one would be very careful not to

lose'[47]. As a consequence of the monetary policy from the reign of Septimius Severus to Philip I the numbers of *asses* decreased significantly. As the number of minted *denarii* and *antoniniani* grew, the *as* denomination has lost its role in transactions and became scarcely minted."

In the case of the larger bronze denominations, *sestertius* and *dupondius* their fluctuations is slightly different. It decreases proportionally starting for the reign of Trajan and Marcus Aurelius but increases for the reigns of Antoninus Pius and Marcus Aurelius (tab 1). The 50% percentage for the reign of Commodus is not relevant due to the low number of *sestertii* (2) (catalogue nos. 357-358, tab. 1). These denominations are scarcely found in the later reigns. In fact, the *dupondius* was not found after Commodus reign while the *sestertius* turned up for the reign of Severus Alexander, Gordian III and Philip I. In all three cases the number is very low number (2 pieces) (catalogue nos. 424, 14 (Silviu Papiriu-Pop collection), 431, 435, 431, 435, 439-440; tab. 1). As already mentioned above, unlike the other sites from Dacia, at Buciumi the coinage 'PROVINCIA DACIA' seems to have arrived in a much lower quantity.

Other bronze denominations issued by the mint of Rome found at Buciumi are the *semis* (1) and the *quadrans* (2), all of Trajan (catalogue nos. 140, 141, 223; tab. 1). Such a low number for these denominations is not a surprise. The smallest bronze denominations of the Roman imperial monetary system may not have had a large production and, on the other hand, their sizes did not make them an easy artefact to be found.

Greek imperial coins

The proportion of the Greek Imperial coins from the total number of coins found at Buciumi is very small (13 coins that equal 2.7 % of the total number of site finds) (tab. 1). Like in the case of the auxiliary fort from *Arcobadara*, the topography and the location of the auxiliary fort of Buciumi – on the *limes*, right on the NW frontier of the province – that makes it a remote area for a possible long distance trade – could be an explanation for such a low number of coins. The similar situation of the urban-military site of *Porolissum* situated in the very close vicinity (maps 2-3) may support this hypothesis[48]. The directions from which these few Greek Imperial coins come are given by various cities, provinces or rulers (Nikopolis ad Istrum, Philippopolis, Perinthos, Philippi, Stobi, Thessalonica, Corinth, Ankyra, Nikaea, koinon Bithynia, Rhoemetalkes I) (catalogue nos.: 316, 317, 224, 282, 344, 16, 89-90, 446, 345, 283, 19).

Regarding the presence and the mints for these Greek civic coins found at the auxiliary fort from Buciumi it must be pointed out some particular features. In comparison with

---

[38] GĂZDAC 2010, 200-201.
[39] GĂZDAC 2010, CD, tab. R4, pl. K1, Q2.
[40] GĂZDAC/ALFÖLDY-GĂZDAC 2001, 137-154; GĂZDAC 2009, 1487-1498.
[41] KING 1996, 237-263.
[42] GĂZDAC/ALFÖLDY-GĂZDAC 2001, 153-154; GĂZDAC 2009, 1496-1497.
[43] GĂZDAC/COCIŞ 2004, 119-121.
[44] GĂZDAC/SUCIU/ALFÖLDY-GĂZDAC 2009, 233-234.
[45] GĂZDAC/GUDEA 2006, 164.
[46] GĂZDAC/GAIU 2011, 226.

[47] GĂZDAC/GUDEA 2006, 25.
[48] At *Porolissum* the percentage of Greek civic coins is 0.9% of the coin finds (GĂZDAC/GUDEA 2006, 166).

the other sites from Roman Dacia the Greek civic coins from Buciumi belong to 'early' chronological sequences (Republic to Marcus Aurelius)[49] (catalogue, tab. 1). On the other hand, at the moment, no coins of the military series with standards issued at Nikaea Bithyniae in the period of Elagabalus – Gordian III were found, although they are very common and overwhelming the other Greek civic issues at the majority of the well-researched Roman sites from Dacia, especially for the reign of Severus Alexander[50].

Cast coins

Amongst the coins discovered within the auxiliary fort of Buciumi one can noticed the cast coins. The archaeological field research brought to light 8 of such cast coins: 3 *asses* depicting Domitian (catalogue, nos. 82-84); 1 *sestertius* and 2 *asses* bearing the portrait of Trajan (catalogue nos. 210, 221-222) and 2 *asses* illustrating Hadrian (catalogue nos. 262-263). The archaeological contexts from where these coins were retrieved may offer some hints on the date of production. While the cast coins with the portraits of Trajan and Hadrian were discovered in contexts belonging to phase Ib (the beginning of Hadrian's reign – 1st quarter of the 3rd century AD) the 3 asses with Domitian's portrait are all coming from layers of phase Ia (AD 106 – the beginning of Hadrian's reign) (catalogue).

Counterfeited coins

Apart from the large number of plated silver coins discovered within the auxiliary for of Buciumi, a consequence of a specific monetary policy of the state, there are some coins which by their design could be products of clandestine minting workshops.

These are coins catalogue nos. 28, 174, 338 (catalogue; pl. I/6, III/1, IV/8). The first piece, an *as* depicting Nero shows the N from Nero reversed spelt: ИERO (catalogue no. 28; pl. I/6). The second piece, a plated *denarius* with the portrait of Trajan, *o*n the reverse has the '*PRINCIPI*' misspelled as *PRINCII* with a possible second 'P' engraved as a longer 'I': PRINCII (catalogue no. 174; pl. III/1). The third piece is a *denarius* bearing the portrait of Marcus Aurelius. The obverse does not match the reverse. On both sides appears the tribunician power with different values. The portrait of M. Aurelius is slightly modified while the name ANTONINVS is misspelled as ANTDNINVS (catalogue no. 338; pl. IV/8).

2. Coins and the archaeological context

Following the technique used during the excavations to record the archaeological evidence from this site (in some cases, still in use nowadays): findspot, trench/meter/ quadrant/, depth – measured from the top soil, the study of coin finds in archaeological contexts must be done with extreme caution. The results presented below can show certain conclusions but, at the same time, some aspects are still left under the question mark.

From 446 coins coming from the systematic excavations in the auxiliary fort of Buciumi (the 16 unidentified coins and the 15 pieces of the Silviu Papiriu-Pop are not included): 51 coins are coming from excavated ground; 54 coins are without a dated archaeological context; and 8 coins are stray finds during the excavations (catalogue). In fact 25.3% of the coin finds from the auxiliary fort are helpless regarding the analysis of coins within the archaeological context.

At the same time, the coins which do have an 'archaeological' context (marked by depth from the top soil) were separated by phases owing to the information provided by one of the participants to the excavations, N. Gudea[51]. According to this scholar the existence phases are established by depth as follows:

phase Ia (-0.90-1.20 m);
phase Ib (-0.30-0.90 m);
phase II (0-0.30 m)[52].

The chronological sequences for these phases are established as AD 106-114 for phase Ia[53]; AD 114/115 – beginning of the 3rd century AD for phase Ib[54]; beginning of the 3rd century AD – AD 275 for phase II[55].

Following this chronological structure of building phases/depth we tried to organize the numismatic evidence – where possible – by phases (catalogue, figs. 9-11).

The result of this approach came out with interesting aspect for the history of this auxiliary fort, the coin period of circulation, as well as for the methodology of excavation technique and the recording of artefacts. We must point here that some of the coins with 'context' were even more 'precise' placed in context according to specific mentions that on certain areas (e.g. barrack 2)[56] the depths may contradict the general scheme of phases by depth mentioned above.

The large majority of coin finds from phase Ia were issued in the period of AD 96-117, mainly to Trajan (see figs. 9-11). In fact the coefficient/period for AD 96-117 represents over 40% of the coin finds from this phase (fig. 11). If this spectrum – a massive presence of Trajan's coins and a much lower number of pre-Trajan coins just left in

---

[49] The pseudo-autonomous minted in Akyra Phrygiae maybe an exception but it is largely dated in the 2nd-3rd centuries (catalogue, no. 446).
[50] *Ulpia Traiana Sarmizegetusa* (GĂZDAC/COCIŞ 2004, 118), *Apulum* (GĂZDAC/SUCIU/ALFÖLDY-GĂZDAC 2009, 235), *Porolissum* (GĂZDAC/GUDEA 2006, 163), the overall situation of Roman Dacia (GĂZDAC 2010, 156, 183; CD, tab. Q1).

[51] GUDEA 1997, 35.
[52] GUDEA 1997, 35.
[53] GUDEA 1997, 26-27.
[54] GUDEA 1997, 34, 37.
[55] GUDEA 1997, 54-55.
[56] GUDEA 1997, 24, 26, 29, 50, 51.

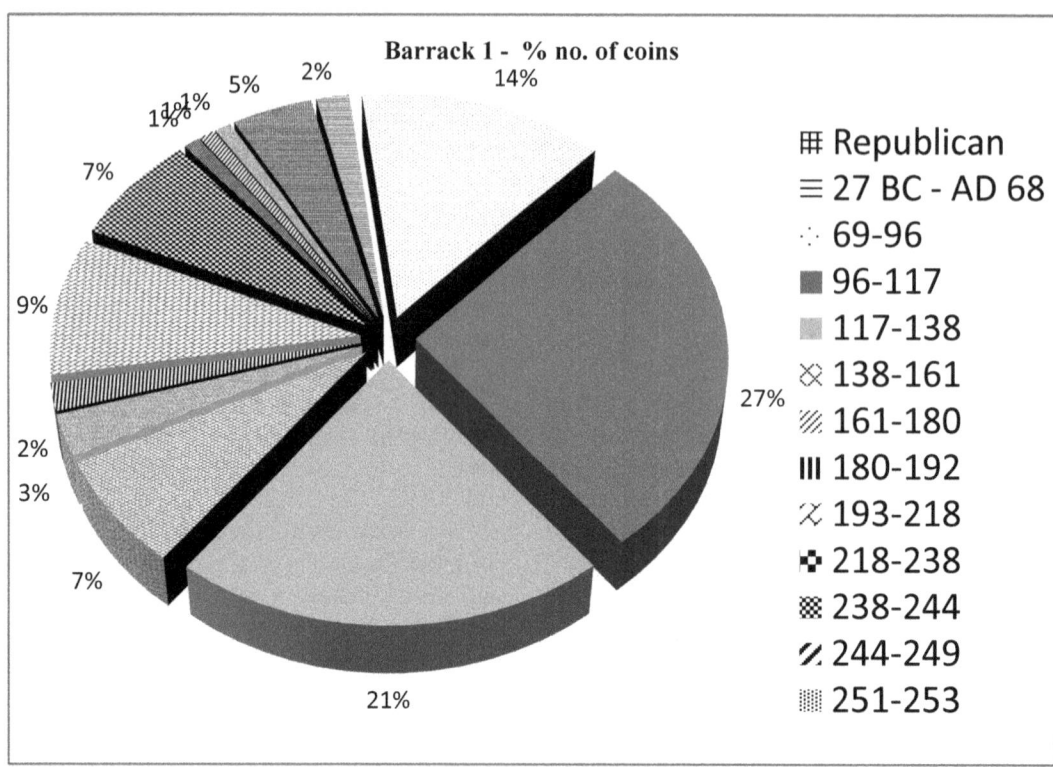

Fig. 4a. Barrack 1 - % no. of coins

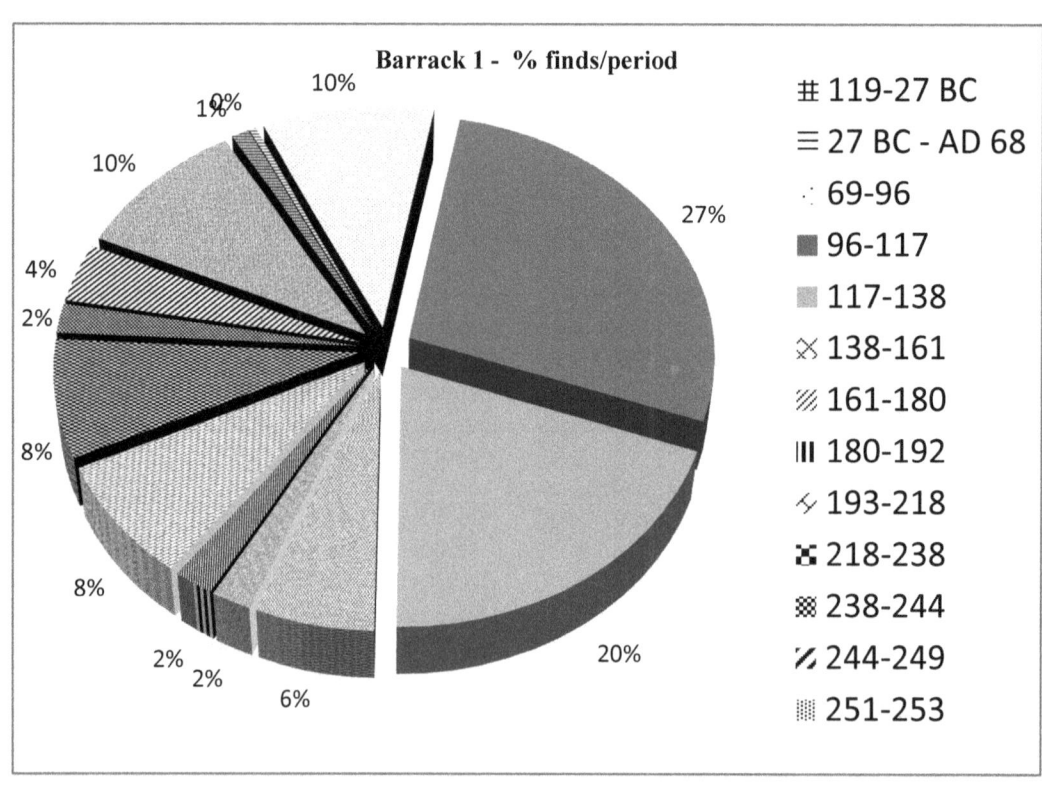

Fig. 4b. Barrack 1 - % finds/period

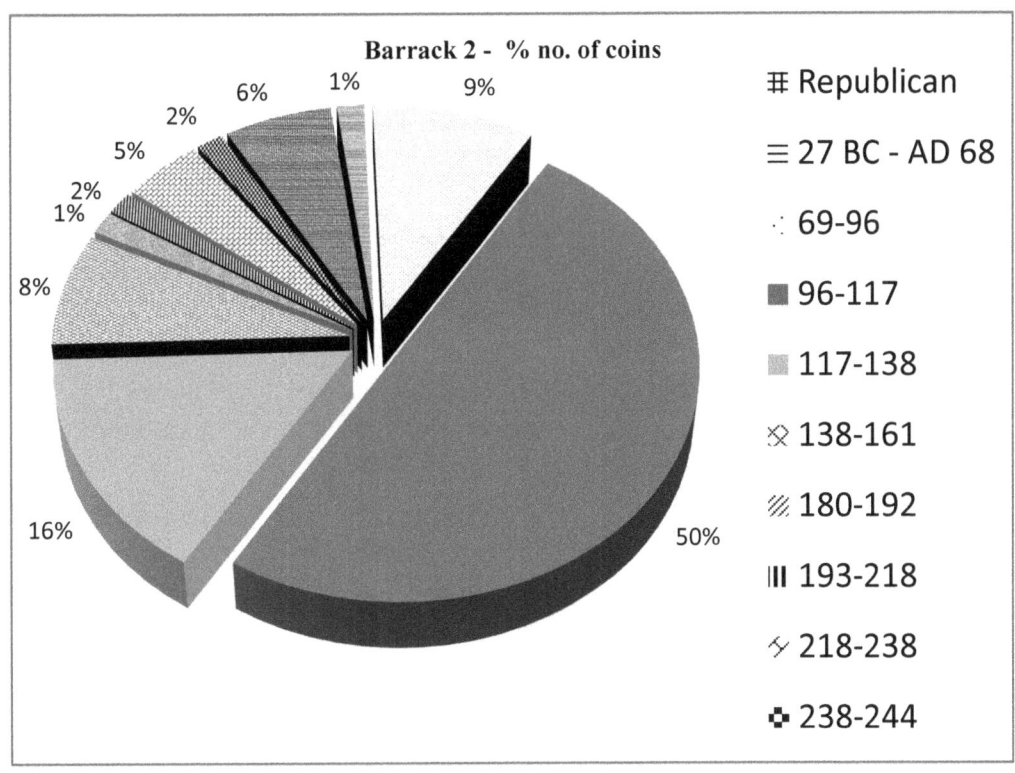

FIG. 5A. BARRACK 2 - % NO. OF COINS

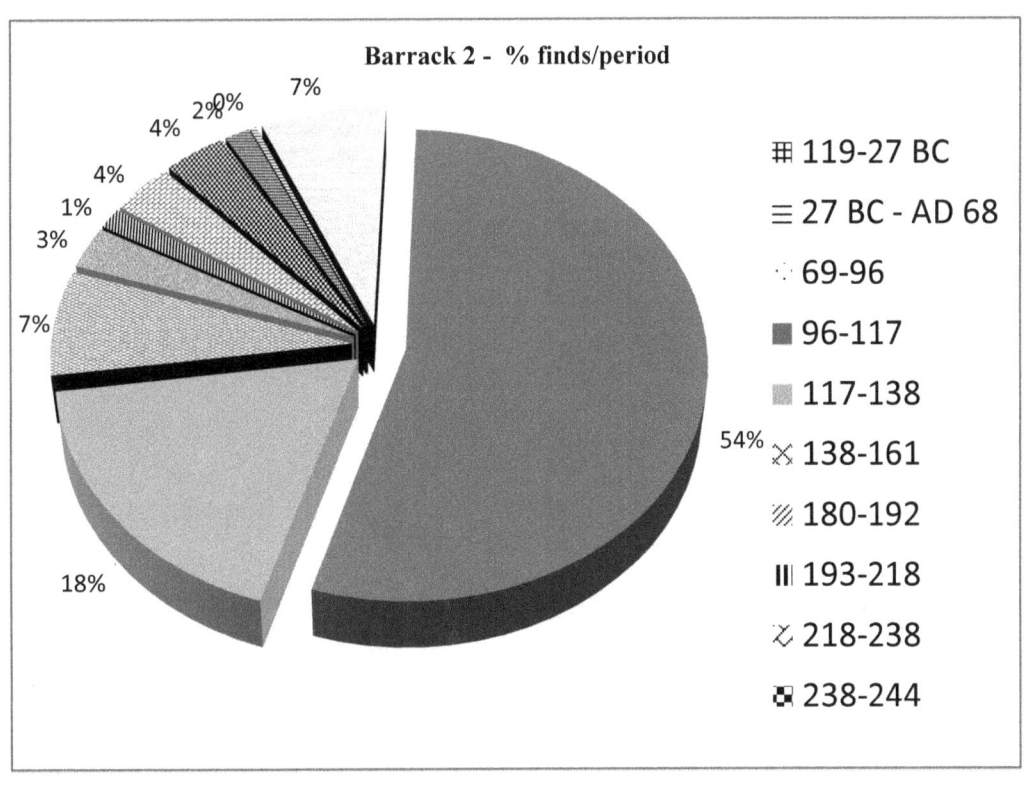

FIG. 5B. BARRACK 2 - % FINDS/PERIOD

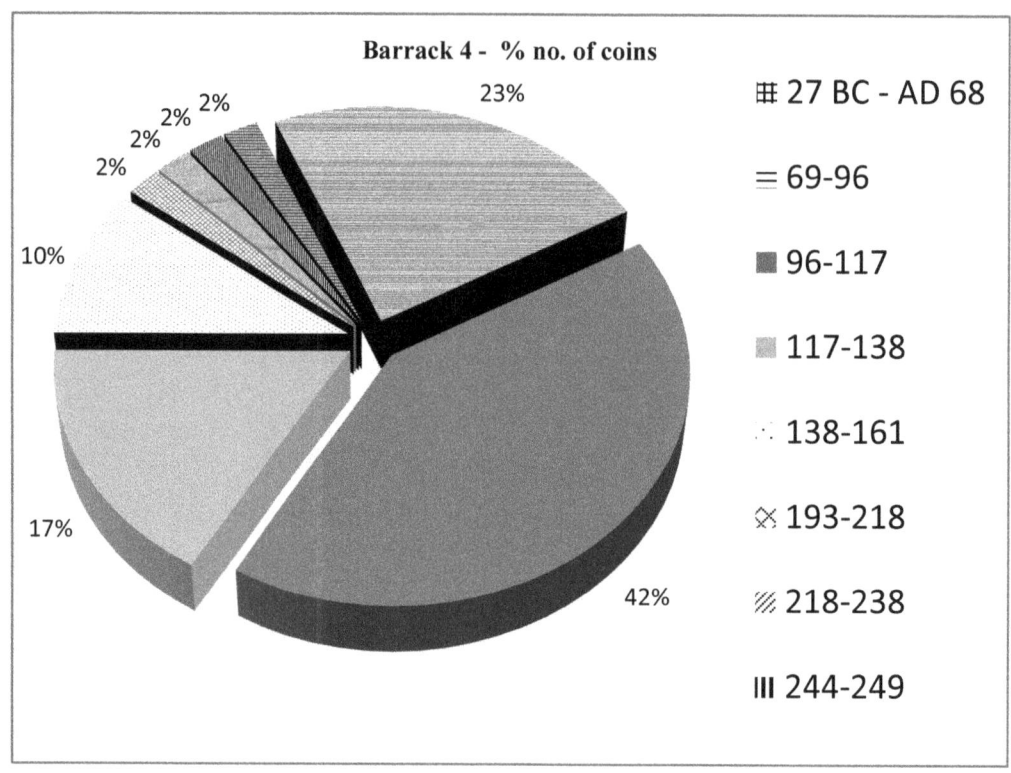

FIG. 6A. BARRACK 4 - % NO. OF COINS

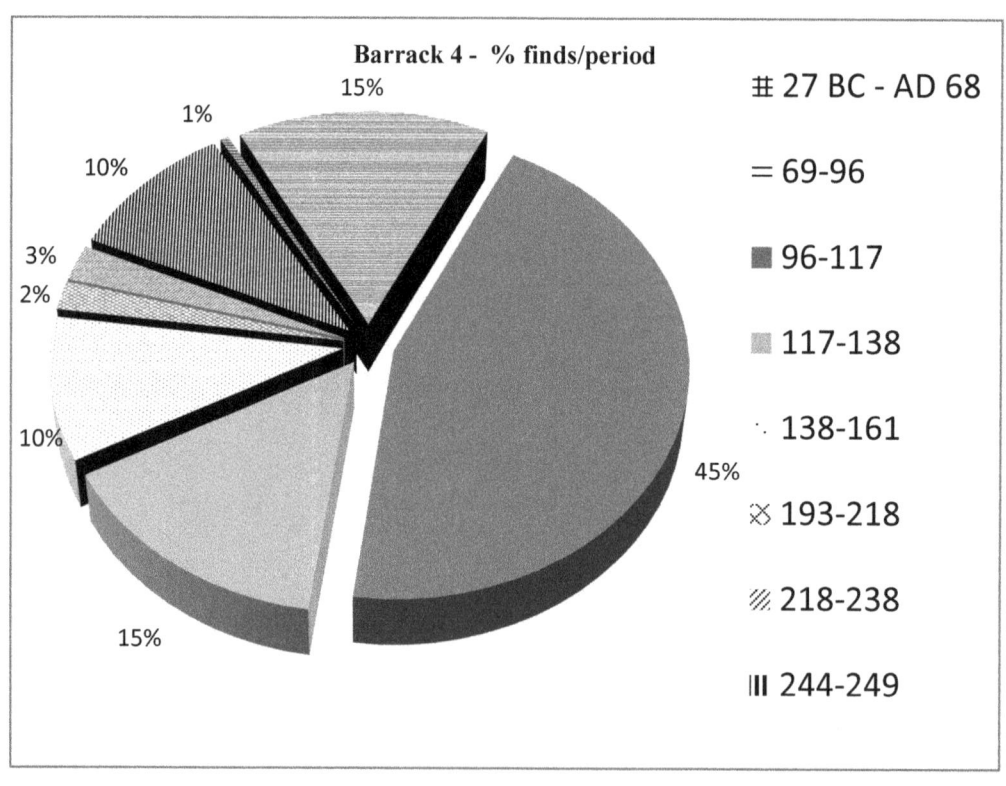

FIG. 6B. BARRACK 4 - % FINDS/PERIOD

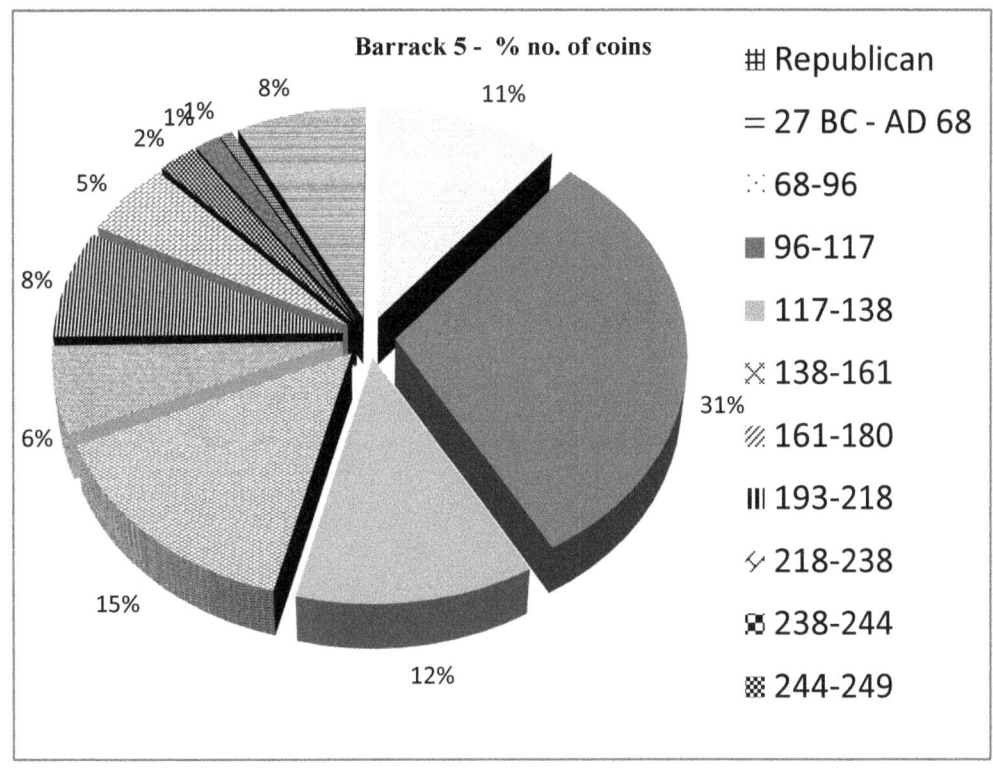

FIG. 7A. BARRACK 5 - % NO. OF COINS

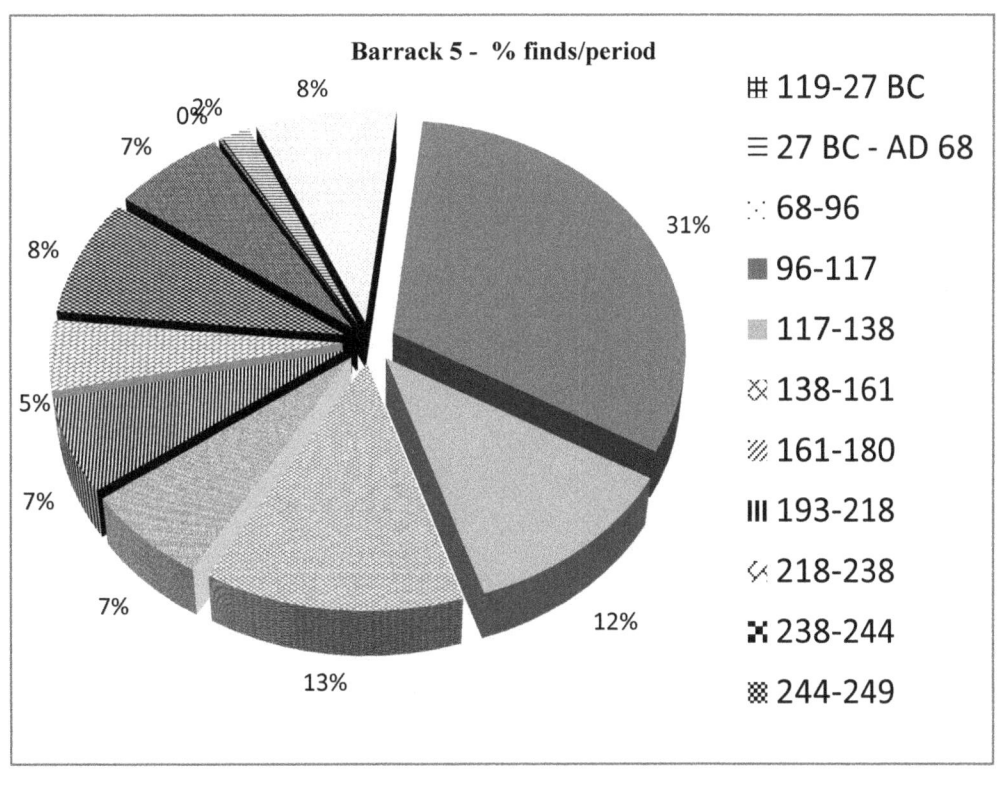

FIG. 7B. BARRACK 5 - % FINDS/PERIOD

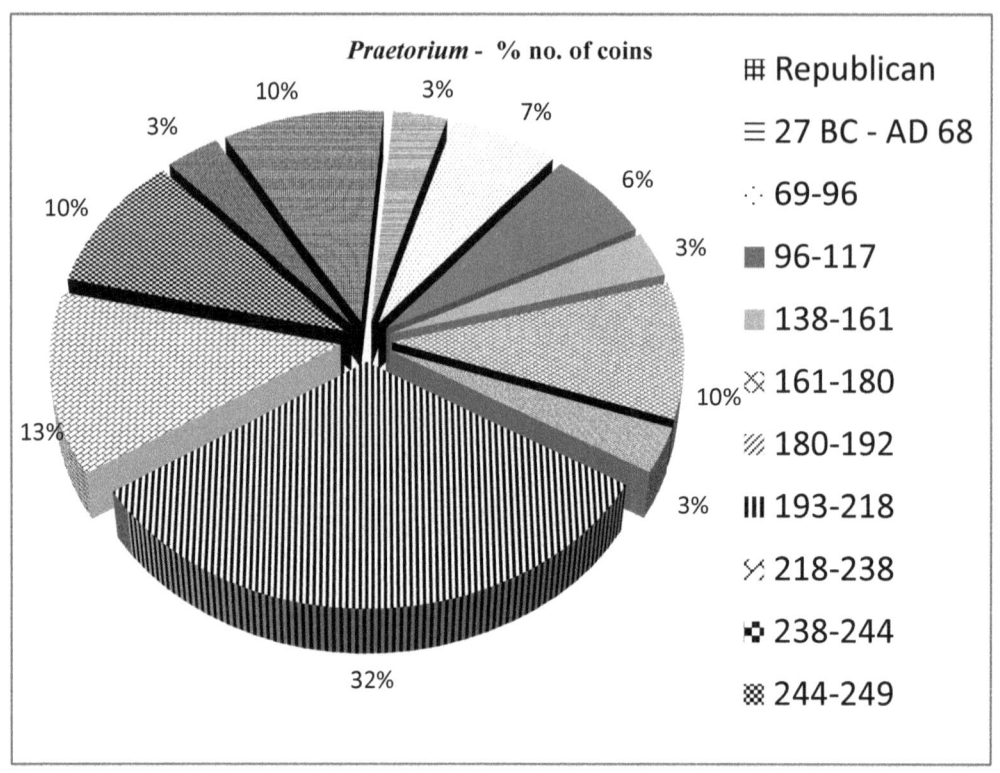

FIG. 8A. *PRAETORIUM* - % NO. OF COINS

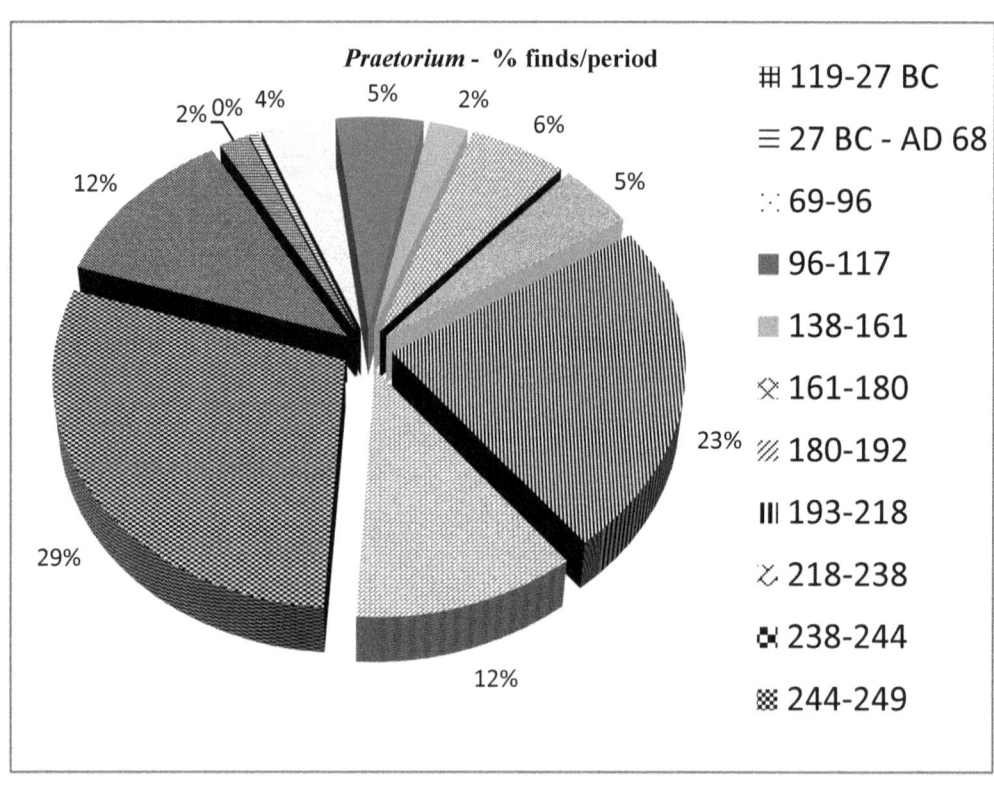

FIG. 8B. *PRAETORIUM* - % FINDS/PERIOD

The Roman Auxiliary Fort at Buciumi (Roman Dacia, Romania): Coins in archaeological context

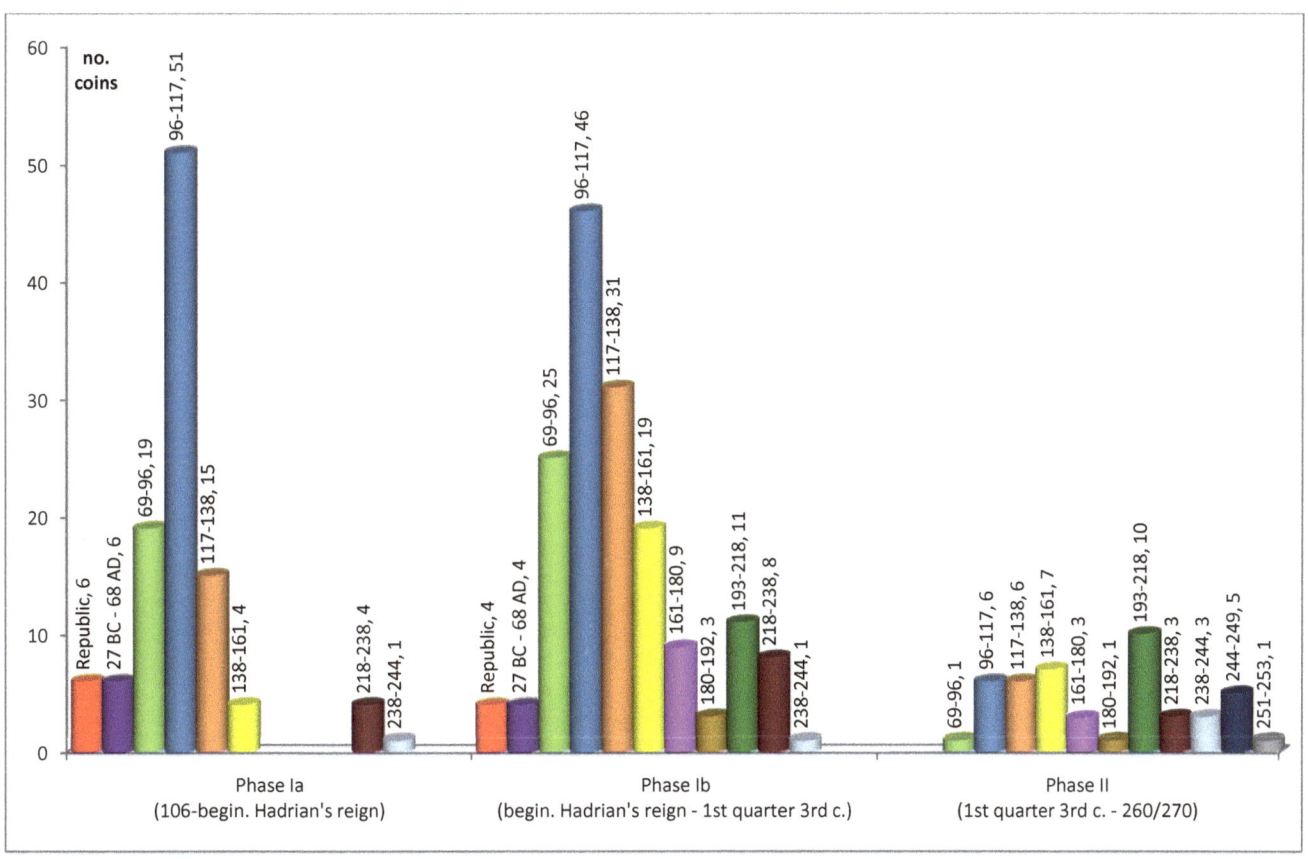

Fig. 9. Graph of the coin finds by phases for the auxiliary fort of Buciumi

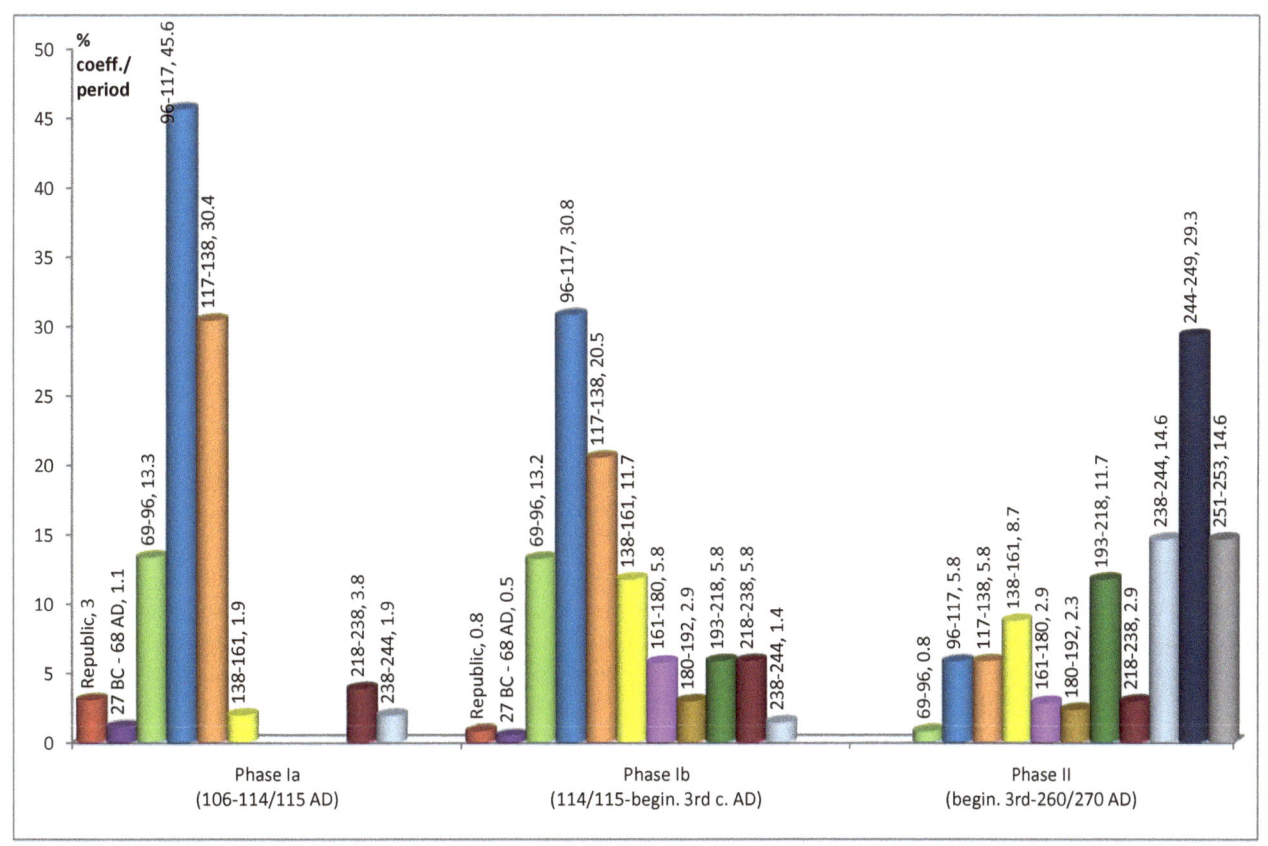

Fig. 10. Graph of the single coin finds by phases and periods for the auxiliary fort from Buciumi

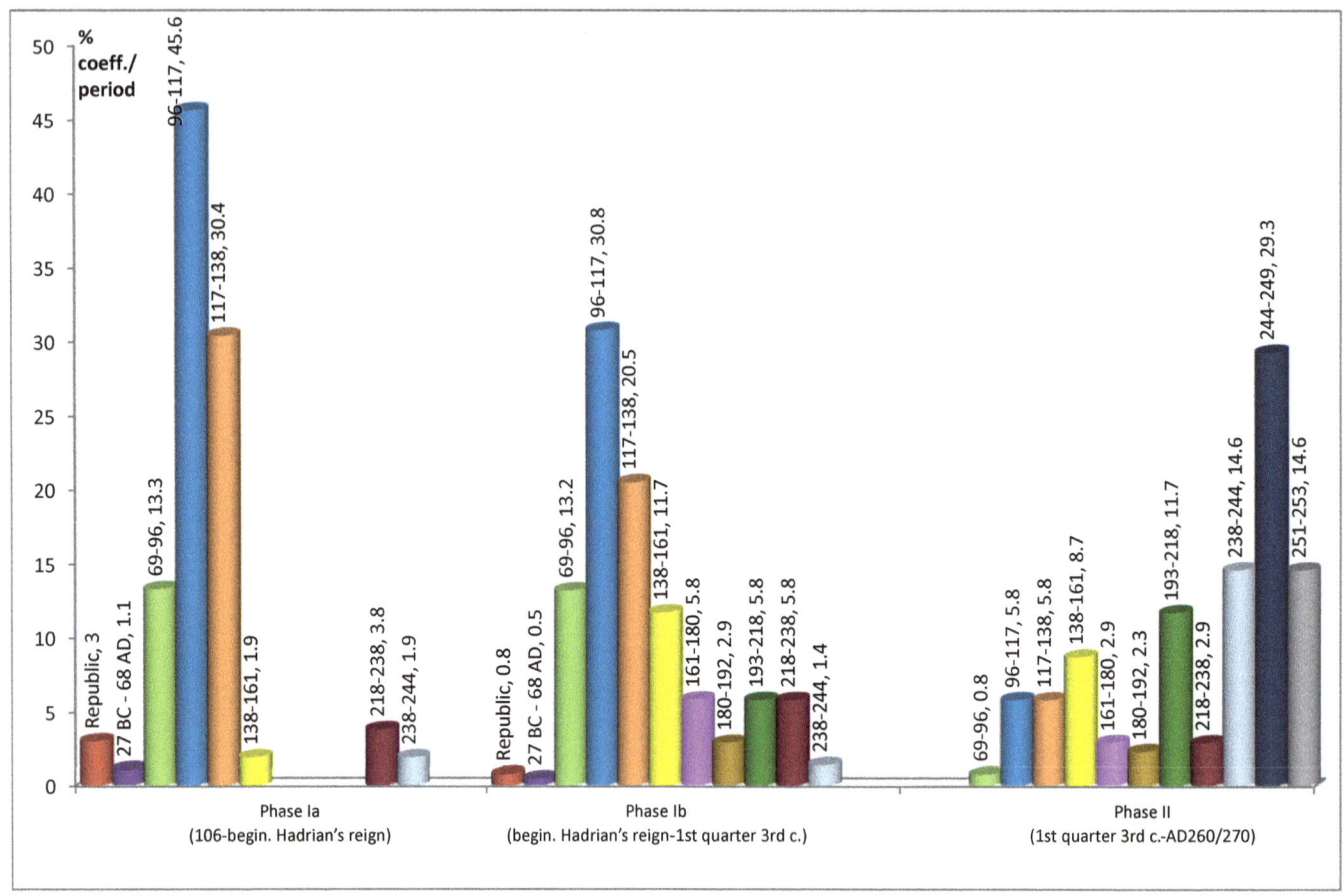

FIG. 11. GRAPH OF THE PERCENTAGE OF THE COEFFICIENT/PERIOD BY PHASES FOR THE AUXILIARY FORT FROM BUCIUMI

circulation – it is a common pattern for Roman Dacia[57], still, there are some aspects that must be discussed.

Firstly, for a phase that has been considered to end around AD 114/115[58] there is a large number of Hadrian's coins found in the layers of this phase – 15 coins, and 30.4% of the coefficient/period for this phase (catalogue, figs. 9-11). Except for two coins of Hadrian issued after AD 122 (catalogue nos. 269, 273) the other ones found in the Phase Ia layers were minted in the period of AD 119-122 (see catalogue, Hadrian).

It has been demonstrated that the frequency of coin loss increased during the times of construction/demolishing activities[59].

This situation may indicate that in fact the building phase Ib may have started only at the beginning of the Hadrian's reign. This hypothesis may also leads us to reconsider the date of arrival (AD 114) of the *cohors II Augusta Nervia Brittonum Pacensis* – the unit that has been considered as the one that reorganized the fort from Buciumi in phase Ib[60]. If we agree that the phase Ib started only with the first years of Hadrian's reign then the old theory that this unit came to Dacia in the time of Hadrian may be valid again[61]. At the moment the first mention of this unit in Dacia is the military diploma dated AD 126[62].

The second particularity of this coin spectrum of phase Ia aspect is one of methodological nature which shows the precariousness character of the method of establishing a general rule about dating phases by depth measurement. Whenever the first phase of this fort ends (either AD 114/115 or the beginning of Hadrian's reign) coins of later emperors (Antoninus Pius) or even much later ones (Elagabalus, Severus Alexander and Gordian III) (catalogue, figs 9-11) cannot belong to this phase. Their presence in this phase may be a consequence of multiple reasons: the terrain configuration, measurement error, writing mistake, etc.

The numismatic spectrum of phase Ib indicates a dominance of Trajan's coins, a consequence of strong injection with coins into a new province together with the army payment and the building of the fort of Buciumi. The strong increase of Hadrian's coins as well as those of the next emperors is a normal aspect for a phase mainly covering the 2nd century AD.

The only 'anomaly' for this phase, considered by scholars to end at the beginning of the 3rd century AD, is the large

---

[57] GĂZDAC 2008, 272-273; GĂZDAC 2010, CD, Tab. F1-12, K1-9.
[58] GUDEA 1997, 27.
[59] REECE 1986, 103.
[60] GUDEA 1997, 31.

[61] For the bibliography on this subject see GUDEA 1997, 31.
[62] GUDEA 1997, 31.

presence of coins issued in the period of AD 218-244. One may consider the 1 coin of Gordian III assigned to this phase – following the depth measurement and the synchronization with the general scheme – as a measurement error. Still, there are 8 coins issued in the period of AD 218-238, and a percentage of coefficient/period similar to other issuers assigned, for certain, to this phase Ib. This aspect may suggest that this phase Ib may be prolonged, in fact, to the first quarter of the 3rd century AD (catalogue, figs. 9-11).

The phase II, the last one, presents the similar patterns for the numismatic picture as the majority of the sites – civilian and military – from Roman Dacia, a province already in troubles after AD 260[63]. The number of coins is much lower compared to the other two phases with no items from the issuers when Dacia is has been still considered as part of the Roman Empire (Valerianus I – Aurelian ?) (catalogue, figs. 9-11).

At this stage of research we can suggest the following chronological segments for the three main phases of the auxiliary fort from Buciumi:

Phase Ia: AD 106 – the beginning of Hadrian's reign
Phase Ib: the beginning of Hadrian's reign – 1st quarter of the 3rd century AD
Phase II: 1st quarter of the 3rd century AD – AD 260/270

Still, as it has been pointed out by other scholars, these are the main phases. Some of the edifices show traces of intermediary phases (e.g. *principia, praetorium*, etc.)[64].

There is another aspect that may point out a specific pattern of the coin finds from this auxiliary fort and, at the same time, could help for a better understanding of the meaning of a numismatic spectrum.

The arrangements of numismatic evidence by findspots/edifices with a higher coin frequency – the barracks and the *praetorium* – indicate the dominance of Trajan's coins followed by those of Hadrian. A normal pattern considering the moment of the beginning of the existence of this fort and the changes in planning produced at the end of Trajan's or the early years of Hadrian's reign (tabs. 2-5, figs. 4a-7b).

A specific pattern comes from the numismatic spectrum for the *praetorium*. In this case the percentages indicate a dominance of the coins issued after AD 193 up to the reign of Philip I (AD 244-249) (tab. 6, figs. 8a-8b). The explanation consists in the historical background and the research method of this edifice. During all the phases this building was placed on the same location and the excavations, despite the fact that they revealed previous phases, were not able to provide us with the information on the presence or absence of various changes of the architecture[65]. Reading in details the archaeological reports we reached the conclusion that, in fact, the excavations at the *praetorium* were focused on unveiling areas than going deeper, mainly unveiling the last phase of existence together with the late additions to this edifice[66].

Thus, the numismatic spectrum of the *praetorium* is a consequence of the methodology of archaeological excavations applied to this findspot.

---

[63] GĂZDAC 2010, 163, 165-167, 170, 191-192, 198-200.
[64] GUDEA 1997, 61; MARCU 2009, 38-42.
[65] BUCIUMI 1972, 30; GUDEA 1997, 48-49; MARCU 2009, 41-42.
[66] BUCIUMI 1972, 27-31; GUDEA 1997, 49; MARCU 2009, 42.

TABLES 2-6. COIN FINDS BY FEATURE

Tab.2. Barrack 1

PERIOD OF MINTING	D	Ant	Plated/Copy	S	Dp	As	Cast	Prov. Issues	Semis	Qd	Total	finds/period
	No	No	No	No	No	No	No	No	No	No		
Republican	5										5	0.05
27 BC - AD 68						2					2	0.02
69-96	4		1		1	6	2	1			15	0.5
96-117	3				8	13	2	2	1	1	30	1.4
117-138	3		1	3		15	1				23	1
138-161			1	2	1	3		1			8	0.3
161-180				1	1	1					3	0.1
180-192				2							2	0.1
193-218	4		6								10	0.4
218-238	4		4								8	0.4
238-244		1									1	0.1
244-249			1								1	0.2
251-253			1								1	0.5
TOTAL	23	1	15	8	11	40	5	4	1	1.0	109	5.07

Tab. 3. Barrack 2

PERIOD OF MINTING	D	Plated/ Copy	S	Dp	As	Cast	Prov. Issues	Qd	Total	finds/ period
	No	No	No	No	No	No	No	No		
Republican	3						1		4	0.04
27 BC - AD 68					1				1	0.01
69-96	2	1			2	1			6	0.2
96-117	3	2	5	3	18			1	32	1.5
117-138			1	1	7		1		10	0.5
138-161	1	2	1				1		5	0.2
180-192		1							1	0.08
193-218		1							1	0.04
218-238	2	1							3	0.1
238-244	1								1	0.1
TOTAL	12	8	7	4	28	1	3	1	64	2.77

Tab. 4. Barrack 4

PERIOD OF MINTING	D	Plated/ Copy	S	Dp	As	Cast	Total	finds/ period
	No	No	No	No	No	No		
27 BC - AD 68					1		1	0.01
69-96	3	1	1		6		11	0.3
96-117	3	1	1	4	10	1	20	0.9
117-138			3		5		8	0.3
138-161	1		2	1	1		5	0.2
193-218	1						1	0.04
218-238	1						1	0.05
244-249			1				1	0.2
TOTAL	9	2	8	5	23	1	48	2

Tab. 5. Barrack 5

PERIOD OF MINTING	Au	D	Ant	Plated/	S	Dp	As	Prov. Issues	Total	finds/ period
	No	No	No	No	No	No	No	No		
Republican		1							1	0.01
27 BC - AD 68						1	8	1	10	0.1
69-96	1	2		3	1		7		14	0.5
96-117		5		2	7	7	19		40	1.9
117-138					1		14	1	16	0.7
138-161		4		1	5	3	6		19	0.8
161-180		2		4	2				8	0.4
193-218		3		7					10	0.4
218-238		7							7	0.3
238-244			1	2					3	0.5
244-249			1	1					2	0.4
TOTAL	1	24	2	20	16	11	54	2	130	6.01

Tab. 6. *Praetorium*

PERIOD OF MINTING	D	Ant	Plated/ Copy	S	Dp	As	Prov. Issues	Total	finds/ period
	No	No	No	No	No	No	No		
Republican	3							3	0.03
27 BC - AD 68						1		1	0.01
69-96				1		1		2	0.07
96-117			1		1			2	0.09
138-161			1					1	0.04
161-180			1	1			1	3	0.1
180-192	1							1	0.08
193-218	2		8					10	0.4
218-238	4							4	0.2
238-244		1	1	1				3	0.5
244-249		1						1	0.2
TOTAL	10	2	12	3	1	2	1	31	1.72

Coin finds from archaeological excavations

ROMAN REPUBLICAN COINS

M. FOURIUS L. F. PHILUS (Pl. I, 1)
1. Denomination: denarius
Axis: 6; D: 19 x 17.9 mm; W: 3.4 g.
Mint: Rome
Dating: 119 BC
Obv: Laureate head of Janus; M•FO[uri•l•]F around.
Rv: Roma standing left erecting trophy, Gallic arms around.
Reference: RRC, 281/1.
Findspot: 1970, barrack 5, excavated ground.
Inv. No: c.c. 32/1970.
BUCIUMI 1972, no. 1

D. SILANUS L. f. (Pl. I, 2)
2. Denomination: denarius
Axis: 2; D: 18.3 x 17.1 mm; W: 3.2 g.
Mint: Rome
Dating: 91 BC
Obv: Helmeted head of Roma, right; behind, control-mark.
Rv: Victory in biga right, holding reins in both hands; in exergue, D • SILAN[us l f]/ ROMA.
Reference: RRC, 337/3.
Findspot: 1973, barrack 2, -1 m; phase Ia.
Inv. No: c.c. 157/1973.

MN. CORDIUS (Pl. I, 3)
3. Denomination: denarius
Axis: 5; D: 17.6 x 16.2 mm; W: 3.6 g.
Mint: Rome
Dating: 46 BC
Obv: Jugate heads of Dioscuri right, wearing pilei, around RVFVS IIIVIR
Rv: Venus standing left. Holding scales in right hand sceptre in left hand; behind ...CORDIVS.
Reference: RRC, 463/1a.
Findspot: 1964, *praetorium*, room G, excavated ground.
Inv. No: c.c. 79/1964.
BUCIUMI 1972, no. 2

MARCUS ANTONIUS
4. Denomination: denarius
Axis: 6; D: 17.2 x 15.7 mm; W: 3.1 g.
Mint: Itinerant mint
Dating: 32-31 BC
Obv: ...IIIVIR R P C...
Galley, right.
Rv: [leg] - XIII
Silhouettes of the standards.
Reference: RRC, 544/27.
Findspot: 1970, barrack 3, -0.70 m; phase Ib.
Inv. No: c.c. 60/1970.
BUCIUMI 1972, no. 5

MARCUS ANTONIUS
5. Denomination: denarius
Axis: 11; D: 17 mm; W: 2.8 g.
Mint: Itinerant mint
Dating: 32-31 BC
Obv: ...IIIVIR R P C
Vague silhouette of galley, right.
Rv: Silhouettes of the standards.
Reference: cf. RRC, 544.
Findspot: 1966, barrack 2.
Inv. No: c.c. 25/1966.
BUCIUMI 1972, no. 4

MARCUS ANTONIUS
6. Denomination: denarius
Axis: -; D: 17.6 x 15.6 mm; W: 2.9 g.
Mint: Itinerant mint
Dating: 32-31 BC
Obv: ...IIIVIR R P C
Galley, right.
Rv: erased.
Reference: cf. RRC, 544.
Findspot: 1974, barrack 2, trench 26, -1 m; phase Ia.
Inv. No: c.c. 35/1974.

MARCUS ANTONIUS
7. Denomination: denarius
Axis: 5; D: 17.7 x 16.5 mm; W: 2.6 g.
Mint: Itinerant mint
Dating: 32-31 BC
Obv: ...IIIVIR...
Vague silhouette of galley, right.
Rv: Silhouettes of the standards.
Reference: cf. RRC, 544.
Findspot: 1973, barrack 1, m 7, -0.80 m; phase Ib.
Inv. No: c.c. 112/1973.

MARCUS ANTONIUS
8. Denomination: denarius
Axis: 7; D: 16.7 mm; W: 2.5 g.
Mint: Itinerant mint
Dating: 32-31 BC
Obv: Legend erased.
Galley, right.
Rv: LEG...
Silhouettes of the standards.
Reference: cf. RRC, 544.
Findspot: 1973, barrack 2, quadrant 40, -1.20 m; phase Ia.
Inv. No: c.c. 158/1973.

MARCUS ANTONIUS
9. Denomination: denarius
Axis: 6; D: 16.2 mm; W: 2.1 g.
Mint: Itinerant mint
Dating: 32-31 BC
Obv: Silhouette of galley, right.
Rv: Silhouette of eagle on standard.
Reference: cf. RRC, 544.
Findspot: 1968, barrack 5.
Inv. No: c.c. 17/1968.
BUCIUMI 1972, no. 3

MARCUS ANTONIUS
10. Denomination: denarius
Axis: 3; D: 17.4 x 15.3 mm; W: 2.7 g.
Mint: Itinerant mint
Dating: 32-31 BC
Obv: Vague silhouette of galley, right.
Rv: Vague silhouette of one of the standards.
Reference: cf. RRC, 544.
Findspot: 1964, *praetorium*, room G, -1 m; phase Ia.
Inv. No: c.c. 80/1964.
BUCIUMI 1972, p. 26; no. 6

MARCUS ANTONIUS
11. Denomination: denarius
Axis: -; D: 17.1 x 15.5 mm; W: 2.5 g.
Mint: Itinerant mint
Dating: 32-31 BC
Obv: Vague silhouette of galley, right.
Rv: erased.
Reference: cf. RRC, 544.
Findspot: 1968, *praetorium*, excavated ground.
Inv. No: c.c. 7/1968.
BUCIUMI 1972, no. 7

MARCUS ANTONIUS
12. Denomination: denarius
Axis: -; D: 17.5 mm; W: 3 g.
Mint: Itinerant mint
Dating: 32-31 BC
Obv: Galley, right.
Rv: erased.
Reference: cf. RRC, 544.
Findspot: 1973, barrack 1, m 3, -0.80 m; phase Ib.
Inv. No: c.c. 113/1973.

MARCUS ANTONIUS
13. Denomination: denarius
Axis: -; D: 19.6 x 16.4 mm; W: 2.4 g.
Mint: Itinerant mint
Dating: 32-31 BC
Obv: Galley, right.
Rv: erased.
Reference: cf. RRC, 544.
Findspot: 1997, *principia*, C1/97, m 6-7, room I, -0.72 m; phase Ib.
Inv. No: c.c. 88/2001.
BUCIUMI 2000, p. 346, no. 1 (but male head)

MARCUS ANTONIUS
14. Denomination: denarius
Axis: -; D: 15.5 mm; W: 2.3 g.
Mint: Itinerant mint
Dating: 32-31 BC
Obv: erased.
Rv: Two of the three standards.
Reference: cf. RRC, 544.
Findspot: 1971, barrack 1, excavated ground.
Inv. No: c.c. 71/1971.

MARCUS ANTONIUS
15. Denomination: denarius
Axis: -; D: 17.1 mm; W: 2.4 g.
Mint: Itinerant mint
Dating: 32-31 BC
Obv: erased.
Rv: One of the three standards.
Reference: cf. RRC, 544.
Findspot: 1973, barrack 1, m 18.80/5.80, -0.90 m; phase Ia.
Inv. No: c.c. 98/1973.

MARCUS ANTONIUS & OCTAVIANUS
16. Denomination: ½ as, provincial
Axis: 12; D: 19.3 mm; W: 5.9 g.
Mint: Thessalonica Macedoniae
Dating: 37 BC
Obv: Legend erased.
    Damaged head of Homonoia, right
Rv: [ΘΕΣ]ΣΑΛ[ΟΝ] ΡΩ[Μ]
    Horse galloping right.
Reference: RPC I, 1553.
Findspot: 1972, barrack 2, -0.90 m; phase Ia.
Inv. No: c.c. 370/1972.

ROMAN IMPERIAL COINS

AVGVSTVS
Moneyer: M. Maecilius Tullus
17. Denomination: as, half
Axis: 6; D: 25.2 mm; W: 5.5 g.
Mint: Rome
Dating: 7 BC
Obv: Legend erased.
    Augustus, head bare, left.
Rv: [m maec]ILIV[s tvllvs iii vir aaa f f], around large S C.
Reference: RIC I^2, 435
Findspot: 1970, barrack 5, the NE end of the inner barrack, -1.10 m; phase Ia.
Inv. No: c.c. 20/1970.
BUCIUMI 1972, no. 9

AVGVSTVS (Pl. I, 4)
18. Denomination: as
Axis: -; D: 25.6 mm; W: 7.5 g.
Mint: Rome
Dating: 27 BC – AD 9?
Obv: Legend erased.

Upper part oh head, right.
Countermarks: on left side, male draped bust, bare head in oval punch; on right side, countermark VAR(us).
Rv: erased.
Countermark: large wheel.
Reference: -
For the countermarks: VAR, Pangerl = MPC 52; large wheel Pangerl = MPC 38; male draped bust, similar to Howgego 125 (first half of the 2nd century AD?)
Findspot: 1969, barrack 5, -1.30 m; phase Ia.
Inv. No: c.c. 123/1969.
BUCIUMI 1972, no. 260

RHOEMETALKES I
19. Denomination: AE20
Axis: 12; D: 19.6 mm; W: 4.4 g.
Mint: Thrace
Dating: 11 BC – AD 12
Obv: Legend erased.
Head of Rhoemetalkes, right.
Rv: Head of Augustus, right
Reference: RPC I, 1718
Findspot: 1969, barrack 5, -1.10 m; phase Ia.
Inv. No: c.c. 116/1969.

TIBERIUS: Divus Augustus
20. Denomination: as
Axis: 6; D: 27.5 mm; W: 8.3 g.
Mint: Rome
Dating: AD 22-30
Obv: [divus augus]TVS P[ater]
Head bare, left.
Rv: S - C either side of large altar;
exergue: PROVIDENT
Reference: RIC I^2, 81
Findspot: 1964, *praetorium*, room J, -0.45 m; phase Ib.
Inv. No: c.c. 81/1964.
BUCIUMI 1972, no. 8

TIBERIUS: Divus Augustus
21. Denomination: as
Axis: -; D: 27.9 mm; W: 7.1 g.
Mint: Rome
Dating: AD 14 and later
Obv: [divus augus]TVS [pater]
Head bare, left.
Rv: Erased.
Reference: -
Findspot: 1973, barrack 1, m 7.5/2, -0.50 m; phase Ib.
Inv. No: c.c. 66/1973.

TIBERIUS: Divus Augustus
22. Denomination: as
Axis: -; D: 26.1 mm; W: 5.9 g.
Mint: Rome
Dating: AD 14 and later
Obv: Corroded.
Rv: S - C either side of large altar;
exergue: [pro]VID[ent]

Reference: cf. RIC I^2, 81
Findspot: 1976, fort area, stray find.
Inv. No: c.c. 159/1976.

CLAUDIUS I
23. Denomination: as
Axis: 7; D: 29.6 x 26.8 mm; W: 6.3 g.
Mint: Rome
Dating: AD 50-54
Obv: TI CLAVDIVS CAESAR AVG CAESAR AVG P M TR P IMP P P
Head bare, left.
Rv: Legend corroded; S – C
Vague silhouette of Constantia standing left, leaning on scepter.
Reference: RIC I^2, 111
Findspot: 1966, barrack 5.
Inv. No: c.c. 18/1966.
BUCIUMI 1972, no. 11

CLAUDIUS I
24. Denomination: as
Axis: -; D: 27.8 mm; W: 8.5 g.
Mint: Rome
Dating: AD 41-54
Obv: [ti claudiu]S CAESAR [aug caesar aug p m tr p] IM[p]
Head bare, left.
Rv: erased.
Reference: -
Findspot: 1969, barrack 5, -0.70 m; phase Ib.
Inv. No: c.c. 129/1969.
BUCIUMI 1972, no. 13 (but Nero)

CLAUDIUS I
25. Denomination: as
Axis: -; D: 28.8 x 26.3 mm; W: 9.2 g.
Mint: Rome
Dating: AD 41-54
Obv: [ti claudiu]S CAESAR AVG [aug caesar aug p m tr p imp]
Head bare, left.
Rv: erased.
Reference: -
Findspot: 1972, barrack 1, m 5-6/5-6, -0.60 m; ; phase Ib.
Inv. No: c.c. 22/1973.

CLAUDIUS I: Antonia (Pl. I, 5)
26. Denomination: dupondius
Axis: 7; D: 29.3 mm; W: 12.2 g.
Mint: Rome
Dating: AD 41-42
Obv: [antonia] – AVG[usta]
Bust draped, right; head bare, hair in long plait.
Countermark: on left side, N C A P R (Nerva Caesar Augustus Probavit).
Rv: [ti claudius] CAESAR AVG [p m t]R [p imp c]; S – C
Claudius, togate, standing left, holding simpulum.
Reference: RIC I^2, 92

For the countermark: most recently see MPC 20[67]
Findspot: 1969, barrack 5, -1.30 m; phase Ia.
Inv. No: c.c. 110/1969.
BUCIUMI 1972, no. 261 (but Tiberius)

NERO
27.   Denomination: as
Axis: 6; D: 22.4 mm; W: 3.7 g.
Mint: Rome
Dating: AD 65 or later
Obv: [nero claud ca]ESAR AVG GE[r p m tr p imp p p]
       Head laureate, right.
Rv: S – C
       Silhouette of Victory with shield to left.
Reference: RIC I^2, 314
Findspot: 1970, barrack 2, east side, excavated ground.
Inv. No: c.c. 8/1970.
BUCIUMI 1972, no. 15

NERO (Pl. I, 6)
28.   Denomination: as
Axis: 4; D: 28.6 x 27.4 mm; W: 6.7 g.
Mint: -
Dating: AD 65 or later
Obv: ИERO CLAVD CAESAR AVG G[er p m tr p imp p p]
       Head laureate, right.
Rv: S – C
       Vague silhouette of Victory with shield to left.
Reference: RIC I^2, 314
Findspot: 1969, barrack 5, -1 m; phase Ia.
Inv. No: c.c. 125/1969.
BUCIUMI 1972, no. 12
Remark: Ancient fake, the N from Nero spelt in reverse.

Julio-Claudian dynasty?
29.   Denomination: as
Axis: -; D: 26.1 mm; W: 4.2 g.
Mint: -
Dating: 1st half of the 1st c. AD
Obv: Legend erased.
       Vague silhouette of head, left.
Rv: erased.
Reference: -
Findspot: 1966, barrack 5.
Inv. No: c.c. 34/1966.
BUCIUMI 1972, no. 16 (but Nero semis)

Julio-Claudian dynasty?
30.   Denomination: as
Axis: -; D: 27.5 x 25.8 mm; W: 9.7 g.
Mint: -
Dating: 1st half of the 1st c. AD
Obv: Legend erased.
       Vague silhouette of head, left.
Rv: erased.
Reference: -
Findspot: 1970, barrack 4, -1.20 m; phase Ia.
Inv. No: c.c. 64/1970.
BUCIUMI 1972, no. 262

Julio-Claudian dynasty?
31.   Denomination: as
Axis: -; D: 26.3 x 23.9 mm; W: 6.1 g.
Mint: -
Dating: 1st half of the 1st c. AD
Obv: Legend erased.
       Vague silhouette of head, right.
Rv: erased.
Reference: -
Findspot: 1966, barrack 5.
Inv. No: c.c. 20/1966.
BUCIUMI 1972, no. 264

Julio-Claudian dynasty?
32.   Denomination: as
Axis: -; D: 25.7 mm; W: 7.1 g.
Mint: -
Dating: 1st half of the 1st c. AD
Obv: Legend erased.
       Vague silhouette of head, left.
Rv: erased.
Reference: -
Findspot: 1966, barrack 5.
Inv. No: c.c. 29/1966.
BUCIUMI 1972, no. 261

GALBA
33.   Denomination: denarius, plated
Axis: 6; D: 18.3 mm; W: 2.2 g.
Mint: Rome
Dating: AD 68-69 or later
Obv: IMP SER [galba au]G
       Head laureate, right.
Rv: S P Q R/ OB / C S within laurel wreath
Reference: RIC I^2, 168
Findspot: 1968, barrack 5, m 30.
Inv. No: c.c. 209/1968.
BUCIUMI 1972, no. 17

VESPASIANUS (Pl. I, 7)
34.   Denomination: denarius
Axis: 6; D: 17.7 mm; W: 2.7 g.
Mint: Rome
Dating: AD 70
Obv: IMP CAESAR VESPASIANVS AVG
       Head laureate, right.
Rv: COS IT[er] TR POT
Pax seated left, holding branch and caduceus.
Reference: RIC II.1, 29
Findspot: 1965, near building 2 beneath the pavement near older wall; phase Ia.
Inv. No: c.c. 100/1965.
MUZEU 1968, no. 28; BUCIUMI 1972, p. 27; no. 23

---

[67] Martini Pangerl Collection, http://www.romancoins.info/CMK-Nero&later.html.

VESPASIANUS (Pl. I, 8)
35.	Denomination: denarius
Axis: 6; D: 18.1 x 17.4 mm; W: 2.9 g.
Mint: Rome
Dating: AD 70
Obv:	IMP CAESAR VESPASIANVS AVG
	Head laureate, right.
Rv:	COS IT-ER T-R POT
	Pax seated left, holding branch and caduceus.
Reference: RIC II.1, 29
Findspot: 1970, barrack 4, -1.10 m; phase Ia.
Inv. No: c.c. 53/1970.
BUCIUMI 1972, no. 24

VESPASIANUS (Pl. I, 9)
36.	Denomination: denarius
Axis: 6; D: 17.6 x 16.5 mm; W: 2.9 g.
Mint: Rome
Dating: AD 70
Obv:	IMP CAESAR VESPASIANVS AVG
	Head laureate, right.
Rv:	[cos iter] TR POT
	Pax seated left, holding branch and caduceus.
Reference: RIC II.1, 29
Findspot: 1973, barrack 1, m 3/3, -0.50 m; phase Ib.
Inv. No: c.c. 68/1973.

VESPASIANUS (Pl. I, 10)
37.	Denomination: denarius
Axis: 6; D: 17.7 mm; W: 3 g.
Mint: Rome
Dating: AD 71
Obv:	IMP CAE VE-SP AVG P M
	Head laureate, right.
Rv:	in field: TRI - POT
	Vesta seated left, holding simpulum.
Reference: RIC II.1, 46
Findspot: 1970, barrack 5, excavated ground.
Inv. No: c.c. 26/1970.
BUCIUMI 1972, no. 22

VESPASIANUS (Pl. I, 11)
38.	Denomination: denarius
Axis: 6; D: 18.1 mm; W: 3 g.
Mint: Rome
Dating: AD 72-73
Obv:	IMP CAES VESP AVG P M COS IIII
	Head laureate, right.
Rv:	VES – TA
	Vesta standing left, holding simpulum and scepter.
Reference: RIC II.1, 360
Findspot: 1970, barrack 4, -1.40 m; phase Ib.
Inv. No: c.c. 66/1970.
BUCIUMI 1972, no. 26

VESPASIANUS (Pl. I, 12)
39.	Denomination: aureus
Axis: 6; D: 18.8 mm; W: 6.1 g.
Mint: Rome
Dating: AD 73
Obv:	IMP CAES VESP AVG P M COS IIII CEN
	Head laureate, right.
Rv: PAX – AVG
	Pax standing left, leaning on column with caduceus over tripod and branch.
Reference: RIC II.1, 521
Findspot: 1968, barrack 5, -0.80 m; phase Ib.
Inv. No: c.c. 33/1968.
BUCIUMI 1972, no. 19

VESPASIANUS (Pl. I, 13)
40.	Denomination: denarius
Axis: 12; D: 20.2 x 17.2 mm; W: 2.8 g.
Mint: Rome
Dating: AD 73
Obv: IMP CAES VESP - AVG CENS ∩
	Head laureate, right.
Rv: PONTIF – MAXIM ∩
Vespasian seated right, holding scepter and branch.
Reference: RIC II.1, 546
Findspot: 1965, barrack 5, -0.80 m; phase Ib.
Inv. No: c.c. 9/1965.
MUZEU 1968, no. 24; BUCIUMI 1972, no. 25

VESPASIANUS
41.	Denomination: denarius, plated
Axis: 11; D: 19.7 x 18 mm; W: 2 g.
Mint: -
Dating: AD 73 or later
Obv:	[imp] CAES VESP - AVG CENS ∩
	Head laureate, right.
Rv:	PONTIF – MAXIM ∩
	Vespasian seated right, holding scepter and branch.
Reference: cf. RIC II.1, 546
Findspot: 1969, barrack 5, excavated ground.
Inv. No: c.c. 102/1969.
BUCIUMI 1972, no. 21

VESPASIANUS (Pl. I, 14)
42.	Denomination: denarius
Axis: 6; D: 18.4 x 16.6 mm; W: 2.6 g.
Mint: Rome
Dating: AD 74
Obv:	IMP CAES VESPASIANVS AVG ∩
	Head laureate, right.
Rv:	PONT MAX – TR P COS V ∩
	Caduceus, winged.
Reference: RIC II.1, 703
Findspot: 1976, fort area, excavated ground.
Inv. No: c.c. 167/1976.

VESPASIANUS
43.	Denomination: denarius, plated
Axis: -; D: 18.4 x 17.4 mm; W: 3.3 g.
Mint: Rome
Dating: AD 74
Obv:	IMP [caes vesp aug] COS V CENS ∩
	Head laureate, right.
Rv:	erased.
Reference: -

Findspot: 1966, *porta praetoria*, E tower, -0.80 m; phase Ib.
Inv. No: c.c. 39/1966.
BUCIUMI 1972, p. 19; no. 27

VESPASIANUS (Pl. I, 15)
44.   Denomination: denarius
Axis: 6; D: 18.3 x 17.2 mm; W: 2.8 g.
Mint: Rome
Dating: AD 75
Obv: IMP CAESAR - VESPASIANVS AVG ↷
       Head laureate, right.
Rv: [pon] MAX – TR P [c]OS VI
       Victory standing left on prow of ship, holding wreath and palm.
Reference: RIC II.1, 777
Findspot: 1970, barrack 4, -0.60 m; phase Ib.
Inv. No: c.c. 58/1970.
BUCIUMI 1972, no. 28

VESPASIANUS (Pl. I, 16)
45.   Denomination: denarius
Axis: 6; D: 18.4 x 15.9 mm; W: 3.1 g.
Mint: Rome
Dating: AD 76
Obv: IMP CAESAR – VESPASIANVS [aug]
       Head laureate, right.
Rv: COS – VI[i]
       Eagle standing on an altar, head left.
Reference: RIC II.1, 847
Findspot: 1971, barrack 1, -0.50 m; phase Ib.
Inv. No: c.c. 24/1971.

VESPASIANUS
46.   Denomination: as
Axis: 6; D: 26.3 x 25.2 mm; W: 8.5 g.
Mint: Rome
Dating: AD 76
Obv: [imp ca]ES VESP AVG P M [t p co]S VII
       Head radiate, right.
Rv: FELICI[tas public]A; S - C
       Felicitas standing left, holding caduceus and cornucopiae.
Reference: RIC II.1, 887
Findspot: 1972, barrack 1, -0.80 m; phase Ib.
Inv. No: c.c. 348/1972.

VESPASIANUS (Pl. I, 17)
47.   Denomination: denarius
Axis: 6; D: 18.7 x 17.4 mm; W: 2.8 g.
Mint: Rome
Dating: AD 77-78
Obv: CAESAR – [ve]SPASIANVS AVG ↷
       Head laureate, right.
Rv: ANNONA - AVG
       Annona seated left holding bundle of corn ears in her lap.
Reference: RIC II.1, 964
Findspot: 1973, barrack 1, m 42/3.50, -0.40 m; phase Ib.
Inv. No: c.c. 52/1973.

VESPASIANUS
48.   Denomination: as
Axis: 6; D: 25.8 x 24.2 mm; W: 7.8 g.
Mint: Rome
Dating: AD 77-78
Obv: IMP CAES V[espasian aug cos viii p p]
       Head laureate, right.
Rv: S – C
       Large altar.
Reference: cf. RIC II.1, 1234
Findspot: 1968, barrack 5, -1 m; phase Ia.
Inv. No: c.c. 40/1968.
BUCIUMI 1972, no. 31

VESPASIANUS
49.   Denomination: sestertius
Axis: -; D: 33.5 mm; W: 23.4 g.
Mint: Rome
Dating: AD 69-79
Obv: Legend erased.
       Silhouette of head, left.
Rv: erased.
Reference: -
Findspot: 1970, barrack 4, -1.20 m; phase Ia.
Inv. No: c.c. 63/1970.
BUCIUMI 1972, no. 44 (but Domitian)

VESPASIANUS
50.   Denomination: as
Axis: 6; D: 27.1x 25.1 mm; W: 8.7 g.
Mint: Rome
Dating: AD 69-79
Obv: [imp caes]AR VESPASIAN[…]
       Head bare, right.
Rv: erased.
Reference: -
Findspot: 1972, barrack 2, -1 m; phase Ia.
Inv. No: c.c. 366/1972.

VESPASIANUS
51.   Denomination: as
Axis: -; D: 25.8 mm; W: 7.2 g.
Mint: Rome
Dating: AD 69-79
Obv: […v]ESP AVG […]
       Silhouette of head, left.
Rv: erased.
Reference: -
Findspot: 1971, barrack 1, -0.40 m; phase Ib.
Inv. No: c.c. 29/1971.

VESPASIANUS
52.   Denomination: as
Axis: -; D: 26.4 mm; W: 7.6 g.
Mint: Rome
Dating: AD 69-79
Obv: Legend erased.
       Silhouette of head, right.
Rv: erased.
Reference: -

Findspot: 1970, barrack 4, -0.30 m; phase Ib.
Inv. No: c.c. 44/1970.
BUCIUMI 1972, no. 42 (but Domitian)

VESPASIANUS
53. Denomination: as
Axis: 6; D: 25.2 mm; W: 6 g.
Mint: Rome
Dating: AD 69-79
Obv: Legend erased.
 Silhouette of head, left.
Rv: Legend erased.
 Silhouette standing.
Reference: -
Findspot: 1970, barrack 4, -1.20 m; phase Ia.
Inv. No: c.c. 76/1970.

VESPASIANUS
54. Denomination: as
Axis: 6; D: 27.6 mm; W: 10.7 g.
Mint: Rome
Dating: AD 69-79
Obv: Legend erased.
 Silhouette of head, right.
Rv: Legend erased.
 Silhouette standing, holding sceptre.
Reference: -
Findspot: 1973, barrack 1, m 26/3, -0.85 m; phase Ia.
Inv. No: c.c. 56/1973.

VESPASIANUS
55. Denomination: as
Axis: 6; D: 26.2 mm; W: 8.3 g.
Mint: Rome
Dating: AD 69-79
Obv: Legend erased.
 Silhouette of head, right.
Rv: Legend erased.
 Silhouette standing.
Reference: -
Findspot: 1976, fort area, stray find.
Inv. No: c.c. 158/1976.

VESPASIANUS
56. Denomination: as/dupondius
Axis: -; D: 28.5 mm; W: 11.1 g.
Mint: Rome
Dating: AD 69-79
Obv: […cae]S VE[sp…]
 Vague silhouette of head, left.
Rv: erased.
Reference: -
Findspot: 1971, barrack 1, -0.60 m; phase Ib.
Inv. No: c.c. 31/1971.

VESPASIANUS: Titus (Caesar)
57. Denomination: as
Axis: 6; D: 26.2 mm; W: 7.3 g.
Mint: Rome
Dating: AD 72-73

Obv: [t caesar vespa]SIAN IMP IIII PON TR POT II COS II
 Head laureate, right.
Rv: F[id]ES - PVBLICA
 exergue: S C
 Clasped hands holding caduceus and two wheat stalks.
Reference: RIC II.1, 507
Findspot: 1975, Building C 1, -0.70 m; phase Ib.
Inv. No: c.c. 40/1975.

TITUS (Pl. I, 18)
58. Denomination: denarius
Axis: 6; D: 17.3 mm; W: 3.1 g.
Mint: Rome
Dating: AD 80
Obv: IMP TITVS CAES VESPASIAN AVG P M ↷
 Head laureate, right.
Rv: TR P IX IMP XV – [co]S VIII P P
 Dolphin coiled around an anchor.
Reference: RIC II.1, 112
Findspot: 1965, barrack 1, -0.80 m; phase Ib.
Inv. No: c.c. 5/1965.
MUZEU 1968, no. 29; BUCIUMI 1972, no. 32 (but barrack 5)

TITUS: Divus Vespasianus (Pl. II, 1)
59. Denomination: denarius
Axis: 6; D: 16.5 mm; W: 2.6 g.
Mint: Rome
Dating: AD 80-81
Obv: DIVVS AVGVSTVS VESPASIANVS ↷
 Head laureate, right.
Rv: S C inscribed on shield supported by two Capricorns, orb with crosshatching below.
Reference: RIC II.1, 357
Findspot: 1965, trench following the N wall near *via principalis*, m 23.60 towards NE, -0.70 m; phase Ib.
Inv. No: c.c. 106/1965.
MUZEU 1968, no. 25; BUCIUMI 1972, no. 30

TITUS: Divus Vespasianus
60. Denomination: denarius
Axis: ?; D: ?; W: 3.1 g.
Mint: Rome
Dating: AD 80-81
Obv: DIVVS AVGVSTVS VESPASIANVS ↷
 Head laureate, right.
Rv: EX - S C
 Victory standing left, holding shield on palm; seated captive.
Reference: RIC II.1, 364
Findspot: fort area
Inv. No: c.c. ?
BUCIUMI 1972, no. 29

TITUS: Domitianus (Caesar)
61. Denomination: denarius
Axis: 6; D: 17.9 x 16.3 mm; W: 2.9 g.
Mint: Rome

Dating: AD 79
Obv: CAESAR AVG F DOMITIANVS COS V[i] ↷
Head laureate, right.
Rv: PRINCE[ps] - IVENTVTIS
Vesta seated left, holding palladium and scepter.
Reference: RIC II.1, 334b
Findspot: 1964, trench XIII, m 32, excavated ground.
Inv. No: c.c. 12/1964.
BUCIUMI 1972, no. 33

TITUS: Domitianus (Caesar)
62. Denomination: as
Axis: -; D: 26.9 x 24.3 mm; W: 7.1 g.
Mint: Rome
Dating: AD 80-81
Obv: [caes divi] VESP F DOMIT[ian]…
Silhouette of head, right.
Rv: erased.
Reference: -
Findspot: 1970, barrack 4, -0.60 m; phase Ib.
Inv. No: c.c. 61/1970.
BUCIUMI 1972, no. 36 (but dupondius)

DOMITIANUS
63. Denomination: as
Axis: 6; D: 26.5 mm; W: 9.6 g.
Mint: Rome
Dating: AD 85
Obv: IMP CAE[s do]MIT AVG GER[m] COS XI CENS POT P P
Head laureate, right.
Rv: MON[eta au]GVSTI; S – C
Moneta standing left, holding scales and cornucopiae.
Reference: RIC II.1, 384.
Findspot: 1966, barrack 5, near *via sagularis*, -1.60 m; phase Ia.
Inv. No: c.c. 30/1966.
BUCIUMI 1972, p. 22, no. 39

DOMITIANUS
64. Denomination: as
Axis: -; D: 27.2 mm; W: 9.1 g.
Mint: Rome
Dating: AD 87
Obv: …COS XIII CENS…
Head laureate, right.
Rv: erased.
Reference: -
Findspot: 1964, *praetorium*, room F, -0.45 m; phase Ib.
Inv. No: c.c. 75/1964.
BUCIUMI 1972, p. 26; no. 38

DOMITIANUS
65. Denomination: denarius, plated
Axis: 6; D: 19.5 x 18.2 mm; W: 3.4 g.
Mint: Rome
Dating: AD 90 or later
Obv: [imp caes d]OMIT [aug germ p m t]R P VIIII
Head laureate, right.
Rv: IMP XXI C[os xv] CENS P P P
Minerva standing left, holding spear & thunderbolt, shield resting against back of leg.
Reference: cf. RIC II.1, 691
Findspot: 1968, barrack 5.
Inv. No: c.c. 44/1968.
BUCIUMI 1972, no. 34

DOMITIANUS
66. Denomination: denarius, plated
Axis: 6; D: 26.3 x 24.4 mm; W: 9.5 g.
Mint: -
Dating: AD 90-91 or later
Obv: IMP CAES DOMITIAN AVG GERM [cos xv cens per p] P
Head laureate, right.
Rv: Legend corroded.
Virtus standing right, holding parazonium and sceptre, left foot on helmet.
Reference: cf. RIC II.1, 691
Findspot: 1970, barrack 4, -0.60 m; phase Ib.
Inv. No: c.c. 43/1970.
BUCIUMI 1972, no. 37

DOMITIANUS (Pl. II, 2)
67. Denomination: denarius
Axis: 6; D: 17.8 x 16.7 mm; W: 2.9 g.
Mint: Rome
Dating: AD 92-93
Obv: IMP CAES DOMIT AVG - GERM P M TR P XII
Head laureate, right.
Rv: IMP XXII COS XVI CENS P P P
Minerva standing right on capital of rostral column, holding spear and shield, owl at feet.
Reference: RIC II.1, 741
Findspot: 1973, barrack 2, *via sagularis*, m 47, -1.10 m; phase Ia.
Inv. No: c.c. 141/1973.

DOMITIANUS
68. Denomination: denarius, plated
Axis: 6; D: 17.7 mm; W: 2.5 g.
Mint: -
Dating: AD 92-93 or later
Obv: IMP [caes] DOMIT [aug ger]M P M TR P XII
Head laureate, right.
Rv: I MP XXII [cos xvi cen]S P P P
Minerva standing left, holding spear.
Reference: cf. RIC II.1, 742
Findspot: 1971, barrack 1, excavated ground.
Inv. No: c.c. 10/1971.

DOMITIANUS
69. Denomination: denarius, plated
Axis: 6; D: 18.3 mm; W: 1.6 g.
Mint: -
Dating: AD 94 or later
Obv: IMP CAES DOMIT AVG GERM P M TR P XIIII
Head laureate, right.
Rv: IMP XXII COS XVI CENS P P P

Minerva advancing right, brandishing a javelin and holding a shield.
Reference: RIC II.1, 766.
Findspot: 1973, barrack 2, -0.75 m; phase Ib.
Inv. No: c.c. 137/1973.

DOMITIANUS (Pl. II, 3)
70. Denomination: denarius
Axis: 6; D: 19.1 mm; W: 3.1 g.
Mint: Rome
Dating: AD 94
Obv: IMP CAES DOMIT AVG GERM P M TR P XIIII
    Head laureate, right.
Rv: IMP XXII COS XVII CENS P P P
    Minerva standing left holding spear.
Reference: RIC II.1, 769.
Findspot: 1972, barrack 2, -0.90 m; phase Ia.
Inv. No: c.c. 353/1972.
Remark: Found stuck to the coin inv. no. 354/1972.

DOMITIANUS
71. Denomination: as
Axis: 5; D: 27.1 mm; W: 9 g.
Mint: Rome
Dating: AD 85-94.
Obv: Legend erased.
    Head laureate, right.
Rv: VIRTV[ti augusti]; S - C
    Virtus standing right, foot on a helmet, holding spear and parazonium.
Reference: RIC II.1 – Domitian, type of *Virtuti Augusti*
Findspot: 1972, barrack 1, -0.75 m; phase Ib.
Inv. No: c.c. 349/1972.

DOMITIANUS
72. Denomination: sestertius
Axis: 6; D: 31.5 x 29.4 mm; W: 18.7 g.
Mint: Rome
Dating: AD 81-96
Obv: Legend erased.
    Head laureate, left.
Rv: Legend erased.
    Vagus silhouette standing left, holding cornucopiae.
Reference: -
Findspot: 1966, barrack 5, near *via sagularis*, -1.80 m; phase Ia.
Inv. No: c.c. 35/1966.
BUCIUMI 1972, no. 45

DOMITIANUS
73. Denomination: sestertius
Axis: -; D: 33.2 mm; W: 21.5 g.
Mint: Rome
Dating: AD 81-96
Obv: Legend erased.
    Head laureate, right.
Rv: Corroded.
Reference: -
Findspot: 1968, *praetorium*.
Inv. No: c.c. 6/1968.
BUCIUMI 1972, no. 43

DOMITIANUS
74. Denomination: dupondius
Axis: -; D: 26.2 mm; W: 8.2 g.
Mint: Rome
Dating: AD 81-96
Obv: Legend erased.
    Head radiate, right.
Rv: Corroded.
Reference: -
Findspot: 1973, barrack 1, m 2/5.50 m, -0.70 m; phase Ib.
Inv. No: c.c. 87/1973.

DOMITIANUS
75. Denomination: as
Axis: -; D: 27 x 26.1 mm; W: 7.5 g.
Mint: Rome
Dating: AD 81-96
Obv: Legend erased.
    Silhouette head, right.
Rv: Corroded.
Reference: -
Findspot: 1968, barrack 5.
Inv. No: c.c. 8/1968.
BUCIUMI 1972, no. 10 (but Claudius I)

DOMITIANUS
76. Denomination: as
Axis: 6; D: 27.6 mm; W: 8.5 g.
Mint: Rome
Dating: AD 81-96
Obv: Legend erased.
    Silhouette of head, right.
Rv: Vague silhouette standing.
Reference: -
Findspot: 1969, *porta principalis sinistra*, excavated ground.
Inv. No: c.c. 113/1969.
BUCIUMI 1972, no. 195 (but Commodus)

DOMITIANUS
77. Denomination: as
Axis: -; D: 26.2 mm; W: 8.4 g.
Mint: Rome
Dating: AD 81-96
Obv: Legend erased.
    Silhouette of head, right.
Rv: erased.
Reference: -
Findspot: 1969, barrack 5, -1.30 m; phase Ia.
Inv. No: c.c. 124/1969.
BUCIUMI 1972, no. 14 (but Nero)

DOMITIANUS
78. Denomination: as
Axis: -; D: 27.6 x 25.9 mm; W: 7.5 g.
Mint: Rome
Dating: AD 81-96
Obv: Legend erased.

Silhouette of head, right.
Rv: erased.
Reference: -
Findspot: 1969, barrack 5, -1.20 m; phase Ia.
Inv. No: c.c. 139/1969.
BUCIUMI 1972, no. 41

DOMITIANUS
79. Denomination: as
Axis: 7; D: 26.2 x 25.3 mm; W: 8.3 g.
Mint: Rome
Dating: AD 81-96
Obv: …[dom]ITIAN…
Silhouette of head, right.
Rv: Legend erased.
Female silhouette standing left, holding cornucopiae.
Reference: -
Findspot: 1970, barrack 4, -1 m; phase Ia.
Inv. No: c.c. 59/1970.
BUCIUMI 1972, no. 40 (but dupondius)

DOMITIANUS
80. Denomination: as
Axis: -; D: 23.6 mm; W: 6.3 g.
Mint: Rome
Dating: AD 81-96
Obv: Legend corroded.
Silhouette of head, right.
Rv: erased.
Reference: -
Findspot: 1970, barrack 4, -1.10 m; phase Ia.
Inv. No: c.c. 81/1970.
BUCIUMI 1972, no. 35

DOMITIANUS
81. Denomination: as
Axis: -; D: 25.7 mm; W: 8.6 g.
Mint: Rome
Dating: AD 81-96
Obv: Legend corroded.
Silhouette of head, right.
Rv: erased.
Reference: -
Findspot: 1970, barrack 4, -1.20 m; phase Ia.
Inv. No: c.c. 82/1970.

DOMITIANUS
82. Denomination: as, *cast*, fragmentary
Axis: 6; D: 23.1 mm; W: 5.1 g.
Mint: -
Dating: AD 81-96 or later
Obv: Legend unreadable.
Head laureate, right.
Rv: Legend unreadable; S – C.
Aequitas/Moneta standing left, holding scales and cornucopia.
Reference: -
Findspot: 1973, barrack 1, m 27-28/5-6, -0.90 m; phase Ia.
Inv. No: c.c. 101/1973.

DOMITIANUS
83. Denomination: as, *cast*
Axis: -; D: 26.9 mm; W: 7.8 g.
Mint: -
Dating: AD 81-96 or later
Obv: Legend corroded.
Silhouette of head, right.
Rv: erased.
Reference: -
Findspot: 1972, barrack 2, -0.90 m; phase Ia.
Inv. No: c.c. 364/1972.

DOMITIANUS
84. Denomination: as, *cast*, fragmentary
Axis: 6; D: 23.6 mm; W: 3.7 g.
Mint: -
Dating: AD 81-96 or later
Obv: Legend corroded.
Silhouette of head, right.
Rv: Legend erased; S – [c].
Silhouette standing.
Reference: -
Findspot: 1973, barrack 1, m 55.9/4, -1.10 m; phase Ia.
Inv. No: c.c. 63/1973.

DOMITIANUS?
85. Denomination: as
Axis: -; D: 27 mm; W: 11.6 g.
Mint: -
Dating: AD 81-96
Obv: Legend erased.
Vague silhouette of head, right.
Rv: Corroded.
Reference: -
Findspot: 1968, barrack 5, m 25, -0.80 m, near wall; phase Ib.
Inv. No: c.c. 37/1968.
BUCIUMI 1972, no. 18 (but Galba)

DOMITIANUS?
86. Denomination: as
Axis: -; D: 26.6 mm; W: 9 g.
Mint: -
Dating: AD 81-96
Obv: Legend corroded.
Silhouette of Domitian head, right.
Rv: erased.
Reference: -
Findspot: 1971, barrack 1, -0.30 m; phase II.
Inv. No: c.c. 20/1971.

DOMITIANUS?
87. Denomination: as
Axis: -; D: 27.8 x 26.6 mm; W: 8.2 g.
Mint: -
Dating: AD 81-96
Obv: Legend corroded.
Vague silhouette of Domitian head, right.
Rv: erased.
Reference: -

Findspot: 1973, barrack 2, -0.80 m; phase Ib.
Inv. No: c.c. 139/1973.

DOMITIANUS?
88. Denomination: as
Axis: -; D: 26 mm; W: 6.3 g.
Mint: -
Dating: AD 81-96
Obv: Legend corroded.
Vague silhouette of Domitian head, right.
Rv: erased.
Reference: -
Findspot: 1997, *principia*, C2/97, quadrant 18-19, room I, -0.40 m; phase Ib.
Inv. No: c.c. 78/2001.

DOMITIANUS
89. Denomination: as, provincial
Axis: 12; D: 26.1 x 23.6 mm; W: 6.7 g.
Mint: Corinth
Dating: AD 85-87
Obv: [imp] CAE[s domitianus augustus ger]
Laureate head of Domitian.
Rv: [col iul] AVG [cor]
Poseidon standing left, foot on rock, holding dolphin and trident.
Reference: RPC II, 186
Findspot: 1970, barrack 5, between the SE walls, -0.50 m; phase Ib.
Inv. No: c.c. 12/1970.
BUCIUMI 1972, no. 212 (but Julia Domna)

DOMITIANUS
90. Denomination: as, provincial
Axis: 12; D: 22.5 mm; W: 6.1 g.
Mint: Corinth
Dating: AD 85-87
Obv: Legend corroded.
Laureate head of Domitian.
Rv: [col] I[ul aug cor]
Poseidon standing left, foot on rock, holding dolphin and trident.
Reference: RPC II, 186
Findspot: 1971, barrack 1, excavated ground.
Inv. No: c.c. 15/1971.

NERVA (Pl. II, 4)
91. Denomination: denarius
Axis: 6; D: 17.7 mm; W: 3.3 g.
Mint: Rome
Dating: AD 97
Obv: IMP NERVA CAES AVG P M TR P COS III P P
Head laureate, right.
Rv: CONCORDIA - EXERCITVVM
Two clasped hands holding aquila set on prow.
Reference: RIC II, 15
Findspot: 1970, barrack 4.
Inv. No: c.c. 71/1970.
BUCIUMI 1972, no. 46

NERVA
92. Denomination: as
Axis: 5; D: 26.7 mm; W: 8.7 g.
Mint: Rome
Dating: AD 96-97
Obv: Legend erased.
Head laureate, right.
Rv: Legend erased.
Aequitas standing left, holding scales in right hand, cornucopiae in left.
Reference: RIC II, 51, 77, 94
Findspot: 1973, barrack 1, m 4-5/5, -0.80 m; phase Ib.
Inv. No: c.c. 94/1973.

NERVA
93. Denomination: as
Axis: 6; D: 26.1 mm; W: 8.2 g.
Mint: Rome
Dating: AD 96-97
Obv: Legend erased.
Head laureate, right.
Rv: Legend erased.
Clasped hands.
Reference: RIC II, 53, 69, 79, 95
Findspot: 1970, barrack 5, between the SE walls, -0.80 m; phase Ib.
Inv. No: c.c. 13/1970.
BUCIUMI 1972, no. 47

NERVA
94. Denomination: as
Axis: 6; D: 25.5 mm; W: 10.2 g.
Mint: Rome
Dating: AD 96-97
Obv: Legend corroded.
Silhouette of head, right.
Rv: Legend corroded.
Fortuna standing left, holding rudder and cornucopiae.
Reference: RIC II, 60, 73, 83, 98
Findspot: 1973, barrack 2, m 6/1, -1 m; phase Ia.
Inv. No: c.c. 146/1973.

NERVA
95. Denomination: as
Axis: -; D: 26.2 x 25.1 mm; W: 8.9 g.
Mint: Rome
Dating: AD 96-98
Obv: …AVG…
Head laureate, right.
Rv: corroded.
Reference: -
Findspot: 1973, barrack 2, -0.75 m; phase Ib.
Inv. No: c.c. 138/1973.

TRAIANUS
96. Denomination: as
Axis: -; D: 24.5 mm; W: 8 g.
Mint: Rome
Dating: AD 98-102

Obv: [imp caes nerva traian aug] GERM P M
  Bust laureate, draped on left shoulder, right.
Rv: corroded.
Reference: -
Findspot: 1966, barrack 5.
Inv. No: c.c. 14/1966.
BUCIUMI 1972, no. 110

TRAIANUS
97. Denomination: as
Axis: -; D: 28.1 x 25.3 mm; W: 6.8 g.
Mint: Rome
Dating: AD 98-102
Obv: [imp caes nerva traian aug germ] P M
  Silhouette of head laureate, right.
Rv: corroded.
Reference: -
Findspot: 1973, barrack 1, m 28-29/2-3, -0.50 m; phase Ib.
Inv. No: c.c. 51/1973.

TRAIANUS
98. Denomination: as
Axis: 6; D: 27.6 x 26.4 mm; W: 10.3 g.
Mint: Rome
Dating: AD 100
Obv: IMP CAES NERVA TRA-IAN AVG [germ p m]
  Head laureate, right.
Rv: TR POT [cos iii p p]
  Mars standing right, holding spear and shield.
Reference: MIR 14, 74a,
Findspot: 1970, barrack 4,-0.80 m; phase Ib.
Inv. No: c.c. 57/1970.
BUCIUMI 1972, no. 62

TRAIANUS
99. Denomination: denarius, plated
Axis: 5; D: 18.3 mm; W: 1.9 g.
Mint: -
Dating: AD 101-102
Obv: IMP CAES NERVA TRAIAN AVG GERM
  Head laureate, right.
Rv: P M TR POT COS IIII [p p]
  Mars advancing right, carrying spear and trophy.
Reference: MIR 14, 104a
Findspot: 1970, *praetorium*, room F, -0.30 m; phase Ib.
Inv. No: c.c. 19/1970.
BUCIUMI 1972, p. 28; no. 49

TRAIANUS (Pl. II, 5)
100. Denomination: dupondius
Axis: 6; D: 27.2 mm; W: 11.3 g.
Mint: Rome
Dating: AD 101-102
Obv: IMP CAES NERVA TRAIAN AVG GERM P M
  Head radiate, right.
Rv: TR POT - COS IIII P P
  exergue: S C
  Abundantia seated left on chair with cornucopiae as armrests, holding sceptre.
Reference: MIR 14, 96a
Findspot: 1971, barrack 1, -0.60 m; phase Ib.
Inv. No: c.c. 26/1971.

TRAIANUS
101. Denomination: as
Axis: 6; D: 27.2 x 26.7 mm; W: 9 g.
Mint: Rome
Dating: AD 101-102
Obv: IMP CAES NERVA TRAIAN AVG GERM P M
  Head laureate, right.
Rv: TR POT COS IIII P P
  Victory walking left, carrying shield inscribed S P/Q R.
Reference: MIR 14, 113a
Findspot: 1970, barrack 5, hearth 3, -1 m; phase Ia.
Inv. No: c.c. 18/1970.
BUCIUMI 1972, no. 61

TRAIANUS (Pl. II, 6)
102. Denomination: denarius
Axis: 6; D: 18.2 mm; W: 2.9 g.
Mint: Rome
Dating: AD 102
Obv: IMP CAES NERVA TRAIAN AVG GERM
  Head laureate, right.
Rv: P M TR P COS IIII P P
  Victory standing to front, head turned left, half-draped, holding wreath and palm.
Reference: MIR 14, 128a
Findspot: 1972, barrack 2, -0.90 m; phase Ia.
Inv. No: c.c. 362/1972.

TRAIANUS (Pl. II, 7)
103. Denomination: sestertius
Axis: 6; D: 34.8 mm; W: 22 g.
Mint: Rome
Dating: AD 103
Obv: IMP NERVA TRAIANVS AVG GER DACICVS
  Bust laureate, draped on left shoulder, right.
Rv: TR P VII IMP IIII - COS V P P
  exergue: S C
  Trajan in slow quadriga left, holding branch and sceptre.
Reference: MIR 14, 157c
Findspot: 1969, barrack 5, excavated ground.
Inv. No: c.c. 107/1969.
BUCIUMI 1972, no. 63

TRAIANUS
104. Denomination: sestertius
Axis: 6; D: 32 mm; W: 24.4 g.
Mint: Rome
Dating: AD 103-104
Obv: Legend erased.
  Silhouette of bust laureate, right.
Rv: S P Q R O[ptimo principi]
  Trajan standing left, crowned by a flying Victory.
Reference: cf. MIR 14, 184a-h
Findspot: 1969, barrack 5, -1 m; phase Ia.
Inv. No: c.c. 118/1969.

BUCIUMI 1972, no. 64

TRAIANUS
105.   Denomination: dupondius
Axis: 6; D: 27 mm; W: 11.5 g.
Mint: Rome
Dating: AD 103-107
Obv: [imp caes nervae traian]O AVG GER D[ac p m tr p cos v p p]
Bust radiate, right.
Rv: S P Q R OP[timo] PRINCIPI; S - C
Trophy, two shields at base.
Reference: MIR 14, 196
Findspot: 1969, barrack 5, -1.50 m; phase Ia.
Inv. No: c.c. 137/1969.
BUCIUMI 1972, no. 72

TRAIANUS
106.   Denomination: dupondius
Axis: 6; D: 27.3 mm; W: 11.8 g.
Mint: Rome
Dating: AD 103-107
Obv: [imp caes nervae traiano aug g]ER D[ac p m tr p cos v p p]
Bust radiate, right.
Rv: S P Q R [optimo princi]PI; S - C
Facing cuirass, consisting of lorica decorated with, lappettes and pteryges.
Reference: MIR 14, 188a
Findspot: 1969, barrack 5, -1 m; phase Ia.
Inv. No: c.c. 127/1969.
BUCIUMI 1972, no. 70

TRAIANUS
107.   Denomination: sestertius
Axis: 6; D: 32.7 mm; W: 21.3 g.
Mint: Rome
Dating: AD 104-107
Obv: IMP CAES [nervae traiano] AVG GER DAC P M TR P COS V P P
Bust laureate, draped on left shoulder, right.
Rv: S P Q R OPTIMO [principi]; S - C
Pax standing left, holding branch and cornucopiae, foot on Dacian captive.
Reference: MIR 14, 200c
Findspot: 1969, barrack 5, -1.20 m; phase Ia.
Inv. No: c.c. 104/1969.
BUCIUMI 1972, no. 69

TRAIANUS
108.   Denomination: dupondius
Axis: 6; D: 26.5 mm; W: 10.1 g.
Mint: Rome
Dating: AD 104-107?
Obv: [imp caes nervae trai]ANO AVG GER DAC [p m tr p] COS V P P
Bust radiate, draped on left shoulder, right.
Rv: [s p q r] OPTIMO PRINC[ipi]; S - C
Pax standing left, holding branch and cornucopiae, foot on Dacian captive.
Reference: MIR 14, 201b
Findspot: 1972, barrack 1, -0.80 m; phase Ib.
Inv. No: c.c. 350/1972.

TRAIANUS
109.   Denomination: dupondius
Axis: 7; D: 26.9 mm; W: 12.7 g.
Mint: Rome
Dating: AD 104-107?
Obv: [imp caes nervae traiano] AVG GER DAC P M TR P COS V P P
Bust radiate, draped on left shoulder, right.
Rv: [s p q r optimo princ]IPI; S - C
Pax standing left, holding branch and cornucopiae, foot on Dacian captive.
Reference: MIR 14, 201b
Findspot: 1973, barrack 1, m 47.5/3, -1.30 m; phase Ia.
Inv. No: c.c. 64/1973.
Remark: found together with coin inv. no. 65/1973.

TRAIANUS
110.   Denomination: dupondius
Axis: 6; D: 28.3 x 25.7 mm; W: 11.6 g.
Mint: Rome
Dating: AD 104-107?
Obv: [imp caes ne]RVAE TRAIANO AVG GER DAC P M TR P COS V P P
Bust radiate, draped on left shoulder, right.
Rv: S P Q R [optimo] PRINCIPI; S - C
Pax standing left, holding branch and cornucopiae, foot on Dacian captive.
Reference: MIR 14, 201b
Findspot: 1973, barrack 1, m 4/4.5, -0.70 m; phase Ib.
Inv. No: c.c. 95/1973.

TRAIANUS
111.   Denomination: as
Axis: 6; D: 26.4 mm; W: 9.7 g.
Mint: Rome
Dating: AD 104-107?
Obv: [imp caes nervae] TRAIANO AVG GER DAC [p m tr p cos v p p]
Bust radiate, draped on left shoulder, right.
Rv: [s p q r] OPTIMO PRINCIPI; S - C
Pax standing left, holding branch and cornucopiae, foot on Dacian captive.
Reference: MIR 14, 207b
Findspot: 1973, barrack 2, -0.60 m; phase Ib.
Inv. No: c.c. 131/1973.

TRAIANUS
112.   Denomination: as
Axis: 6; D: 26.5 mm; W: 8.3 g.
Mint: Rome
Dating: AD 104-107?
Obv: Legend corroded.
Bust radiate, draped on left shoulder, right.
Rv: Legend corroded; S - C
Pax standing left holding branch and cornucopiae, foot on Dacian captive.

Reference: MIR 14, 207b
Findspot: 1973, barrack 2, quadrant 35, -1 m; phase Ia.
Inv. No: c.c. 132/1973.

TRAIANUS
113.   Denomination: as
Axis: 6; D: 30.5 x 27.4 mm; W: 10.7 g.
Mint: Rome
Dating: AD 104-107?
Obv: [imp caes] NERVAE TRAIANO [aug ger dac p m tr p cos v p p]
       Bust radiate, draped on left shoulder, right.
Rv: S P [q r optimo princip]I; S - C
       Pax standing left holding branch and cornucopiae, foot on Dacian captive.
Reference: MIR 14, 207b
Findspot: 1973, barrack 2, excavated ground.
Inv. No: c.c. 148/1973.

TRAIANUS
114.   Denomination: as
Axis: 6; D: 27.4 x 26.3 mm; W: 8.7 g.
Mint: Rome
Dating: AD 104-107?
Obv: [imp caes nervae trai]ANO AVG GER [dac] P M TR P COS V P P
       Bust laureate, draped on left shoulder, right.
Rv: [s p q r optimo prin]CIPI; S - C
       Pax standing left, holding branch and cornucopiae, foot on Dacian captive.
Reference: MIR 14, 207b
Findspot: 1965, barrack 1, -0.80 m; phase Ib.
Inv. No: c.c. 6/1965.
MUZEU 1968, no. 58; BUCIUMI 1972, no. 75 (but barrack 5)

TRAIANUS
115.   Denomination: as
Axis: 6; D: 26.7 mm; W: 10.5 g.
Mint: Rome
Dating: AD 104-107?
Obv: [imp caes nervae traiano] AVG [ger dac p m tr p cos v p p]
       Bust laureate, draped on left shoulder, right.
Rv: [s p] Q R [optimo principi]; S - C
       Pax standing left, holding branch and cornucopiae, foot on Dacian captive.
Reference: MIR 14, 207b
Findspot: 1966, barrack 5.
Inv. No: c.c. 13/1966.
BUCIUMI 1972, no. 68

TRAIANUS
116.   Denomination: as
Axis: 6; D: 27.3 x 25.5 mm; W: 9.1 g.
Mint: Rome
Dating: AD 104-107?
Obv: [imp caes nervae traiano aug ger dac p m tr p] COS V P P
       Bust laureate, draped on left shoulder, right.
Rv: [s] P Q R OPTIMO PRINCIPI; S - C
       Pax standing left, holding branch and cornucopiae, foot on Dacian captive.
Reference: MIR 14, 207b
Findspot: 1971, barrack 1, excavated ground.
Inv. No: c.c. 16/1971.

TRAIANUS
117.   Denomination: as
Axis: 6; D: 26.9 mm; W: 8.7 g.
Mint: Rome
Dating: AD 104-107?
Obv: Legend corroded.
       Bust laureate, draped on left shoulder, right.
Rv: [s p q r optimo] PR[i]NCIPI; S - C
       Pax standing left, holding branch and cornucopiae, foot on Dacian captive.
Reference: MIR 14, 207b
Findspot: 1971, barrack 2, -1 m; phase Ia.
Inv. No: c.c. 355/1972.

TRAIANUS
118.   Denomination: as
Axis: 6; D: 26 x 25.1 mm; W: 9.7 g.
Mint: Rome
Dating: AD 104-107?
Obv: Legend corroded.
       Bust laureate, draped on left shoulder, right.
Rv: Legend corroded
       Silhouette of Pax standing left, holding branch and cornucopiae, probably, foot on Dacian captive.
Reference: cf. MIR 14, 207b
Findspot: 1970, barrack 5, excavated ground.
Inv. No: c.c. 24/1970.
BUCIUMI 1972, no. 80

TRAIANUS
119.   Denomination: as
Axis: 6; D: 26.6 mm; W: 8.6 g.
Mint: Rome
Dating: AD 104-107?
Obv: Legend corroded.
       Bust laureate, draped on left shoulder, right.
Rv: [s p q r optimo prin]CIPI; S - C
       Silhouette of Pax standing left, holding branch and cornucopiae, probably, foot on Dacian captive.
Reference: cf. MIR 14, 207b
Findspot: 1972, barrack 2, -0.85 m; phase Ia.
Inv. No: c.c. 367/1972.

TRAIANUS
120.   Denomination: as
Axis: 6; D: 26.5 x 25 mm; W: 11.1 g.
Mint: Rome
Dating: AD 104-107?
Obv: Legend corroded.
       Bust laureate, draped on left shoulder, right.
Rv: S P Q R OPTIMO PRINCIPI; S - C
       Pax standing left, holding branch and cornucopiae, foot on Dacian captive.

Reference: MIR 14, 207b
Findspot: 1973, barrack 1, m 4.25/3, -0.50 m; phase Ib.
Inv. No: c.c. 69/1973.

TRAIANUS
121. Denomination: as
Axis: 6; D: 26.9 mm; W: 8.8 g.
Mint: Rome
Dating: AD 104-107?
Obv: Legend corroded.
    Bust laureate, draped on left shoulder, right.
Rv: [s p q r opti]MO PRINCIPI; S - C
    Pax standing left, holding branch and cornucopiae, foot on Dacian captive.
Reference: MIR 14, 207b
Findspot: 1973, barrack 1, m 43/4, -1 m; phase Ia.
Inv. No: c.c. 75/1973.

TRAIANUS
122. Denomination: as
Axis: 6; D: 28.4 mm; W: 10.6 g.
Mint: Rome
Dating: AD 104-107?
Obv: Legend corroded.
    Bust laureate, draped on left shoulder, right.
Rv: Legend corroded.
    Pax standing left, holding branch and cornucopiae, foot on Dacian captive.
Reference: MIR 14, 207b
Findspot: 1975, barrack 2, trench 26, m 13.60, -0.95 m; phase Ia.
Inv. No: c.c. 49/1975.

TRAIANUS
123. Denomination: as
Axis: 6; D: 26.3 mm; W: 8.8 g.
Mint: Rome
Dating: AD 104-107?
Obv: Legend corroded.
    Bust laureate, draped on left shoulder, right.
Rv: Legend corroded
    Silhouette of Pax standing left, holding branch and cornucopiae, probably, foot on Dacian captive.
Reference: cf. MIR 14, 207b
Findspot: 1973, barrack 1, m 4.70/2.50, -0.60 m; phase Ib.
Inv. No: c.c. 74/1973.

TRAIANUS
124. Denomination: as
Axis: 6; D: 25.8 x 24.8 mm; W: 9.2 g.
Mint: Rome
Dating: AD 104-107?
Obv: Legend corroded.
    Bust laureate, draped on left shoulder, right.
Rv: Legend corroded
    Silhouette of Pax standing left, holding branch and cornucopiae, probably, foot on Dacian captive.
Reference: cf. MIR 14, 207b
Findspot: 1973, barrack 1, m 4-5/5, -0.80 m; phase Ib.
Inv. No: c.c. 92/1973.

TRAIANUS
125. Denomination: as
Axis: 6; D: 26 x 25 mm; W: 11 g.
Mint: Rome
Dating: AD 104-107?
Obv: Legend corroded.
    Bust laureate, draped on left shoulder, right.
Rv: Legend corroded
    Silhouette of Pax standing left, holding branch and cornucopiae, probably, foot on Dacian captive.
Reference: cf. MIR 14, 207b
Findspot: 1973, barrack 1, m 4, -0.80 m; phase Ib.
Inv. No: c.c. 114/1973.

TRAIANUS
126. Denomination: denarius, plated
Axis: 6; D: 16.6 mm; W: 2.4 g.
Mint: -
Dating: AD 106-107
Obv: IMP TRAIANO AVG GER DAC P M TR P [cos V p p]
    Head laureate, right.
Rv: S P Q R OPTIMO PRINCIPI
    Felicitas standing left, holding caduceus and cornucopia, lighted altar at feet.
Reference: cf. MIR 14, 214
Findspot: 1969, barrack 5, -0.50 m; phase II.
Inv. No: c.c. 101/1969.
BUCIUMI 1972, no. 50

TRAIANUS (Pl. II, 8)
127. Denomination: denarius
Axis: 6; D: 19.2 mm; W: 2.7 g.
Mint: Rome
Dating: AD 106-107
Obv: IMP TRAIANO AVG GER DAC P M TR P COS V P P
    Bust laureate draped on left shoulder, right.
Rv: S P Q R OPTIMO PRINCIPI
    Pax seated left, holding olive branch, Dacian kneeling in supplication before.
Reference: MIR 14, 220b
Findspot: 1972, barrack 2, -0.90 m; phase Ia.
Inv. No: c.c. 354/1972.
Remark: Found stuck to the coin inv. no. 353/1972.

TRAIANUS (Pl. II, 9)
128. Denomination: denarius, plated
Axis: 6; D: 18 mm; W: 2.9 g.
Mint: Rome
Dating: AD 107
Obv: IMP TRAIANO AVG GER DAC P M TR P COS V P P
    Bust laureate draped on left shoulder, right.
Rv: S P Q R OPTIMO PRINCIPI
    Aequitas standing left, holding scales and cornucopia.
Reference: MIR 14, 228b
Findspot: 1975, barrack 2, m 10.50, -1.15 m; phase Ia.
Inv. No: c.c. 43/1975.

TRAIANUS
129.   Denomination: as
Axis: 6; D: 26 x 25 mm; W: 8.8 g.
Mint: Rome
Dating: AD 106-107
Obv: Legend erased.
        Bust laureate, draped on left shoulder, right.
Rv: Legend erased.
        Vague silhouette of Dacia seated left, trophy before
Reference: cf. MIR 14, 245b
Findspot: 1970, barrack 4, -0.60 m; phase Ib.
Inv. No: c.c. 52/1970.
BUCIUMI 1972, no. 66

TRAIANUS
130.   Denomination: as
Axis: 6; D: 26.7 mm; W: 11.7 g.
Mint: Rome
Dating: AD 106-107
Obv: Legend erased.
        Bust laureate, draped on left shoulder, right.
Rv: Legend erased.
        Vague silhouette of Dacia seated left, trophy before
Reference: cf. MIR 14, 245b
Findspot: 1973, barrack 1, m 3/5, -0.90 m; phase Ia.
Inv. No: c.c. 97/1973.

TRAIANUS
131.   Denomination: as
Axis: 6; D: 25.8 mm; W: 10.3 g.
Mint: Rome
Dating: AD 106-107
Obv: Legend erased.
        Silhouette of bust, right.
Rv: Legend erased.
        Silhouette of Dacia seated left, trophy before
Reference: cf. MIR 14, 245b
Findspot: 1973, barrack 2, quadrant 30, -1 m; phase Ia.
Inv. No: c.c. 134/1973.

TRAIANUS
132.   Denomination: sestertius
Axis: 5; D: 33.7 mm; W: 21 g.
Mint: Rome
Dating: AD 106-107
Obv: IMP CAES NERVAE TRAIANO AVG GER DAC
        P M TR P CO[s v p p]
        Bust laureate, draped on left shoulder, right.
Rv: S P Q R O[ptimo principi]
        exergue: S C
        Victory standing left, holding palm and erecting trophy; shields at base.
Reference: MIR 14, 256b
Findspot: 1969, barrack 5, -1.20m; phase Ia.
Inv. No: c.c. 119/1969.
BUCIUMI 1972, no. 73

TRAIANUS (Pl. II, 10)
133.   Denomination: denarius
Axis: 6; D: 19.4 x 17 mm; W: 3.2 g.
Mint: Rome
Dating: AD 107-108
Obv: IMP TRAIANO AVG GER DAC P M TR P
        Bust laureate, draped on left shoulder, right.
Rv: COS V P P S P Q R OPTIMO PRINC
        Mars advancing left carrying Victory and trophy.
Reference: MIR 14, 265b
Findspot: 1973, barrack 1, m 39/6.5, -0.50 m; phase Ib.
Inv. No: c.c. 106/1973.

TRAIANUS (Pl. II, 11)
134.   Denomination: denarius
Axis: 7; D: 18.6 x 17 mm; W: 2.8 g.
Mint: Rome
Dating: AD 107-108
Obv: IMP TRAIANO AVG GER DAC P M TR P
        Bust laureate, draped on left shoulder, right.
Rv: COS V P P [s p q r opt]IMO PRINC
        Trophy on stump; shields and spears at base.
Reference: MIR 14, 268b
Findspot: 1970, barrack 5, the room between the NW walls, -0.80 m; phase Ib.
Inv. No: c.c. 9/1970.
BUCIUMI 1972, no. 53

TRAIANUS
135.   Denomination: dupondius
Axis: 7; D: 27.9 mm; W: 10.1 g.
Mint: Rome
Dating: AD 107-108
Obv: IMP CAES NERVAE TRAIANO AVG GER DAC
        P M TR P COS V P P
        Bust radiate, draped on left shoulder, right.
Rv: S P Q R OPTIMO PRINCIPI
        exergue: S C
        Trajan in slow quadriga left, holding branch and sceptre.
Reference: MIR 14, 309b
Findspot: 1970, barrack 5, excavated ground.
Inv. No: c.c. 31/1970.
BUCIUMI 1972, no. 77

TRAIANUS
136.   Denomination: denarius
Axis: 6; D: 17.9 x 16.7 mm; W: 2.9 g.
Mint: Rome
Dating: AD 108-109
Obv: IMP [traiano a]VG GER DAC P M TR P
        Bust laureate, draped on left shoulder, right.
Rv: COS V P P S P Q R OPTIMO PRINC
        Aequitas seated left, holding scales and cornucopiae.
Reference: MIR 14, 279b
Findspot: 1973, barrack 2, m 18, beneath the S wall, -0.80 m; phase Ia.
Inv. No: c.c. 154/1973.

TRAIANUS (Pl. II, 12)
137.   Denomination: denarius
Axis: 6; D: 19.4 x 17.5 mm; W: 3.3 g.
Mint: Rome

Dating: AD 108-109
Obv: IMP TRAIANO AVG GER DAC P M TR P
  Bust laureate, draped on left shoulder, right.
Rv: COS V P P S P Q R OPTIMO PRINC
  Roma seated left with Victory and spear.
Reference: MIR 14, 281b
Findspot: 1966, barrack 5.
Inv. No: c.c. 21/1966.
BUCIUMI 1972, no. 55

TRAIANUS (Pl. II, 13)
138. Denomination: denarius, plated
Axis: 7; D: 19.4 x 18.3 mm; W: 2.5 g.
Mint: Rome
Dating: AD 108-109
Obv: IMP TRAIANO AVG GER DAC P M TR P
  Bust laureate, draped on left shoulder, right.
Rv: COS V P P S P Q R OPTIMO PRINC
  Victory, standing left on shields, holding wreath and palm.
Reference: cf. MIR 14, 282b
Findspot: 1966, barrack 5.
Inv. No: c.c. 15/1966.
BUCIUMI 1972, no. 54

TRAIANUS (Pl. II, 14)
139. Denomination: denarius
Axis: 6; D: 18.8 x 16.6 mm; W: 3 g.
Mint: Rome
Dating: AD 108-109
Obv: IMP TRAIANO AVG GER DAC P M TR P
  Bust laureate, draped on left shoulder, right.
Rv: COS V P P S P Q R OPTIMO PRINC
  Victory, standing left on shields, holding wreath and palm.
Reference: MIR 14, 282b
Findspot: 1968, barrack 5, -0.60 m; phase II.
Inv. No: c.c. 12/1968.
BUCIUMI 1972, no. 52

TRAIANUS
140. Denomination: semis
Axis: 7; D: 17.2 mm; W: 2.6 g.
Mint: Rome
Dating: AD 107-109
Obv: Legend unreadable.
  Head laureate, right.
Rv: No legend.
  exergue: S C
  Gaming table with vase and wreath.
Reference: MIR 14, 596, 597
Findspot: 1973, barrack 1, m 35/6, -1 m; phase Ia.
Inv. No: c.c. 104/1973.

TRAIANUS (Pl. II, 15)
141. Denomination: quadrans
Axis: 7; D: 15.6 mm; W: 2.1 g.
Mint: Rome
Dating: post AD 109
Obv: Legend unreadable.
  Head laureate draped on left shoulder, right.
Rv: No legend.
  exergue: S C
  She-wolf crouching left.
Reference: MIR 14, 600b
Findspot: 1973, barrack 1, excavated ground.
Inv. No: c.c. 115/1973.

TRAIANUS
142. Denomination: as
Axis: 6; D: 26.8 mm; W: 6.6 g.
Mint: Rome
Dating: AD 107-110
Obv: [imp caes] NERVAE TRAIANO [aug ger dac p m tr p cos v p p]
  Bust laureate, draped on left shoulder, right.
Rv: Legend erased
  exergue: S C
  Bridge.
Reference: MIR 14, 316b
Findspot: 1969, barrack 5, -0.80 m; phase Ib.
Inv. No: c.c. 136/1969.
BUCIUMI 1972, no. 87

TRAIANUS (Pl. II, 17)
143. Denomination: dupondius
Axis: 7; D: 25.9 mm; W: 10.6 g.
Mint: Rome
Dating: AD 108-110
Obv: [imp caes nervae traiano avg ger da]C P M TR P COS V P P
  Bust laureate, draped on left shoulder, right.
Rv: S P Q R OPTIMO PRINCIPI
  exergue: S C
  Roma seated left on cuirass, holding Victory and spear..
Reference: MIR 14, 333b
Findspot: 1973, barrack 1, m 47.5/3, -1.30 m; phase Ia.
Inv. No: c.c. 65/1973.
Remark: found together with coin inv. no. 64/1973.

TRAIANUS
144. Denomination: as
Axis: 5; D: 25.9 x 24.7 mm; W: 8.5 g.
Mint: Rome
Dating: AD 108-110
Obv: IMP CAESTRAIANO AVG GER DAC P M TR [p cos v p p]
  Bust laureate, draped on left shoulder, right.
Rv: [s p q r o]P[timo principi]; S - C
  Annona standing left, holding grain ears and cornucopiae; modius with grain ears and prow at her feet.
Reference: cf. MIR 14, 325b
Findspot: 1973, fort area, stray find.
Inv. No: c.c. 160/1973.

TRAIANUS
145. Denomination: as
Axis: 6; D: 27.3 x 25.4 mm; W: 10.8 g.

Mint: Rome
Dating: AD 108-110
Obv: Legend corroded.
　　　Bust laureate, draped on left shoulder, right.
Rv: S P Q R [optimo principi]; S - C
　　　Annona standing left, holding grain ears and cornucopiae; modius with grain ears and prow at her feet.
Reference: cf. MIR 14, 325b
Findspot: 1970, barrack 4, -0.60 m; phase Ib.
Inv. No: c.c. 49/1970.
BUCIUMI 1972, no. 79

TRAIANUS
146.　　Denomination: as
Axis: 6; D: 26.7 mm; W: 10.6 g.
Mint: Rome
Dating: AD 108-110
Obv: Legend unreadable.
　　　Bust laureate, draped on left shoulder, right.
Rv: [s p q r opti]MO PRINCIPI; S - C
　　　Annona standing left, holding grain ears and cornucopiae; modius with grain ears and prow at her feet.
Reference: MIR 14, 325b
Findspot: 1973, barrack 2, quadrant 30, -1 m; phase Ia.
Inv. No: c.c. 136/1973.

TRAIANUS
147.　　Denomination: as
Axis: 6; D: 27.1 x 25.4 mm; W: 14.1 g.
Mint: Rome
Dating: AD 108-110
Obv: IMP [caes nervae trai]ANO AVG GER DAC P M TR P COS V P P
　　　Bust laureate, draped on left shoulder, right.
Rv: [s p q r optimo] PRINCIPI; S - C
　　　Fortuna standing, head left, with rudder and cornucopia, prow behind.
Reference: MIR 14, 331b
Findspot: 1966, barrack 5.
Inv. No: c.c. 22/1966.
BUCIUMI 1972, no. 88

TRAIANUS
148.　　Denomination: as
Axis: 5; D: 26.3 x 25.2 mm; W: 10.5 g.
Mint: Rome
Dating: AD 108-110
Obv: [imp caes nervae] TRAIANO AVG GER DAC [p m tr p cos v p p]
　　　Bust laureate, draped on left shoulder, right.
Rv: Legend corroded; [s] - C
　　　Fortuna standing, head left, with rudder and cornucopia, prow behind.
Reference: MIR 14, 331b
Findspot: 1970, barrack 4, -0.60 m; phase Ib.
Inv. No: c.c. 48/1970.
BUCIUMI 1972, no. 91

TRAIANUS
149.　　Denomination: as
Axis: 6; D: 26.2 x 25.3 mm; W: 8.8 g.
Mint: Rome
Dating: AD 108-110
Obv: Legend corroded.
　　　Bust laureate, draped on left shoulder, right.
Rv: [s p q r opt]IMO PRINCIPI; S - C
　　　Fortuna standing, head left, with rudder and cornucopia, prow behind.
Reference: MIR 14, 331b
Findspot: 1966, barrack 5.
Inv. No: c.c. 36/1966.
BUCIUMI 1972, no. 89

TRAIANUS
150.　　Denomination: as
Axis: 4; D: 27.1 x 25.9 mm; W: 11.5 g.
Mint: Rome
Dating: AD 108-110
Obv: Legend corroded.
　　　Bust laureate, draped on left shoulder, right.
Rv: [s p q r optimo pri]NCIPI; S - C
　　　Fortuna standing, head left, with rudder and cornucopia, prow behind.
Reference: MIR 14, 331b
Findspot: 1972, barrack 2, -0.75 m; phase Ib.
Inv. No: c.c. 345/1972.

TRAIANUS (Pl. II, 18)
151.　　Denomination: as
Axis: 6; D: 27.6 mm; W: 10.7 g.
Mint: Rome
Dating: AD 108-110
Obv: IMP CAES NERVAE TRAIANO AVG GE[r d]AC P M TR P COS V P P
　　　Bust laureate, draped on left shoulder, right.
Rv: [s] P Q R OP[timo principi]
　　　exergue: S C
　　　Roma seated left on cuirass, holding Victory and spear.
Reference: MIR 14, 334b
Findspot: 1970, barrack 5, the NE end, -1.20 m; phase Ia.
Inv. No: c.c. 22/1970.
BUCIUMI 1972, no. 82

TRAIANUS
152.　　Denomination: as
Axis: 6; D: 27.4 x 26.3 mm; W: 8.7 g.
Mint: Rome
Dating: AD 108-110
Obv: [imp caes nervae traian]O AVG GE[r d]AC P M TR P COS V P P
　　　Bust laureate, draped on left shoulder, right.
Rv: [s] P Q R OPTI[mo principi];
　　　exergue: S C
　　　Roma seated left on cuirass, holding Victory and spear.
Reference: MIR 14, 334b

Findspot: 1963, the *porta principalis sinistra*; in the layer of red sand from the *via principalis*; D-5/1963-1.
Inv. No: c.c. 97/1963.
MUZEU 1968, no. 57; BUCIUMI 1972, no. 86

TRAIANUS
153. Denomination: as
Axis: 6; D: 26.2 mm; W: 10.5 g.
Mint: Rome
Dating: AD 108-110
Obv: [imp caes] NERVAE TRAIANO AVG GER DAC P M TR P [cos v p p]
Bust laureate, draped on left shoulder, right.
Rv: [s] P Q R OPTI[mo principi];
exergue: S C
Roma seated left on cuirass, holding Victory and spear.
Reference: MIR 14, 334b
Findspot: 1969, barrack 5, -1.50 m; phase Ia.
Inv. No: c.c. 131/1969.
BUCIUMI 1972, no. 85

TRAIANUS
154. Denomination: as
Axis: 6; D: 28.8 x 27.3 mm; W: 11.4 g.
Mint: Rome
Dating: AD 108-110
Obv: [imp] CAES NERVAE TRAIANO AVG GER DAC P M TR P COS V P P
Bust laureate, draped on left shoulder, right.
Rv: S P Q R [optimi princi]PI
exergue: S C
Roma seated left on cuirass, holding Victory and spear.
Reference: MIR 14, 334b
Findspot: 1970, barrack 4, -0.70 m; phase Ib.
Inv. No: c.c. 50/1970.
BUCIUMI 1972, no. 84

TRAIANUS
155. Denomination: as
Axis: 6; D: 26.6 x 25 mm; W: 10.9 g.
Mint: Rome
Dating: AD 108-110
Obv: [imp] CAES NERVAE TRAIANO AVG GER [dac p m tr p cos v p p]
Bust laureate, draped on left shoulder, right.
Rv: S P Q R OPTIM[i principi]
exergue: broken
Roma seated left on cuirass, holding Victory and spear.
Reference: MIR 14, 334b
Findspot: 1970, barrack 4, -0.80 m; phase Ib.
Inv. No: c.c. 55/1970.
BUCIUMI 1972, no. 83

TRAIANUS
156. Denomination: as
Axis: 6; D: 27.8 x 26.4 mm; W: 9.1 g.
Mint: Rome
Dating: AD 108-110
Obv: [imp caes nervae] TRAIANO A[ug ger] DAC P M TR P COS V P P
Bust laureate, draped on left shoulder, right.
Rv: S P Q R OPTIM[i principi]
exergue: S C
Roma seated left on cuirass, holding Victory and spear.
Reference: MIR 14, 334b
Findspot: 1972, barrack 2, -1 m; phase Ia.
Inv. No: c.c. 356/1972.

TRAIANUS
157. Denomination: sestertius
Axis: 5; D: 33.7 x 32.4 mm; W: 25 g.
Mint: Rome
Dating: AD 109-110
Obv: [imp] CAES NERVAE TRAIANO AVG GER DAC P M TR P COS V P P
Bust laureate, right.
Rv: [s p q r optimo pri]NCI[pi]; S - C
Spes standing left with flower and raising hem of skirt.
Reference: MIR 14, 338a
Findspot: 1969, barrack 5, -1.20 m; phase Ia.
Inv. No: c.c. 120/1969.
BUCIUMI 1972, no. 101

TRAIANUS
158. Denomination: dupondius
Axis: 6; D: 26.6 mm; W: 9.9 g.
Mint: Rome
Dating: AD 109-110
Obv: Legend corroded.
Bust laureate draped on left shoulder, right.
Rv: [s p q r] OPTIMO [principi]; S - C
Spes standing left with flower and raising hem of skirt.
Reference: cf. MIR 14, 339b
Findspot: 1970, barrack 4, excavated ground.
Inv. No: c.c. 84/1970.
BUCIUMI 1972, no. 94

TRAIANUS
159. Denomination: as
Axis: 6; D: 27.7 mm; W: 9 g.
Mint: Rome
Dating: AD 109-110
Obv: Legend corroded.
Bust laureate with paludamentum on left shoulder, right.
Rv: legend corroded; S - C
Spes standing left with flower and raising hem of skirt.
Reference: MIR 14, 340b
Findspot: 1970, barrack 5, between the NW walls, north side, -1.50 m; phase Ia.
Inv. No: c.c. 21/1970.
BUCIUMI 1972, no. 109

TRAIANUS
160. Denomination: as
Axis: 6; D: 27.4 x 25.4 mm; W: 11.3 g.
Mint: Rome
Dating: AD 109-110
Obv: [imp caes nervae t]RAIANO AVG GER DAC [p m tr p cos v p p]
Bust laureate with paludamentum on left shoulder, right.
Rv: [S P Q R] [optimo princ]IPI; S - C
Spes standing left with flower and raising hem of skirt.
Reference: MIR 14, 340b
Findspot: 1970, barrack 4, -0.50 m; phase Ib.
Inv. No: c.c. 41/1970.
BUCIUMI 1972, no. 95

TRAIANUS
161. Denomination: as
Axis: 6; D: 27 x 24.9 mm; W: 10.2 g.
Mint: Rome
Dating: AD 109-110
Obv: [imp caes nervae traiano aug ger dac] P M TR P COS V P P
Bust laureate with paludamentum on left shoulder, right.
Rv: S P Q R OPTIMO PRINCIPI; S - C
Spes standing left with flower and raising hem of skirt.
Reference: MIR 14, 340b
Findspot: 1972, barrack 2, -0.80 m; phase Ia.
Inv. No: c.c. 369/1972.

TRAIANUS
162. Denomination: as
Axis: 6; D: 27.6 x 26.1 mm; W: 9.6 g.
Mint: Rome
Dating: AD 109-110
Obv: IMP CAES NERVAE TRAIANO AVG GER DAC [p m tr p cos v p p]
Bust laureate with paludamentum on left shoulder, right.
Rv: [s p q r optimo] PRINCIPI; S - C
Spes standing left with flower and raising hem of skirt.
Reference: MIR 14, 340b
Findspot: 1973, barrack 1, m 3/6, -0.80 m; phase Ib.
Inv. No: c.c. 89/1973.

TRAIANUS
163. Denomination: as
Axis: 6; D: 27.6 x 25.9 mm; W: 10.9 g.
Mint: Rome
Dating: AD 109-110
Obv: [imp caes nervae tra]IANO [aug] GER DAC P M TR P COS V P P
Bust laureate with paludamentum on left shoulder, right.
Rv: [s p q r optimo princ]IPI; S - C
Spes standing left with flower and raising hem of skirt.
Reference: MIR 14, 340b
Findspot: 1973, barrack 1, m 30, -1 m; phase Ia.
Inv. No: c.c. 135/1973.

TRAIANUS
164. Denomination: as
Axis: 6; D: 26.4 x 24.9 mm; W: 10.5 g.
Mint: Rome
Dating: AD 109-110
Obv: Legend erased.
Bust laureate, right.
Rv: Legend erased.
Spes standing left with flower and raising hem of skirt.
Reference: cf. MIR 14, 340b
Findspot: 1970, barrack 4, -0.60 m; phase Ib.
Inv. No: c.c. 56/1970.
BUCIUMI 1972, no. 67

TRAIANUS
165. Denomination: as
Axis: 6; D: 27.7 x 26 mm; W: 11.2 g.
Mint: Rome
Dating: AD 109-110
Obv: Legend erased.
Bust laureate, right.
Rv: Legend erased; S - C.
Spes standing left with flower and raising hem of skirt.
Reference: cf. MIR 14, 340b
Findspot: 1970, barrack 4, -1.20 m; phase Ia.
Inv. No: c.c. 77/1970.
BUCIUMI 1972, no. 100

TRAIANUS
166. Denomination: as
Axis: 6; D: 28.7 x 26.4 mm; W: 9.5 g.
Mint: Rome
Dating: AD 109-110
Obv: Legend erased.
Bust laureate, right.
Rv: Legend erased; S - C.
Spes standing left with flower and raising hem of skirt.
Reference: cf. MIR 14, 340b
Findspot: 1973, barrack 2, m 30/4, -1.20 m; phase Ia.
Inv. No: c.c. 150/1973.

TRAIANUS (Pl. II, 19)
167. Denomination: denarius
Axis: 6; D: 17.1 mm; W: 2.6 g.
Mint: Rome
Dating: AD 110
Obv: IMP TRAIANO AVG GER DAC P M TR P
Bust laureate, draped on left shoulder, right.
Rv: COS V P P S P Q R OPTIMO PRINC
Roma standing left, holding Victory and spear.
Reference: MIR 14, 287b

Findspot: 1971, barrack 1, -0.50 m; phase Ib.
Inv. No: c.c. 25/1971.

TRAIANUS
168.   Denomination: denarius, plated
Axis: 6; D: 18.6 x 16.9 mm; W: 1.5 g.
Mint: Rome
Dating: AD 110 or later
Obv: [imp tra]IANO AVG GER DAC [p m tr p]
        Bust laureate, draped on left shoulder, right.
Rv: Legend erased.
        Roma standing left, holding Victory and spear.
Reference: cf. MIR 14, 287b
Findspot: 1975, building C 1, 3 m from the E wall and 4 m from the N wall, -0.50 m; phase Ib.
Inv. No: c.c. 41/1975.

TRAIANUS
169.   Denomination: dupondius
Axis: 7; D: 26.7 x 24.9 mm; W: 13 g.
Mint: Rome
Dating: AD 111
Obv: IMP CAES NERVAE TRAIANO AVG GER DAC P M TR P COS V P P
        Bust laureate, draped on left shoulder, right.
Rv: SP QR [opt]IMO PRINCIPI; S - C
Exergue: [ali]M/ITAL
        River god reclining left in arched grotto, resting on urn and holding reed.
Reference: MIR 14, 355b
Findspot: 1966, barrack 5.
Inv. No: c.c. 16/1966.
BUCIUMI 1972, no. 98

TRAIANUS
170.   Denomination: dupondius
Axis: 6; D: 26.4 mm; W: 9.8 g.
Mint: Rome
Dating: AD 111
Obv: IMP CAES NERVAE TRAIANO AVG GER DAC P M TR P COS V P P
        Bust laureate, draped on left shoulder, right.
Rv: SP QR OPTIMO PRINCIPI
Exergue: S – C flanking AQVA/TRAIANA
        River god reclining left in arched grotto, resting on urn and holding reed.
Reference: MIR 14, 360a
Findspot: 1965, barrack 1, -1.05 m; phase Ia.
Inv. No: c.c. 1b/1965.
MUZEU 1968, no. 54; BUCIUMI 1972, no. 96 (but barrack 5)

TRAIANUS (Pl. II, 20)
171.   Denomination: denarius
Axis: 7; D: 19.3 x 17.8 mm; W: 2.8 g.
Mint: Rome
Dating: AD 112
Obv: IMP TRAIANO AVG GER P M TR P COS VI P P
        Bust laureate, draped on left shoulder, right.
Rv: S P Q R OPTIMO PRINCIPI
        Victory standing right inscribing DA/C/ICA on shield.
Reference: MIR 14, 389b
Findspot: 1970, barrack 4, -0.50 m; phase Ib.
Inv. No: c.c. 45/1970.
BUCIUMI 1972, no. 57

TRAIANUS
172.   Denomination: dupondius
Axis: 6; D: 27.7 x 26.4 mm; W: 11.8 g.
Mint: Rome
Dating: AD 112-113
Obv: IMP CAES NERVAE TRAIANO AVG GER P M TR P COS VI P P
        Bust radiate, draped on left shoulder, right.
Rv: S P Q R OPTIMO PRINCIPI; S - C
        exergues: [arab] ADQ
        Arabia standing facing, head left, holding branch and bundle of sticks; camel at feet left.
Reference: MIR 14, 455b
Findspot: 1969, barrack 5, -0.80 m; phase Ib.
Inv. No: c.c. 121/1969.
BUCIUMI 1972, no. 78

TRAIANUS
173.   Denomination: dupondius
Axis: 6; D: 27.5 mm; W: 9.9 g.
Mint: Rome
Dating: AD 112-113
Obv: [imp caes ne]RVAE TRAIANO AVG GER P M TR P C[os vi p p]
        Bust radiate, draped on left shoulder, right.
Rv: [s P Q r] OPTIMO PRINCIPI; S - C
        exergues: [ar]AB ADQ
        Arabia standing facing, head left, holding branch and bundle of sticks; camel at feet left.
Reference: MIR 14, 455b
Findspot: 1969, barrack 5, hearth 3; phase II.
Inv. No: c.c. 128/1969.
BUCIUMI 1972, no. 93

TRAIANUS (Pl. III, 1)
174.   Denomination: denarius, plated
Axis: 6; D: 19.7 x 18.6 mm; W: 3.3 g.
Mint: Rome
Dating: AD 113-114 or later
Obv: IMP TRAIANO AVG GER DAC P M TR P COS VI P P
        Bust laureate, draped, right.
Rv: S P Q R OPTIMO PRINCII
        Legionary eagle between two standards, one surmounted by a wreath, the other by a hand.
Reference: cf. MIR 14, 419v
Findspot: 1973, barrack 2, near the *via sagularis*, -0.60 m; phase Ib.
Inv. No: c.c. 122/1973.
Remark: *On the reverse PRINCII with a possible second P as a longer I.*

TRAIANUS
175.   Denomination: denarius, plated
Axis: 7; D: 17.8 mm; W: 2.2 g.
Mint: Rome
Dating: AD 113-114 or later
Obv: IMP TRAIANO AVG GER [dac p m tr p cos vi p p]
          Bust laureate, draped, right.
Rv: Legend erased.
          Mars advancing right, holding spear and trophy.
Reference: MIR 14, 423v
Findspot: 1967, between barracks 2 and 3, 2 m from the *via praetoria*.
Inv. No: c.c. 12/1967.
BUCIUMI 1972, no. 48

TRAIANUS
176.   Denomination: sestertius
Axis: 6; D: 33.1 x 30.8 mm; W: 27.1 g.
Mint: Rome
Dating: AD 112-114
Obv: IMP CAES NERVAE TRAIANO AVG GER DAC P M TR P COS VI P P
          Bust laureate, draped on left shoulder, right.
Rv: DACIA AVGVST
          exergue: [pro]VINC[ia]/ [s c]
          Dacia seated left on rock, holding legionary eagle, two naked boys on her laps, one holding bunch of grapes, the other holding two corn-ears.
Reference: MIR 14, 467b
Findspot: 1970, barrack 4, -0.50 m; phase Ib.
Inv. No: c.c. 37/1970.
BUCIUMI 1972, no. 97

TRAIANUS
177.   Denomination: as
Axis: 6; D: 26.5 mm; W: 9.6 g.
Mint: Rome
Dating: AD 112-114
Obv: Legend corroded.
          Bust laureate, draped on left shoulder, right.
Rv: Legend corroded
          Victory walking right, holding wreath and palm.
Reference: cf. MIR 14, 475b
Findspot: 1970, barrack 5, excavated ground.
Inv. No: c.c. 67/1970.
BUCIUMI 1972, no. 104

TRAIANUS
178.   Denomination: sestertius
Axis: 6; D: 33.8 mm; W: 27.7 g.
Mint: Rome
Dating: AD 112-114
Obv: IMP CAES NERVAE TRAIANO AVG GER DAC [p m tr p cos vi p p]
          Bust laureate, draped on left shoulder, right.
Rv: FELI[citas augus]T; S – C
          Felicitas standing left, holding caduceus and cornucopiae.
Reference: MIR 14, 480b
Findspot: 1969, barrack 5, -1.10 m; phase Ia.
Inv. No: c.c. 108/1969.
BUCIUMI 1972, no. 102

TRAIANUS
179.   Denomination: sestertius
Axis: 6; D: 32.8 mm; W: 24.4 g.
Mint: Rome
Dating: AD 112-114
Obv: Legend corroded.
          Bust laureate, draped on left shoulder, right.
Rv: [fel]ICI[tas augus]T; S – C
          Felicitas standing left, holding caduceus and cornucopiae.
Reference: MIR 14, 480b
Findspot: 1966, barrack 2.
Inv. No: c.c. 17/1966.
BUCIUMI 1972, no. 103

TRAIANUS
180.   Denomination: sestertius
Axis: 6; D: 34.7 mm; W: 25.7 g.
Mint: Rome
Dating: AD 114
Obv: IMP CAES TRAIANO OPTIMO AVG GER DAC P M TR P COS VI P P
          Bust laureate, draped on left shoulder, right
Rv: SENATVS POPVLVSQVE ROMANVS; S - C
          Felicitas standing left, holding caduceus and cornucopiae.
Reference: MIR 14, 499b
Findspot: 1975, barrack 2, trench 26, m 59.30, -0.30 m; phase II.
Inv. No: c.c. 44/1975.

TRAIANUS
181.   Denomination: sestertius
Axis: 6; D: 33.5 x 32.5 mm; W: 26.8 g.
Mint: Rome
Dating: AD 114
Obv: IMP CAES NER TRAIANO OPTIMO AVG G[er dac] P M TR P C[os vi p p]
          Bust laureate, draped, right
Rv: [sena]TVS P[opulusqu]E RO[manus]
          exergue: [fo]RT RED/ S – C
          Fortuna Redux seated left, holding rudder and cornucopia.
Reference: MIR 14, 505v
Findspot: 1973, barrack 2, m 39/3, -1.50 m; phase Ia.
Inv. No: c.c. 151/1973.

TRAIANUS
182.   Denomination: dupondius
Axis: 6; D: 26.4 mm; W: 13.2 g.
Mint: Rome
Dating: AD 114
Obv: [imp caes ner tr]AIANO OPTIMO AVG GER DAC [p m tr p cos vi p p]
          Bust radiate, draped, right
Rv: SENATVS POPVLVSQVE ROMANVS; S – C

Felicitas standing left, holding caduceus and cornucopiae.
Reference: MIR 14, 500v
Findspot: 1970, barrack 4, -0.60 m; phase Ib.
Inv. No: c.c. 54/1970.
BUCIUMI 1972, no. 99

TRAIANUS
183. Denomination: sestertius
Axis: 6; D: 33.4 mm; W: 20 g.
Mint: Rome
Dating: AD 114-116
Obv: IMP [caes] NER TRAIANO [optimo aug ger dac p m tr p cos vi p p]
Bust radiate, draped, right
Rv: [s]ENA[tus populusque romanus]; S – C
Felicitas standing left, holding caduceus and cornucopiae.
Reference: MIR 14, 534v
Findspot: 1973, barrack 2, m 50/11, -1.80 m; phase Ia.
Inv. No: c.c. 149/1973.

TRAIANUS
184. Denomination: denarius
Axis: 6; D: 19.6 x 17.9 mm; W: 2.8 g.
Mint: Rome
Dating: AD 114-116
Obv: IMP CAES NER TRAIANO OPTIMO AVG GER DAC
Bust laureate, with paludamentum, right.
Rv: P M TR P – CO-S VI S P Q R
Felicitas standing front, head left, holding caduceus and cornucopiae.
Reference: MIR 14, 519v
Findspot: 1970, barrack 4, -1 m; phase Ia.
Inv. No: c.c. 79/1970.
BUCIUMI 1972, no. 58

TRAIANUS
185. Denomination: denarius, plated
Axis: 7; D: 19.4 x 17.7 mm; W: 2.5 g.
Mint: -
Dating: AD 114-116 or later
Obv: [imp] CAES NER TRAIANO OPTIMO AVG GER DAC
Bust laureate, draped on left shoulder, right.
Rv: P M TR P COS VI S P Q R
Mars advancing right, carrying spear and trophy.
Reference: cf. MIR 14, 520v
Findspot: 1970, barrack 4, -1 m; phase Ia.
Inv. No: c.c. 78/1970.
BUCIUMI 1972, no. 59

TRAIANUS (Pl. III, 2)
186. Denomination: denarius
Axis: 7; D: 19.3 x 17.5 mm; W: 3.1 g.
Mint: Rome
Dating: AD 114-116
Obv: IMP CAES NER TRAIANO OPTIMO AVG GER DAC
Bust laureate, draped, seen 2/3 facing, right.
Rv: P M TR P CO-S VI S P Q R
Virtus standing right, foot on helmet, holding spear and parazonium.
Reference: MIR 14, 524
Findspot: 1971, barrack 1, excavated ground.
Inv. No: c.c. 14/1971.

TRAIANUS
187. Denomination: dupondius
Axis: 6; D: 28.2 x 26.4 mm; W: 10.9 g.
Mint: Rome
Dating: AD 114-116
Obv: [imp caes ner] TRAIANO OPTIMO AVG [ger dac p m tr p cos vi p p]
Bust radiate, draped, right
Rv: SENATVS POP[ulusque roman]V[s]; S – C
Felicitas standing left, holding caduceus and cornucopiae.
Reference: MIR 14, 535v
Findspot: 1972, barrack 2, -1.20 m; phase Ia.
Inv. No: c.c. 359/1972.

TRAIANUS
188. Denomination: dupondius
Axis: 6; D: 26.3 mm; W: 11.3 g.
Mint: Rome
Dating: AD 114-116
Obv: Legend corroded.
Bust radiate, draped, right
Rv: Legend corroded.
Felicitas standing left, holding caduceus and cornucopiae.
Reference: MIR 14, 500, 535
Findspot: 1973, barrack 1, m 2/3/4-5, -0.6 0m; phase Ib.
Inv. No: c.c. 84/1973.

TRAIANUS
189. Denomination: dupondius
Axis: 6; D: 26.5 mm; W: 10.9 g.
Mint: Rome
Dating: AD 114-116
Obv: IMP CAES NER TRAIANO OPTIMO AVG GER DAC [p m tr p cos vi p p]
Bust laureate, draped, seen 2/3 facing, right.
Rv: Legend erased.
Female standing left, holding cornucopia and ?
Reference: cf. MIR 14, p. 587, group 16
Findspot: 1973, barrack 1, m 42/9, -1 m; phase Ia.
Inv. No: c.c. 109/1973.

TRAIANUS
190. Denomination: as
Axis: 6; D: 28 x 25.6 mm; W: 11.3 g.
Mint: Rome
Dating: AD 114-116
Obv: IMP CAES NER TRAIANO OPTIMO AVG GER DAC P M TR P COS VI P P
Bust laureate, draped, right

Rv: [sen]ATVS POPVLVSQVE ROMANVS; S – C
Victory advancing right, wreath in extended right hand and palm over left shoulder.
Reference: MIR 14, 540v
Findspot: 1976, fort area, stray find.
Inv. No: c.c. 156/1976.

TRAIANUS (Pl. III, 3)
191.   Denomination: denarius
Axis: 7; D: 18.6 x 17 mm; W: 3 g.
Mint: Rome
Dating: AD 116-117
Obv: IMP CAES NER TRAIAN OPTIM AVG GERM DAC
Bust laureate, draped on left shoulder, right.
Rv: PARTHICO P M T-R P COS VI S P Q R
Exergue: FORT RED
Fortuna seated left, holding rudder and cornucopia.
Reference: MIR 14, 579v
Findspot: 1968, barrack 5, -0.60 m; phase Ib.
Inv. No: c.c. 29/1968.
BUCIUMI 1972, no. 60

TRAIANUS
192.   Denomination: dupondius
Axis: 6; D: 26.9 mm; W: 11.3 g.
Mint: Rome
Dating: AD 116-117
Obv: [imp caes ner traiano optimo au]G GER DAC [parthico p m tr p cos vi p p]
Bust radiate with *paludamentum*, right.
Rv: Legend erased.
Trajan advancing right between two trophies.
Reference: MIR 14, 586v
Findspot: 1969, barrack 5.
Inv. No: c.c. 115/1969.
BUCIUMI 1972, no. 105

TRAIANUS
193.   Denomination: dupondius
Axis: 6; D: 26.1 mm; W: 12.5 g.
Mint: Rome
Dating: AD 116-117
Obv: Legend unreadable
Bust radiate with *paludamentum*, right.
Rv: Legend erased.
exergue: S C
Trajan advancing right between two trophies.
Reference: MIR 14, 586v
Findspot: 1974, *praetorium*, excavated ground.
Inv. No: c.c. 37/1974.

TRAIANUS
194.   Denomination: dupondius
Axis: 6; D: 27 mm; W: 10.9 g.
Mint: Rome
Dating: AD 116-117
Obv: [imp caes ner traiano op]TIMO AVG GER DAC PART[hico p m tr p cos vi p p]
Bust radiate with *paludamentum* on the left shoulder, seen ¾ facing, right.
Rv: [providentia augusti] S P Q R; S – C
Providentia standing left, resting elbow on column and pointing to globe at feet.
Reference: MIR 14, 592x
Findspot: 1970, barrack 4, -0.50 m; phase Ib.
Inv. No: c.c. 38/1970.
BUCIUMI 1972, no. 106

TRAIANUS
195.   Denomination: sestertius
Axis: 6; D: 33.7 mm; W: 25.4 g.
Mint: Rome
Dating: AD 103-117
Obv: […tr]AIANO AVG GER DAC [p m tr p cos…]
Head laureate, right (portrait after AD 103).
Rv: Legend erased; S - C
Female silhouette standing left, holding cornucopiae and?
Reference: -
Findspot: 1972, barrack 2, -0.95 m; phase Ia.
Inv. No: c.c. 360/1972.

TRAIANUS
196.   Denomination: sestertius
Axis: -; D: 32.1 x 29.8 mm; W: 22.6 g.
Mint: Rome
Dating: AD 103-117
Obv: Legend corroded.
Bust laureate, right (portrait after AD 103).
Rv: Corroded.
Reference: -
Findspot: 1964, trench 13, quadrant 146, -1.35 m; phase Ia.
Inv. No: c.c. -/1964.
BUCIUMI 1972, no. 65

TRAIANUS
197.   Denomination: dupondius
Axis: -; D: 26.6 mm; W: 11.7 g.
Mint: Rome
Dating: AD 103-117
Obv: Legend corroded.
Bust radiate, right (portrait after AD 103).
Rv: Corroded.
Reference: -
Findspot: 1973, barrack 2, m 45/4.5, -1.40 m; phase Ia.
Inv. No: c.c. 147/1973.

TRAIANUS
198.   Denomination: dupondius
Axis: -; D: 26.5 x 24. 8 mm; W: 10.6 g.
Mint: Rome
Dating: AD 103-117
Obv: Legend corroded.
Head radiate, right (portrait after AD 103).
Rv: Erased.
Reference: -

Findspot: 1973, barrack 2, m 42, beneath the S wall, -1.40 m; phase Ia.
Inv. No: c.c. 156/1973.

TRAIANUS
199.   Denomination: as
Axis: 6; D: 26.3 mm; W: 11.8 g.
Mint: Rome
Dating: AD 103-117
Obv: Legend erased.
       Head laureate, right (portrait after AD 103).
Rv: ...OPTIMO...; S - C
       Silhouette standing.
Reference: -
Findspot: 1966, barrack 5.
Inv. No: c.c. 23/1966.
BUCIUMI 1972, no. 71

TRAIANUS
200.   Denomination: as
Axis: 6; D: 26.2 mm; W: 8.3 g.
Mint: Rome
Dating: AD 103-117
Obv: Legend erased.
       Bust laureate, right (portrait after AD 103).
Rv: Legend corroded.
       exergue: S C
       Pax seated left, holding branch.
Reference: -
Findspot: 1976, fort area, stray find.
Inv. No: c.c. 160/1976.

TRAIANUS
201.   Denomination: as, fragmentary
Axis: 6; D: 26.9 mm; W: 8.1 g.
Mint: Rome
Dating: AD 103-117
Obv: Legend erased.
       Silhouette of head laureate, right (portrait after AD 103).
Rv: Legend corroded.
       Silhouette standing.
Reference: -
Findspot: 1973, barrack 1, m 3-4/7, -0.80 m; phase Ib.
Inv. No: c.c. 91/1973.

TRAIANUS
202.   Denomination: as
Axis: 6; D: 26.8 x 24.7 mm; W: 10.6 g.
Mint: Rome
Dating: AD 103-117
Obv: Legend erased.
       Head laureate, right (portrait after AD 103).
Rv: Legend erased; S - C
       Fortuna standing left, holding rudder and cornucopiae.
Reference: -
Findspot: 1968, barrack 5, m 30, -1 m; phase Ia.
Inv. No: c.c. 39/1968.
BUCIUMI 1972, no. 92

TRAIANUS
203.   Denomination: as
Axis: 6; D: 26.8 mm; W: 8.7 g.
Mint: Rome
Dating: AD 103-117
Obv: Legend erased.
       Head laureate, right (portrait after AD 103).
Rv: Legend erased; S - C
       Female silhouette standing left, holding cornucopia and ?.
Reference: -
Findspot: 1973, barrack 2, m 7/13, -0.70 m; phase Ib.
Inv. No: c.c. 140/1973.

TRAIANUS
204.   Denomination: as
Axis: -; D: 28 x 25.1 mm; W: 9.1 g.
Mint: Rome
Dating: AD 103-117
Obv: Legend erased.
       Head laureate, right (portrait after AD 103).
Rv: Erased.
Reference: -
Findspot: 1972, barrack 2, -0.90 m; phase Ia.
Inv. No: c.c. 365/1972.

TRAIANUS
205.   Denomination: as
Axis: -; D: 27.5 x 24 mm; W: 9.8 g.
Mint: Rome
Dating: AD 103-117
Obv: Legend erased.
       Head laureate, right (portrait after AD 103).
Rv: Erased.
Reference: -
Findspot: 1973, barrack 2, m 4/ 0.50, -1.10 m; phase Ia.
Inv. No: c.c. 145/1973.

TRAIANUS
206.   Denomination: as
Axis: -; D: 26.6 mm; W: 10.4 g.
Mint: Rome
Dating: AD 103-117
Obv: Legend erased.
       Head laureate, right (portrait after AD 103).
Rv: Erased.
Reference: -
Findspot: 1973, barrack 1, m 2-3/7-8, -0.80 m; phase Ib.
Inv. No: c.c. 90/1973.

TRAIANUS
207.   Denomination: as
Axis: -; D: 27.1 x 25.7 mm; W: 10.8 g.
Mint: Rome
Dating: AD 103-117
Obv: Legend erased.
       Silhouette of bust, right (portrait after AD 103).
Rv: Corroded.
Reference: -
Findspot: 1973, barrack 2, -0.90 m; phase Ia.

Inv. No: c.c. 123/1973.

TRAIANUS
208. Denomination: denarius
Axis: -; D: 19.2 x 17.7 mm; W: 2 g.
Mint: Rome
Dating: AD 98-117
Obv: Legend erased.
   Silhouette of head, right.
Rv: corroded.
Reference: -
Findspot: 1970, barrack 5, excavated ground.
Inv. No: c.c. 23/1970.

TRAIANUS
209. Denomination: sestertius
Axis: -; D: 31.7 x 30.2 mm; W: 23.4 g.
Mint: Rome
Dating: AD 98-117
Obv: Legend erased.
   Silhouette of head, right.
Rv: corroded.
Reference: -
Findspot: 1968, barrack 5, excavated ground.
Inv. No: c.c. 32/1968.

BUCIUMI 1972, no. 114

TRAIANUS
210. Denomination: sestertius, *cast*
Axis: -; D: 33.5 x 30.2 mm; W: 19.4 g.
Mint: Rome
Dating: AD 98-117
Obv: Legend erased.
   Silhouette of head laureate, right.
Rv: corroded.
Reference: -
Findspot: 1973, barrack 1, m 28/2, -1 m; phase Ib.
Inv. No: c.c. 60/1973.
Remark: A very rudimentary cast coin.

TRAIANUS
211. Denomination: dupondius
Axis: -; D: 28.1 mm; W: 10.7 g.
Mint: Rome
Dating: AD 98-117
Obv: Legend erased.
   Vague silhouette of head radiate, right.
Rv: erased.
Reference: -
Findspot: 1970, barrack 4, -0.60 m; phase Ib.
Inv. No: c.c. 72/1970.
BUCIUMI 1972, no. 74

TRAIANUS
212. Denomination: as
Axis: -; D: 26.1 x 23.9 mm; W: 8.1 g.
Mint: Rome
Dating: AD 98-117
Obv: Legend erased.
   Vague silhouette of head, right.
Rv: corroded.
Reference: -
Findspot: 1967, the path between barracks 1 and 2.
Inv. No: c.c. 18/1967.
BUCIUMI 1972, no. 113

TRAIANUS
213. Denomination: as
Axis: -; D: 26.4 x 24.6 mm; W: 8.8 g.
Mint: Rome
Dating: AD 98-117
Obv: Legend erased.
   Vague silhouette of head, right.
Rv: corroded.
Reference: -
Findspot: 1967, the path between barracks 2 and 3.
Inv. No: c.c. 29/1967.
BUCIUMI 1972, no. 108

TRAIANUS
214. Denomination: as
Axis: -; D: 26.8 x 25 mm; W: 9 g.
Mint: Rome
Dating: AD 98-117
Obv: Legend erased.
   Vague silhouette of head, right.
Rv: Vague silhouette standing
Reference: -
Findspot: 1968, barrack 5.
Inv. No: c.c. 20/1968.
BUCIUMI 1972, no. 111

TRAIANUS
215. Denomination: as
Axis: 6; D: 26.6 x 24.4 mm; W: 5.8 g.
Mint: Rome
Dating: AD 98-117
Obv: Legend erased.
   Vague silhouette of head, right.
Rv: Vague silhouette standing.
Reference: -
Findspot: 1968, barrack 5, -0.50 m; phase II.
Inv. No: c.c. 26/1968.
BUCIUMI 1972, no. 265

TRAIANUS
216. Denomination: as
Axis: 6; D: 25.9 mm; W: 10.2 g.
Mint: Rome
Dating: AD 98-117
Obv: Legend erased.
   Silhouette of bust laureate, right.
Rv: Vague silhouette standing left, right hand extended.
Reference: -
Findspot: 1970, barrack 4, excavated ground.
Inv. No: c.c. 47/1970.
BUCIUMI 1972, no. 90

TRAIANUS
217.   Denomination: as
Axis: 6; D: 28.6 mm; W: 11.5 g.
Mint: Rome
Dating: AD 98-117
Obv: Legend erased.
        Silhouette of head, right.
Rv: [s] - C
        Vague silhouette standing.
Reference: -
Findspot: 1969, barrack 5, -1 m; phase Ia.
Inv. No: c.c. 105/1969.
BUCIUMI 1972, no. 76

TRAIANUS
218.   Denomination: as
Axis: -; D: 25.8 mm; W: 6.6 g.
Mint: Rome
Dating: AD 98-117
Obv: Legend erased.
        Vague silhouette of head, right.
Rv: erased.
Reference: -
Findspot: 1969, barrack 5, -1 m; phase Ia.
Inv. No: c.c. 117/1969.
BUCIUMI 1972, no. 112

TRAIANUS
219.   Denomination: as
Axis: -; D: 26.5 x 25.1 mm; W: 9.7 g.
Mint: Rome
Dating: AD 98-117
Obv: Legend erased.
        Vague silhouette of head, right.
Rv: erased.
Reference: -
Findspot: 1969, barrack 5, -1 m; phase Ia.
Inv. No: c.c. 133/1969.
BUCIUMI 1972, no. 107

TRAIANUS
220.   Denomination: as
Axis: 6; D: 27.6 mm; W: 10 g.
Mint: Rome
Dating: AD 98-117
Obv: Legend erased.
        Vague silhouette of head, right.
Rv: Legend corroded; S – [c].
Reference: -
Findspot: 1972, barrack 2, -0.90 m; phase Ia.
Inv. No: c.c. 371/1972.

TRAIANUS
221.   Denomination: as, *cast*
Axis: 6; D: 27.2 x 26 mm; W: 5.3 g.
Mint: Rome
Dating: AD 98-117 or later
Obv: IMP CAES NER...
        Vague silhouette of head, right.
Rv: Legend erased.
        Silhouette standing left.
Reference: -
Findspot: 1970, barrack 4, -0.80 m; phase Ib.
Inv. No: c.c. 81/1970.
BUCIUMI 1972, no. 81

TRAIANUS
222.   Denomination: as, *cast*
Axis: 6; D: 26.4 mm; W: 5.3 g.
Mint: Rome
Dating: AD 98-117 or later
Obv: Legend erased.
        Vague silhouette of head, right.
Rv: Legend erased: [s] - C.
        Silhouette standing left.
Reference: -
Findspot: 1971, barrack 1, -0.60 m; phase Ib.
Inv. No: c.c. 28/1971.

TRAIANUS
223.   Denomination: quadrans
Axis: -; D: 16 mm; W: 1.4 g.
Mint: Rome
Dating: AD 98-117
Obv: Legend erased.
        Vague silhouette of bust draped, right.
Rv: Corroded.
Reference: -
Findspot: 1975, barrack 2, trench 26, m 56.10, -0.25 m; phase II.
Inv. No: c.c. 48/1975.

TRAIANUS
224.   Denomination: AE20, provincial
Axis: 12; D: 22.7 mm; W: 3 g.
Mint: Perinthos Thraciae
Dating: AD 98-117
Obv: Legend erased.
        Head laureate, right.
Rv: ΠΕΡΙΝΘΙΩΝ
        Dionysus standing left, holding cantharus over lighted altar and thyrsus.
Reference: MOUSHMOV, 4438.
Findspot: 1973, barrack 1, m 41/8, -0.85 m; phase Ib.
Inv. No: c.c. 107/1973.

TRAIANUS
225.   Denomination: AE22, provincial
Axis: -; D: 22.7 mm; W: 3.5 g.
Mint: -
Dating: AD 98-117
Obv: Legend erased.
        Small head laureate, right.
Rv: Corroded
Reference: -
Findspot: 1973, barrack 1, m 32-33/2, -0.60 m; in the adobe layer; phase Ib.
Inv. No: c.c. 78/1973.

HADRIANUS
226. Denomination: sestertius
Axis: 6; D: 33.5 mm; W: 25.9 g.
Mint: Rome
Dating: AD 118
Obv: IMP CAESAR TRAIAN HADRIANVS AVG
Bust laureate, draped on left shoulder, 2/3 turned frontal, right.
Rv: PONT MAX TR P COS II; S – C
exergue: FORT RED
Fortuna seated left, holding cornucopiae and rudder.
Reference: RIC II, 551
Findspot: 1970, barrack 4, excavated ground.
Inv. No: c.c. 65/1970.
BUCIUMI 1972, no. 119

HADRIANUS
227. Denomination: as
Axis: 6; D: 26.3 x 24.8 mm; W: 7.8 g.
Mint: Rome
Dating: AD 118
Obv: Legend corroded.
Bust laureate, draped on left shoulder, 2/3 turned frontal, right.
Rv: Legend corroded.
Three legionary standards.
Reference: RIC II, 546a
Findspot: 1973, barrack 1, m 29, -0.80 m; phase Ib.
Inv. No: c.c. 116/1973.

HADRIANUS
228. Denomination: denarius, plated
Axis: 4; D: 18.1 mm; W: 2.8 g.
Mint: Rome
Dating: AD 119-122 or later
Obv: IMP CAESAR TRAIAN HADRIANVS AVG
Bust laureate, draped on left shoulder, right.
Rv: P M TR - P COS III
Mars advancing right with spear and trophy.
Reference: cf. RIC II, 67
Findspot: 1965, *principia*, near the wall 3, at 1 m from the S wall of trench XIV, -1.10 m; phase Ia.
Inv. No: c.c. 62/1965.
MUZEU 1968, no. 68; BUCIUMI 1972, p. 27; no. 115

HADRIANUS (Pl. III, 4)
229. Denomination: denarius
Axis: 6; D: 17.4 mm; W: 2.5 g.
Mint: Rome
Dating: AD 119-122
Obv: IMP CAESAR TRAIAN - HADRIANVS AVG
Bust laureate, draped on left shoulder, right.
Rv: P M TR - P COS III
Felicitas standing left, holding caduceus and cornucopiae.
Reference: RIC II, 83
Findspot: 1971, barrack 1, -0.40 m; phase Ib.
Inv. No: c.c. 21/1971.

HADRIANUS
230. Denomination: denarius, plated, fragment
Axis: 6; D: -; W: 1.3 g.
Mint: -
Dating: AD 119-122 or later
Obv: Legend corroded.
Bust laureate, right.
Rv: Legend corroded.
Victory flying right with trophy.
Reference: cf. RIC II, 101
Findspot: 1971, barrack 1, excavated ground.
Inv. No: c.c. 13/1971.

HADRIANUS (Pl. III, 5)
231. Denomination: denarius
Axis: 6; D: 18.2 x 17.1 mm; W: 2.8 g.
Mint: Rome
Dating: AD 119-122
Obv: IMP CAESAR TRAIAN - HADRIANVS AVG
Bust laureate, draped on left shoulder, right.
Rv: P M TR P – COS III; in field HI-LAR/ P - R
Hilaritas standing front, lifting veil from face.
Reference: RIC II, 126
Findspot: 1972, barrack 1, excavated ground.
Inv. No: c.c. 344/1972.

HADRIANUS (Pl. III, 6)
232. Denomination: sestertius
Axis: 6; D: 33.4 mm; W: 24.5 g.
Mint: Rome
Dating: AD 119-122
Obv: IMP CAESAR TRAIAN H-ADRIANVS AUG
Bust laureate, draped on left shoulder seen 2/3 turned frontal, right.
Rv: PONT MAX TR P-OT COS III
exergue: S C
Jupiter seated left, holding Victory and scepter.
Reference: RIC II, 561a
Findspot: 1970, barrack 4, -0.60 m; phase Ib.
Inv. No: c.c. 73/1970.
BUCIUMI 1972, no. 126

HADRIANUS
233. Denomination: sestertius
Axis: 6; D: 35 mm; W: 20.3 g.
Mint: Rome
Dating: AD 119-122
Obv: [imp caesa]R TRAIAN H-AD[rianus aug]
Bust laureate, draped and cuirassed seen 2/3 turned frontal, right.
Rv: Legend erased.
Ceres standing left, holding long torch.
Reference: RIC II, 610
Findspot: 1967, barrack 2.
Inv. No: c.c. 14/1967.
BUCIUMI 1972, no. 136

HADRIANUS
234. Denomination: as
Axis: 6; D: 25 mm; W: 7 g.

Mint: Rome
Dating: AD 119-122
Obv: IMP [caesar] TRAIANVS - HADRIANVS AVG
Bust laureate, draped and cuirassed seen 2/3 turned frontal, right.
Rv: [p]ONT [max tr pot cos iii]; S – [c]
Victory advancing right, holding wreath and palm.
Reference: RIC II, 572
Findspot: 1970, barrack 4, N part, -0.50 m; phase Ib.
Inv. No: c.c. 46/1970.
BUCIUMI 1972, no. 127

HADRIANUS
235.   Denomination: as
Axis: 6; D: 25.9 mm; W: 9 g.
Mint: Rome
Dating: AD 119-122
Obv: [imp caesar] TRAIANVS – H[adrianus aug]
Bust laureate, draped and cuirassed seen 2/3 turned frontal, right.
Rv: [pont ma]X TR POT [cos iii]; S – C
Felicitas standing left, holding a caduceus and a cornucopiae.
Reference: RIC II, 573b
Findspot: 1968, barrack 5, -1.25 m; phase Ia.
Inv. No: c.c. 106/1969.
BUCIUMI 1972, no. 128

HADRIANUS
236.   Denomination: as
Axis: 6; D: 25.8 mm; W: 9.1 g.
Mint: Rome
Dating: AD 119-122
Obv: IMP CAESAR TRAIANVS - HADRIANVS AVG
Bust laureate, draped and cuirassed seen 2/3 turned, right.
Rv: PONT MAX TR POT [cos iii]; S – C
Genius standing right, foot on globe, holding scepter and cornucopiae.
Reference: RIC II, 574
Findspot: 1968, barrack 5, m 25, -0.80 m; phase Ib.
Inv. No: c.c. 38/1968.
BUCIUMI 1972, no. 129

HADRIANUS
237.   Denomination: as
Axis: 6; D: 24.3 mm; W: 9.3 g.
Mint: Rome
Dating: AD 119-122
Obv: Legend corroded.
Silhouette of head, right.
Rv: PONT MAX TR [pot cos iii]; S – C
Aequitas standing left, holding scales and rod.
Reference: RIC II, 576
Findspot: 1973, barrack 1, m 8.75/3.50, -0.50 m; phase Ib.
Inv. No: c.c. 70/1973.

HADRIANUS
238.   Denomination: as
Axis: 6; D: 26.2 x 25.1 mm; W: 9.2 g.
Mint: Rome
Dating: AD 119-122
Obv: [imp caesar] TRAIANVS – HADR[ianus aug]
Bust laureate, draped on left shoulder, right.
Rv: [pont max tr pot] COS III; in field, PIE – AVG; S – C
Pietas standing with patera, altar at right.
Reference: RIC II, 579a
Findspot: 1971, barrack 1, quadrant 10 x 3, -0.70 m; phase Ib.
Inv. No: c.c. 32/1971.

HADRIANUS
239.   Denomination: as
Axis: 6; D: 28.6 x 25.4 mm; W: 10.4 g.
Mint: Rome
Dating: AD 119-122
Obv: [imp caesar tra]IAN HA-DRIANVS AVG
Bust laureate, draped and cuirassed seen 2/3 turned, right.
Rv: P M TR P COS III; S – C
Pax standing left, holding branch and cornucopiae.
Reference: RIC II, 616c
Findspot: 1965, barrack 2, -0.80 m; phase Ib.
Inv. No: c.c. 7/1965.
MUZEU 1968, no. 87; BUCIUMI 1972, no. 124

HADRIANUS
240.   Denomination: as
Axis: 6; D: 28.2 mm; W: 10.6 g.
Mint: Rome
Dating: AD 119-122
Obv: [imp caesar tra]IAN HADRIANVS AVG
Bust laureate, draped and cuirassed seen 2/3 turned, right.
Rv: P M [tr p cos] III; S – C
Pax standing left, holding branch and cornucopiae.
Reference: RIC II, 616c
Findspot: 1969, barrack 5, -0.60 m; phase II.
Inv. No: c.c. 111/1969.
BUCIUMI 1972, no. 117

HADRIANUS
241.   Denomination: as
Axis: 5; D: 27.2 x 25.3 mm; W: 9.2 g.
Mint: Rome
Dating: AD 119-122
Obv: IMP CAESAR TRAIAN HADRIANVS AVG
Bust laureate, draped and cuirassed seen 2/3 turned, right.
Rv: Legend corroded; S – C
Pax standing left, holding branch and cornucopiae.
Reference: RIC II, 616c
Findspot: 1971, barrack 1, excavated ground.
Inv. No: c.c. 17/1971.

HADRIANUS
242.   Denomination: as
Axis: 6; D: 24.8 x 23.1 mm; W: 4.8 g.
Mint: Rome

Dating: AD 119-122
Obv: Legend corroded
  Bust laureate, draped and cuirassed seen 2/3 turned, right.
Rv: [p m tr p] - COS III; S – C
  exergue: FORT RED
  Fortuna seated left, holding rudder and cornucopiae.
Reference: RIC II, 617c
Findspot: 1970, barrack 4, in the modern humus, -0.30 m; phase II.
Inv. No: c.c. 70/1970.
BUCIUMI 1972, no. 206 (but Septimius Severus)

HADRIANUS
243.   Denomination: as
Axis: 5; D: 28.4 x 26.4 mm; W: 9.1 g.
Mint: Rome
Dating: AD 119-122
Obv: [imp] CAES[ar tra]IAN HAD[rianus aug]
  Bust laureate, draped and cuirassed seen 2/3 turned, right.
Rv: [p] M TR [p] – [cos iii]; S – C
  Aequitas standing left, holding scales and cornucopiae.
Reference: RIC II, 618 (but quadrans)
Findspot: 1970, barrack 4, -1 m; phase Ia.
Inv. No: c.c. 75/1970.
BUCIUMI 1972, no. 125

HADRIANUS
244.   Denomination: as
Axis: 6; D: 23 mm; W: 4.9 g.
Mint: Rome
Dating: AD 119-122
Obv: Legend erased
  Bust laureate, draped and cuirassed seen 2/3 turned, right.
Rv: Legend erased; S – C
  Aequitas standing left, holding scales and cornucopiae.
Reference: cf. RIC II, 618 (but quadrans)
Findspot: 1972, barrack 2, -1 m; phase Ia.
Inv. No: c.c. 357/1972.

HADRIANUS
245.   Denomination: dupondius
Axis: -; D: 25.9 mm; W: 9.9 g.
Mint: Rome
Dating: AD 119-122
Obv: Legend non-readable (long inscription)
  Bust radiate, draped and cuirassed seen 2/3 turned, right.
Rv: erased.
Reference: -
Findspot: 1972, barrack 2, -1 m; phase Ia.
Inv. No: c.c. 363/1972.

HADRIANUS (Pl. III, 7)
246.   Denomination: denarius
Axis: 4; D: 20.6 x 17.6 mm; W: 2.4 g.
Mint: Rome
Dating: AD 125-128
Obv: HADRIANVS - [augus]TVS
  Head laureate, draped on left shoulder, right.
Rv: CO[s] I[ii]
  Roma seated right on cuirass and shield, holding spear and parazonium; foot on helmet.
Reference: variant of RIC II, 163.
Findspot: 1973, barrack 1, m 3.20/3.75, -0.50 m; phase Ib.
Inv. No: c.c. 72/1973.
Remark: a possible minting error due to the irregular shape of the flan.

HADRIANUS (Pl. III, 8)
247.   Denomination: denarius
Axis: 6; D: 18.8 x 17.9 mm; W: 3 g.
Mint: Rome
Dating: AD 125-128
Obv: HADRIANVS AVGVSTVS
  Head laureate, right.
Rv: CO-S III
  Hercules seated right, holding club on shield, seated upon cuirass and holding Victory.
Reference: RIC II, 148
Findspot: 1968, barrack 5, m 5, -0.90 m; phase Ib.
Inv. No: c.c. 48/1968.
BUCIUMI 1972, no. 118

HADRIANUS
248.   Denomination: as
Axis: 5; D: 27.2 x 25.3 mm; W: 10 g.
Mint: Rome
Dating: AD 125-128
Obv: HADRIANVS - AVGVSTVS
  Head laureate, right.
Rv: COS – III; S – C
  Salus standing, head right, feeding snake held in arms from patera.
Reference: RIC II, 669
Findspot: 1976, fort area, stray find.
Inv. No: c.c. 157/1976.

HADRIANUS
249.   Denomination: as
Axis: 6; D: 25.3 x 23.8 mm; W: 8.6 g.
Mint: Rome
Dating: AD 125-128
Obv: HADRIANVS [august]VS
  Head laureate, right.
Rv: COS – [ii]I; S – C
  Salus standing, head right, feeding snake held in arms from patera.
Reference: RIC II, 669
Findspot: 1968, barrack 5, m 21, -0.70 m; phase Ib.
Inv. No: c.c. 35/1968.
BUCIUMI 1972, no. 123

HADRIANUS
250.   Denomination: as
Axis: 6; D: 26.2 x 24.7 mm; W: 6.4 g.

Mint: Rome
Dating: AD 125-128
Obv: HADRIANVS AVG[ustus]
  Head laureate, right.
Rv: COS – III; S – C
  Salus standing, head right, feeding snake held in arms from patera.
Reference: RIC II, 669
Findspot: 1969, barrack 5, excavated ground.
Inv. No: c.c. 126/1969.
BUCIUMI 1972, no. 133

HADRIANUS
251.   Denomination: as
Axis: 6; D: 26.8 x 25.6 mm; W: 8.3 g.
Mint: Rome
Dating: AD 125-128
Obv: HADRIANVS AVGVST[us]
  Head laureate, right.
Rv: COS – III; S – C
  Salus standing, head right, feeding snake held in arms from patera.
Reference: RIC II, 669
Findspot: 1973, barrack 1, m 29/2, -0.70 m; phase Ib.
Inv. No: c.c. 55/1973.

HADRIANUS
252.   Denomination: as
Axis: 6; D: 27.7 x 26.1 mm; W: 9.6 g.
Mint: Rome
Dating: AD 125-128
Obv: HADRIANVS [augustus]
  Head laureate, right.
Rv: Legend corroded; S – C
  Salus standing, head right, feeding snake held in arms from patera.
Reference: RIC II, 669
Findspot: 1968, barrack 5, -0.90 m; phase Ib.
Inv. No: c.c. 11/1968.
BUCIUMI 1972, no. 121

HADRIANUS
253.   Denomination: as
Axis: 6; D: 27.3 x 24.9 mm; W: 8.3 g.
Mint: Rome
Dating: AD 125-128
Obv: HADRIANVS [augustus]
  Head laureate, right.
Rv: Legend corroded; S – C
  Salus standing, head right, feeding snake held in arms from patera.
Reference: RIC II, 669
Findspot: 1968, barrack 5, m 20, -0.80 m; phase Ib.
Inv. No: c.c. 47/1968.
BUCIUMI 1972, no. 122

HADRIANUS
254.   Denomination: as
Axis: 6; D: 26.3 mm; W: 8.8 g.
Mint: Rome
Dating: AD 125-128
Obv: HADRIANVS AVGVS[tus]
  Head laureate, right.
Rv: COS [iii]; S – C
  Salus standing, head right, feeding snake held in arms from patera.
Reference: RIC II, 669
Findspot: 1969, barrack 5, -0.80 m; phase Ib.
Inv. No: c.c. 138/1969.
BUCIUMI 1972, no. 131

HADRIANUS
255.   Denomination: as
Axis: 6; D: 27.4 mm; W: 9.6 g.
Mint: Rome
Dating: AD 125-128
Obv: HADR[ianus august]VS
  Head laureate, right.
Rv: [c]O[s iii]; S – C
  Salus standing, head right, feeding snake held in arms from patera.
Reference: RIC II, 669
Findspot: 1970, barrack 4, -0.50 m; phase Ib.
Inv. No: c.c. 39/1970.
BUCIUMI 1972, no. 120

HADRIANUS
256.   Denomination: as
Axis: 4; D: 25.7 x 23.7 mm; W: 10.3 g.
Mint: Rome
Dating: AD 125-128
Obv: [hadrianus] AVGVS[tus]
  Head laureate, right.
Rv: [cos i]I[i]; S – C
  Salus standing, head right, feeding snake held in arms from patera.
Reference: RIC II, 669
Findspot: 1972, barrack 2, -0.80 m; phase Ib.
Inv. No: c.c. 361/1972.

HADRIANUS
257.   Denomination: as
Axis: 6; D: 26.9 x 25.3 mm; W: 9.7 g.
Mint: Rome
Dating: AD 125-128
Obv: HADRIANVS AV[ugustus]
  Head laureate, right.
Rv: COS - I[ii]; S – [c]
  Silhouette of Salus standing, head right, feeding snake held in arms from patera.
Reference: RIC II, 669
Findspot: 1973, barrack 1, m 26/2, -0.80 m; phase Ib.
Inv. No: c.c. 59/1973.

HADRIANUS
258.   Denomination: as
Axis: 5; D: 26.5 x 24.7 mm; W: 8.8 g.
Mint: Rome
Dating: AD 125-128
Obv: HADRIANVS AVGVSTVS

Head laureate, right.
Rv: COS - III; S – C
Salus standing, head right, feeding snake held in arms from patera.
Reference: RIC II, 669
Findspot: 1973, barrack 1, m 48, -0.80 m; phase Ib.
Inv. No: c.c. 118/1973.

HADRIANUS
259.   Denomination: as
Axis: 6; D: 26.9 mm; W: 12.4 g.
Mint: Rome
Dating: AD 125-128
Obv: HADRIANVS [august]VS
Head laureate, right.
Rv: COS - III; S – C
Salus standing, head right, feeding snake held in arms from patera.
Reference: RIC II, 669
Findspot: 1973, barrack 2, -0.80 m; phase Ib.
Inv. No: c.c. 126/1973.

HADRIANUS
260.   Denomination: as
Axis: 6; D: 27.1 x 24.3 mm; W: 8.7 g.
Mint: Rome
Dating: AD 125-128
Obv: HADRIANVS [au]GVSTV[s]
Head laureate, right.
Rv: COS - III; S – C
Salus standing, head right, feeding snake held in arms from patera.
Reference: RIC II, 669
Findspot: 1973, barrack 2, -0.80 m; phase Ib.
Inv. No: c.c. 129/1973.

HADRIANUS
261.   Denomination: as
Axis: 6; D: 25.4 x 23.6 mm; W: 6.8 g.
Mint: Rome
Dating: AD 125-128
Obv: Legend erased.
Silhouette of head, right.
Rv: Legend erased.
Salus standing, head right, feeding snake held in arms from patera.
Reference: cf. RIC II, 669
Findspot: 1973, barrack 1, m 2/3.50, -0.40 m; phase Ib.
Inv. No: c.c. 71/1973.

HADRIANUS
262.   Denomination: as, *cast*
Axis: 5; D: 23.6 x 22.6 mm; W: 2.9 g.
Mint: Rome
Dating: AD 125-128
Obv: [hadria]NVS AVGVS[tus]
Head laureate, right.
Rv: COS III; S – C
Salus standing, head right, feeding snake held in arms from patera.
Reference: cf. RIC II, 669
Findspot: 1976, fort area, stray find.
Inv. No: c.c. 166/1976.

HADRIANUS
263.   Denomination: as, *cast*
Axis: 5; D: 23.7 mm; W: 5.1 g.
Mint: -
Dating: AD 125-128 or later
Obv: Legend erased.
Silhouette of head, right.
Rv: [c] O [s iii]; S - C
Salus standing, head right, feeding snake held in arms from patera.
Reference: cf. RIC II, 669
Findspot: 1973, barrack 1, m 2-3/5-6, -0.60 m; phase Ib.
Inv. No: c.c. 85/1973.

HADRIANUS (Pl. III, 9)
264.   Denomination: denarius, fragmentary
Axis: 6; D: 18.4 x 17.7 mm; W: 2.6 g.
Mint: Rome
Dating: AD 134-138
Obv: HADRI[anus] - AVG COS III P P
Head laureate, right.
Rv: FORT – RE[duci]
Fortuna standing left with rudder on globe and cornucopiae, shaking hands with Hadrian.
Reference: RIC II, 243
Findspot: 1973, barrack 1, m 26/3.5, -0.85 m; phase Ib.
Inv. No: c.c. 58/1973.

HADRIANUS
265.   Denomination: sestertius
Axis: 4; D: 31.3 x 30 mm; W: 23.9 g.
Mint: Rome
Dating: AD 134-138
Obv: HADRIANVS - AVG COS III P P
Head bare, right.
Rv: No legend; S - C
Diana standing facing, head left, holding arrow and bow.
Reference: RIC II, 777
Findspot: 1973, barrack 1, m 2-3/4-5, -0.50-0.60 m; phase Ib.
Inv. No: c.c. 83/1973.

HADRIANUS
266.   Denomination: as
Axis: 6; D: 25.3 x 23.1 mm; W: 10.2 g.
Mint: Rome
Dating: AD 134-138
Obv: HAD[rianus aug cos iii] P P
Bust laureate and draped, right.
Rv: SAL[us aug]
exergue: S C
Salus seated left, feeding snake coiled around altar and resting left arm on chair.
Reference: RIC II, 833
Findspot: 1972, barrack 1, -0.80 m; phase Ib.

Inv. No: c.c. 352/1972.

HADRIANUS
267.   Denomination: as
Axis: 6; D: 24.3 x 22.6 mm; W: 9.5 g.
Mint: Rome
Dating: AD 134-138
Obv: HADRIAN[us aug] CO[s iii p p]
       Bust laureate and draped bust, left.
Rv: S – C
       exergue: Dacia
       Dacia seated left on rock, holding vexillum in right hand, curved sword in left.
Reference: RIC II, 849
Findspot: 1971, barrack 1, -0.20 m; phase II.
Inv. No: c.c. 18/1971.

HADRIANUS
268.   Denomination: as, fragmentary
Axis: 6; D: 23.5 mm; W: 3 g.
Mint: Rome
Dating: AD 134-138
Obv: [hadrianus] AVG COS III P P
       Silhouette of head laureate, right.
Rv: Legend corroded; S - C.
       Salus standing right, holding patera, feeding serpent arising from altar.
Reference: cf. RIC II, 832
Findspot: 1973, barrack 1, excavated ground.
Inv. No: c.c. 49/1973.

HADRIANUS
269.   Denomination: as
Axis: 6; D: 24.3 x 22.6 mm; W: 9.5 g.
Mint: Rome
Dating: AD 134-138
Obv: [hadri]ANVS…
       Bust laureate, right.
Rv: Legend erased
       Salus standing right, holding patera, feeding serpent arising from altar.
Reference: RIC II, 832
Findspot: 1965, *porta principalis dextra*, W tower, -1.15 m; phase Ia.
Inv. No: c.c. 112/1965.
MUZEU 1968, no. 89; BUCIUMI 1972, p. 18; no. 138

HADRIANUS
270.   Denomination: as
Axis: 6; D: 25.3 mm; W: 9.4 g.
Mint: Rome
Dating: AD 134-138
Obv: [hadrianus] – AVG C[os iii p p]
       Bust, right.
Rv: Legend erased
       Vague silhouette standing.
Reference: -
Findspot: 1970, barrack 5, excavated ground.
Inv. No: c.c. 33/1970.
BUCIUMI 1972, no. 116

HADRIANUS
271.   Denomination: as
Axis: -; D: 25.1 x 23.9 mm; W: 9.7 g.
Mint: Rome
Dating: AD 122-138
Obv: Legend corroded.
       Bust laureate, right (portrait after AD 122).
Rv: Corroded.
Reference: -
Findspot: 1967, barrack 5, near *via praetoria*.
Inv. No: c.c. 21/1967.
BUCIUMI 1972, no. 137

HADRIANUS
272.   Denomination: as
Axis: 6; D: 25.7 x 24.8 mm; W: 12.3 g.
Mint: Rome
Dating: AD 122-138
Obv: Legend corroded.
       Bust laureate, right (portrait after AD 122).
Rv: Legend corroded.
       Vague silhouette of person seated left.
Reference: -
Findspot: 1973, barrack 2, m 17, beneath de the S wall, -0.80 m; phase Ib
Inv. No: c.c. 155/1973.

HADRIANUS
273.   Denomination: as
Axis: 6; D: -; W: 4.6 g.
Mint: Rome
Dating: AD 122-138
Obv: Legend corroded.
       Silhouette of head, right (portrait after AD 122).
Rv: Legend corroded.
       Vague silhouette of person standing right.
Reference: -
Findspot: 1973, barrack 2, m 50/11, -1.50 m; phase Ia
Inv. No: c.c. 144/1973.

HADRIANUS
274.   Denomination: sestertius
Axis: 6; D: 31.7 mm; W: 22.1 g.
Mint: Rome
Dating: AD 117-138
Obv: Legend corroded.
       Vague silhouette of head, right.
Rv: Legend corroded.
       Female silhouette standing left, holding cornucopiae and ?
Reference: -
Findspot: 1972, barrack 1, -0.75 m; phase Ib.
Inv. No: c.c. 347/1972.

HADRIANUS
275.   Denomination: sestertius
Axis: -; D: 30.9 x 29.8 mm; W: 24.1 g.
Mint: Rome
Dating: AD 117-138
Obv: Legend corroded.

Bust right.
Rv: Corroded.
Reference: -
Findspot: 1970, barrack 4, -1.20 m; phase Ia.
Inv. No: c.c. 62/1970.
BUCIUMI 1972, no. 142

HADRIANUS
276.   Denomination: as, fragmentary
Axis: -; D: -; W: 7.6 g.
Mint: Rome
Dating: AD 117-138
Obv: Legend corroded.
       Bust right.
Rv: Corroded.
Reference: -
Findspot: 1968, barrack 5, m 30.
Inv. No: c.c. 34/1968.

HADRIANUS
277.   Denomination: as
Axis: -; D: 25.9 x 24.1 mm; W: 8.8 g.
Mint: Rome
Dating: AD 117-138
Obv: Legend corroded.
       Bust laureate, right.
Rv: Corroded.
Reference: -
Findspot: 1968, barrack 5, m 30, -0.75m; phase Ib.
Inv. No: c.c. 36/1968.
BUCIUMI 1972, no. 140

HADRIANUS
278.   Denomination: as
Axis: -; D: 26.8 x 25.5 mm; W: 10.3 g.
Mint: Rome
Dating: AD 117-138
Obv: Legend corroded.
       Bust laureate, right.
Rv: Corroded.
Reference: -
Findspot: 1968, barrack 5.
Inv. No: c.c. 42/1968.
BUCIUMI 1972, no. 141

HADRIANUS
279.   Denomination: as
Axis: -; D: 27 mm; W: 10.3 g.
Mint: Rome
Dating: AD 117-138
Obv: Legend corroded.
       Vague silhouette of head, right.
Rv: Corroded.
Reference: -
Findspot: 1973, barrack 1, m 14.80/2, -1 m; phase Ia.
Inv. No: c.c. 76/1973.

HADRIANUS
280.   Denomination: as
Axis: -; D: 26.6 x 25.7 mm; W: 8.2 g.
Mint: Rome
Dating: AD 117-138
Obv: Legend corroded.
       Vague silhouette of head, right.
Rv: Corroded.
Reference: -
Findspot: 1973, barrack 1, m 2/8, -1 m; phase Ia.
Inv. No: c.c. 110/1973.

HADRIANUS
281.   Denomination: as, burnt
Axis: -; D: 25.1 mm; W: 4.3 g.
Mint: Rome
Dating: AD 117-138
Obv: Legend corroded.
       Vague silhouette of head, right.
Rv: Corroded.
Reference: -
Findspot: 1975, barrack 2, m 15.35, -2 m; in the coal and mortar layer that delimited the m 15.50 from the yellow clay.
Inv. No: c.c. 47/1975.

HADRIANUS (Pl. III, 10)
282.   Denomination: AE (as?) provincial
Axis: 6; D: 25.4 mm; W: 8.4 g.
Mint: Philippi Macedoniae
Dating: AD 117-138
Obv: IMP CAES TR[aian had/hadrianus aug cos iii?]
       Laureate head of Hadrian, right.
Rv: COLON [?...phil]I[p]
       Cippus inscribed DIVVS/AVG on which stand statues of Augustus in military dress crowned by Divus Julius; altar on either side.
Reference: cf. MOUSHMOV, 6928 (var.)
Findspot: 1970, barrack 5, between the SE walls, -1 m; phase Ia.
Inv. No: c.c. 17/1970.
BUCIUMI 1972, no. 139

HADRIANUS
283.   Denomination: AE (dupondius?) provincial
Axis: 6; D: 27.5 x 26.6 mm; W: 10.2 g.
Mint: Bithynia
Dating: AD 117-138
Obv: Legend erased.
       Radiate head of Hadrian, right.
Rv: [KOI] – [N]O[N]
       exergue: B[EIΘ]VNIAC
       Octastyle temple with shield in pediment.
Reference: SNG von Aulock, 285
Findspot: 1973, barrack 2, *via sagularis*, m 49, -0.50 m; phase Ib.
Inv. No: c.c. 142/1973.

Posthumous issue?: Hadrianus Augustus P P
284.   Denomination: sestertius
Axis: 6; D: 33.2 x 30.9 mm; W: 26.2 g.
Mint: Rome
Dating: AD 138-139

Obv: HADRIANVS – AVGVSTVS P P
Head laureate, right.
Rv: [cos i]II
exergue: S C
Roma seated left on cuirass, holding Victory and cornucopiae.
Reference: RIC II, 967
Findspot: 1968, barrack 5, m 10, -0.75 m; phase Ib.
Inv. No: c.c. 45/1968.
BUCIUMI 1972, no. 130

Posthumous issue?: Hadrianus Augustus P P
(Pl. III, 11)
285. Denomination: sestertius
Axis: 5; D: 31.6 mm; W: 22.3 g.
Mint: Rome
Dating: AD 138-139
Obv: HADRIANVS – AVGVSTVS P P
Head laureate, right.
Rv: HILAR-I-TAS P R; S - C
exergue: COS III
Hilaritas standing left, holding long palm and cornucopia, small boy and girl to sides.
Reference: RIC II, 970
Findspot: 1966, barrack 2, near the *via sagularis*, -1.35 m; phase Ia.
Inv. No: c.c. 31/1966.
BUCIUMI 1972, p. 22; no. 135

Posthumous issue?: Hadrianus Augustus P P
286. Denomination: sestertius
Axis: 5; D: 34.9 x 31.9 mm; W: 25.4 g.
Mint: Rome
Dating: AD 138-139
Obv: HADRIANVS – AVGVSTVS [p p]
Head laureate, right.
Rv: HILARI-TAS [p r]; S - C
exergue: COS III
Hilaritas standing left, holding long palm and cornucopia, small boy and girl to sides.
Reference: RIC II, 970
Findspot: 1973, barrack 2, m 5/4, -1 m; phase Ia.
Inv. No: c.c. 143/1973.

Posthumous issue?: Hadrianus Augustus P P
287. Denomination: dupondius
Axis: 6; D: 26 mm; W: 10.8 g.
Mint: Rome
Dating: AD 138-139
Obv: HADRIANVS – AVGVSTVS P P
Bust radiate with drapery on left shoulder, right.
Rv: HILARITAS P R; S - C
exergue: COS III
Hilaritas standing left, holding long palm and cornucopia, small boy and girl to sides.
Reference: RIC II, 974
Findspot: 1969, barrack 5, excavated ground.
Inv. No: c.c. 109/1969.
BUCIUMI 1972, no. 134

Posthumous issue?: Hadrianus Augustus P P
288. Denomination: dupondius
Axis: 6; D: 27.8 mm; W: 12.1 g.
Mint: Rome
Dating: AD 138-139
Obv: HADRIANVS – AVGVSTVS P P
Bust radiate, right.
Rv: HILA-RI-T-[as p r]; S - C
exergue: COS III
Hilaritas standing left, holding long palm and cornucopia, small boy and girl to sides.
Reference: RIC II, 974
Findspot: 1969, barrack 5, -0.50 m; phase II.
Inv. No: c.c. 135/1969.
BUCIUMI 1972, no. 132

Posthumous issue?: Hadrianus Augustus P P
289. Denomination: as
Axis: 4; D: 27.1 mm; W: 12.4 g.
Mint: Rome
Dating: AD 138-139
Obv: HADRI[anus – au]GVSTVS P P
Head laureate, right.
Rv: COS – III; S - C
Salus standing right, feeding snake.
Reference: RIC II, 975
Findspot: 1973, barrack 1, -1 m; phase Ia.
Inv. No: c.c. 77/1973.

Posthumous issue?: Hadrianus Augustus P P
290. Denomination: as
Axis: 6; D: 26.8 mm; W: 11.5 g.
Mint: Rome
Dating: AD 138-139
Obv: HADRIANVS – AVGVSTVS P P
Head laureate, right.
Rv: COS – III; S - C
Salus standing right, feeding snake.
Reference: RIC II, 975
Findspot: 1976, fort area, stray find.
Inv. No: c.c. 155/1976.

Posthumous issue?: Hadrianus Augustus P P
291. Denomination: as
Axis: 6; D: 25.8 mm; W: 9.1 g.
Mint: Rome
Dating: AD 138-139
Obv: HADRIANVS – AVGVSTVS [p p]
Head laureate, right.
Rv: COS – III; S - C
Salus standing right, feeding snake.
Reference: RIC II, 975
Findspot: 1997, *principia*, C2/97, m 17-18, -0.40 m; phase II.
Inv. No: c.c. 51/2001.
BUCIUMI 2000, p. 346, no. 3 (but dupondius)

HADRIANUS: Sabina
292. Denomination: as
Axis: 6; D: 27.2 x 25.2 mm; W: 6.6 g.

Mint: Rome
Dating: AD 117-138
Obv: Legend erased.
Diademed draped bust right, with plait down nape of neck, right.
Rv: Legend erased.
Concordia standing left, holding patera and double cornucopiae.
Reference: cf. RIC II, 1047
Findspot: 1970, barrack 4, -0.25 m; phase II.
Inv. No: c.c. 35/1970.
BUCIUMI 1972, no. 143

ANTONINUS PIUS (Pl. III, 13)
293.   Denomination: denarius
Axis: 6; D: 17.4 mm; W: 3.1 g.
Mint: Rome
Dating: AD 139
Obv: ANTONINVS - AVG PIVS P P
Head bare, right.
Rv: TR P – COS II
Pax standing left, holding olive branch and cornucopia.
Reference: RIC III, 42
Findspot: 1973, barrack 2, *via sagularis*, m 51, 0.60 m from the SE wall of the barrack, -0.65 m; phase Ib.
Inv. No: c.c. 127/1973.

ANTONINUS PIUS
294.   Denomination: dupondius
Axis: 11; D: 25.6 x 23.6 mm; W: 11 g.
Mint: Rome
Dating: AD 143-144
Obv: ANTONINVS AVG [pivs p p tr p cos iii]
Head radiate, right.
Rv: [imperator]R II; S - C
Victory advancing right with trophy.
Reference: RIC III, 724
Findspot: 1968, barrack 5, m 5-10, -0.80 m; phase Ib.
Inv. No: c.c. 46/1968.
BUCIUMI 1972, no. 152.

ANTONINUS PIUS
295.   Denomination: dupondius
Axis: 12; D: 26 x 24.2 mm; W: 10.7 g.
Mint: Rome
Dating: AD 140-144
Obv: ANTONINVS AVG PI-VS P P TR P COS III
Head radiate, right.
Rv: [s]ALVS – AVG; S - C
Salus standing left, feeding snake coiled around altar and holding sceptre.
Reference: RIC III, 668
Findspot: 1963, the N tower of the *porta principalis sinistra*.
Inv. No: c.c. 70/1963.
MUZEU 1968, no. 115; BUCIUMI 1972, p. 15; no. 153.

ANTONINUS PIUS
296.   Denomination: as
Axis: 12; D: 25.7 x 24.3 mm; W: 10 g.
Mint: Rome
Dating: AD 140-144
Obv: ANTONINVS AVG PI-VS P P TR P COS III
Head radiate, right.
Rv: ANNO – [na aug]; S – [c]
Abundantia standing right, holding corn-ears and cornucopiae; to left, modius with corn-ears; to right, prow of ship.
Reference: RIC III, 675
Findspot: 1973, barrack 1, m 11.50/5-6, -0.90 m; phase Ib.
Inv. No: c.c. 100/1973.

ANTONINUS PIUS
297.   Denomination: denarius, plated
Axis: 12; D: 17.5 mm; W: 2.6 g.
Mint: Rome
Dating: AD 147-148 or later
Obv: ANTONINVS AVG – PIVS P P TR P XI
Head laureate, right.
Rv: CO-S – III[i]
Annona standing left before modius filled with corn ears, holding two corn ears and anchor.
Reference: cf. RIC III, 162
Findspot: 1973, barrack 1, m 27/2, -0.80 m.
Inv. No: c.c. 57/1973.

ANTONINUS PIUS
298.   Denomination: denarius, plated, 2 fragments
Axis: 12; D: -; W: 1.4 g.
Mint: -
Dating: AD 148-149 or later
Obv: ANTONINVS [aug pius p p tr] P XII
Head laureate, right.
Rv: [cos ii]II
Aequitas standing left, holding scales and cornucopia.
Reference: cf. RIC III, 177
Findspot: 1975, building C1, N corner, -0.30 m; phase II.
Inv. No: c.c. 38/1975.

ANTONINUS PIUS (Pl. III, 14)
299.   Denomination: denarius
Axis: 6; D: 17.9 x 16 mm; W: 3 g.
Mint: Rome
Dating: AD 148-149
Obv: ANTONINVS AVG – PIVS P P TR P XII
Head laureate, right.
Rv: CO-S – IIII
Genius standing left, holding patera and grain ears.
Reference: RIC III, 180
Findspot: 1969, barrack 5, -0.70 m; phase Ib.
Inv. No: c.c. 103/1969.
BUCIUMI 1972, no. 145.

ANTONINUS PIUS
300.   Denomination: sestertius
Axis: 12; D: 30.7 x 30 mm; W: 26 g.
Mint: Rome
Dating: AD 148-149

Obv: [an]TONINVS AVG – [pi]VS P P TR P XII
Head laureate, right.
Rv: TEMPORVM FELICITAS; S - C
exergue: COS IIII
Crossed cornuacopiae each surmounted by busts of two little boys.
Reference: RIC III, 857
Findspot: 1971, barrack 1, -0.40 m; phase Ib.
Inv. No: c.c. 30/1971.

ANTONINUS PIUS (Pl. III, 16)
301.   Denomination: denarius
Axis: 6; D: 17.2 x 16.2 mm; W: 2.8 g.
Mint: Rome
Dating: AD 152-153
Obv: ANTONINVS AVG – PIVS P P TR P XVI
Head laureate, right.
Rv: C-OS IIII
Annona standing left, holding grain-ears and resting hand on modius set on ship.
Reference: RIC III, 221
Findspot: 1974, *principia*, excavated ground.
Inv. No: c.c. 40/1974.

ANTONINUS PIUS
302.   Denomination: sestertius
Axis: 12; D: 32.2 mm; W: 21.1 g.
Mint: Rome
Dating: AD 153-154
Obv: [antoninus aug pius p p] TR P XVII
Head laureate, right.
Rv: LIBERTAS – [aug]; S - C
Libertas standing, head right, holding cap.
Reference: RIC III, 916a
Findspot: 1966, *porta praetoria*, W tower, in the layer of fire; phase II.
Inv. No: c.c. 40/1966.
BUCIUMI 1972, p. 18; no. 159.

ANTONINUS PIUS (Pl. III, 17)
303.   Denomination: denarius
Axis: 6; D: 17 mm; W: 2.7 g.
Mint: Rome
Dating: AD 156-157
Obv: ANTONINVS AVG PIVS P P IMP II
Head laureate, right.
Rv: TR POT – XX COS IIII
Salus seated left, feeding serpent rising from altar.
Reference: RIC III, 264
Findspot: 1970, barrack 5, between the SE walls, -0.70 m; phase Ib.
Inv. No: c.c. 14/1970.
BUCIUMI 1972, no. 147.

ANTONINUS PIUS
304.   Denomination: dupondius
Axis: 12; D: 24.7 mm; W: 9.4 g.
Mint: Rome
Dating: AD 157-158
Obv: [anton]INVS AVG - PIVS [p p imp ii]
Head radiate, right.
Rv: [tr pot xxi] - COS IIII
Abundantia standing right foot on a prow holding rudder on globe
Reference: cf. RIC III, 993
Findspot: 1970, barrack 4, -1.50 m; phase Ia (!).
Inv. No: c.c. 68/1970.
BUCIUMI 1972, no. 160.

ANTONINUS PIUS (Pl. III, 19)
305.   Denomination: denarius
Axis: 12; D: 18.5 x 16.1 mm; W: 2.8 g.
Mint: Rome
Dating: AD 158-159
Obv: ANTONINVS - AVG PIVS P P
Head laureate, right.
Rv: V OT SOL - DECENNAL II
exergue: COS IIII
Antoninus veiled standing left, sacrificing out of patera in right hand over tripod-altar, and holding scroll; prostrate bull beside altar.
Reference: BMC IV, 578
Findspot: 1970, barrack 4, -0.50 m; phase Ib.
Inv. No: c.c. 40/1970.
BUCIUMI 1972, no. 149.

ANTONINUS PIUS
306.   Denomination: denarius, plated
Axis: 11; D: 17.9 x 16.7 mm; W: 2.4 g.
Mint: Rome
Dating: AD 158-160 or later
Obv: ANTONINVS AVG PI[us p p tr p xxii/xxiii]
Head laureate, right.
Rv: SALVS [aug] COS IIII
Salus standing left feeding snake coiled around altar and holding sceptre.
Reference: cf. RIC III, 287, 304
Findspot: 1964, *praetorium*, near room G.
Inv. No: c.c. 78/1964.
BUCIUMI 1972, p. 26; no. 150.

ANTONINUS PIUS (Pl. IV, 1)
307.   Denomination: sestertius
Axis: 12; D: 31.2 x 29.2 mm; W: 25.6 g.
Mint: Rome
Dating: AD 145-161
Obv: ANTONINVS - AVG PIVS P P TR P
Head laureate, right.
Rv: HONORI – AVG – COS [iiii]; S - C
Honos standing front, head left, holding branch and cornucopiae.
Reference: RIC III, 772
Findspot: 1965, barrack 1, -0.60 m; phase Ib.
Inv. No: c.c. 3/1965.
BUCIUMI 1972, no. 155.

ANTONINUS PIUS (Pl. IV, 2)
308.   Denomination: sestertius
Axis: 12; D: 30.9 x 30.4 mm; W: 22.6 g.
Mint: Rome

Dating: AD 145-161
Obv: ANTONINVS AVG PI-VS P P TR P COS IIII
Head laureate, right.
Rv: S - C
Mars advancing right, bearing trophy and spear
Reference: RIC III, 778
Findspot: 1968, barrack 5, -0.50 m; phase II.
Inv. No: c.c. 10/1968.
BUCIUMI 1972, no. 157.

ANTONINUS PIUS
309. Denomination: denarius, burnt
Axis: 12; D: 17.4 mm; W: 1.8 g.
Mint: Rome
Dating: AD 138-161
Obv: Legend corroded.
Silhouette of head, right.
Rv: Legend corroded.
Silhouette standing left.
Reference: -
Findspot: 1966, barrack 5.
Inv. No: c.c. 24/1966.
BUCIUMI 1972, no. 151.

ANTONINUS PIUS
310. Denomination: denarius, plated, fragmentary
Axis: -; D: -; W: 2.4 g.
Mint: -
Dating: AD 138-161 or later
Obv: Legend corroded.
Head laureate, right.
Rv: Corroded.
Reference: -
Findspot: 1973, barrack 2, m 51/?, -1 m; phase Ia (!).
Inv. No: c.c. 130/1973.

ANTONINUS PIUS
311. Denomination: denarius, plated, fragmentary
Axis: 6; D: -; W: 1.7 g.
Mint: -
Dating: AD 138-161 or later
Obv: Legend unreadable.
Head laureate, right.
Rv: Legend corroded.
Female silhouette standing.
Reference: -
Findspot: 1975, barrack 2, trench 26, m 15.35, -1.50 m; phase Ia (!).
Inv. No: c.c. 46/1975.

ANTONINUS PIUS
312. Denomination: sestertius
Axis: 12; D: 29.4 x 27.7 mm; W: 17 g.
Mint: Rome
Dating: AD 138-161
Obv: ANTONINVS AV[g...]
Head laureate, right.
Rv: Legend corroded.
Aequitas standing left, holding scales and cornucopiae.
Reference: -
Findspot: 1970, barrack 4, -0.40 m; phase Ib.
Inv. No: c.c. 42/1970.
BUCIUMI 1972, no. 154.

ANTONINUS PIUS
313. Denomination: sestertius
Axis: 12; D: 29.4 x 27.7 mm; W: 17 g.
Mint: Rome
Dating: AD 138-161
Obv: [anto]NINVS AVG – PIVS...
Head laureate, right.
Rv: Legend corroded; S - C.
Concordia (?) standing left, sacrificing from patera over altar.
Reference: -
Findspot: 1970, barrack 4, -0.80 m; phase Ib.
Inv. No: c.c. 83/1970.
BUCIUMI 1972, no. 161.

ANTONINUS PIUS
314. Denomination: as, fragmentary
Axis: -; D: -; W: 6.2 g.
Mint: Rome
Dating: AD 138-161
Obv: Legend corroded.
Head laureate, right.
Rv: corroded.
Reference: -
Findspot: 1972, barrack 1, -0.80 m; phase Ib.
Inv. No: c.c. 346/1972.

ANTONINUS PIUS
315. Denomination: as
Axis: -; D: 23.4 mm; W: 4.3 g.
Mint: Rome
Dating: AD 138-161
Obv: Legend corroded.
Head laureate, right.
Rv: corroded.
Reference: -
Findspot: 1997, *principia*, C2/97, m 18-19, -0.50 m; phase Ib.
Inv. No: c.c. 74/2001.

ANTONINUS PIUS
316. Denomination: AE provincial
Axis: 6; D: 24.9 mm; W: 7.5 g.
Mint: Nikopolis ad Istrum Moesiae Inferioris
Dating: AD 138-161
Obv: Legend unreadable.
Head laureate, right.
Rv: Legend unreadable.
River god reclining left, holding corn-ears.
Reference: cf. MOUSHMOV, 5118-9, 5121
Findspot: 1972, barrack 2, -1 m; phase Ia (!).
Inv. No: c.c. 358/1972.

ANTONINUS PIUS
317. Denomination: AE provincial

Axis: 12; D: 28.9 mm; W: 17.5 g.
Mint: Philippopolis Thraciae
Dating: AD 138-161
Obv: Legend erased.
Head laureate, right.
Rv: Legend erased.
Nude Heracles? standing, facing, head left, resting arm on club, holding lion-skin.
Reference: cf. RPC IV, temp no. 11065.
Findspot: 1973, barrack 1, m 1.75/3.20, -0.50 m; phase Ib.
Inv. No: c.c. 73/1973.

ANTONINUS PIUS: M. Aurelius (Caesar)
318. Denomination: denarius, plated, fragmentary
Axis: -; D: 18.7 mm; W: 1.5 g.
Mint: -
Dating: AD 140-144 or later
Obv: [aurelius cae]SAR AVG PII F COS
Destroyed by restoration, the lower part of neck.
Rv: [ho]N[os]
Destroyed by restoration.
Reference: cf. RIC III, 423a
Findspot: 1970, barrack 5, excavated ground.
Inv. No: c.c. 28/1970.
BUCIUMI 1972, no. 172.

ANTONINUS PIUS: M. Aurelius (Caesar) (Pl. IV, 3)
319. Denomination: dupondius
Axis: 11; D: 27.5 x 25.5 mm; W: 13.1 g.
Mint: Rome
Dating: AD 140-144
Obv: AVRELIVS CAESAR - AVG PII F COS
Bust bare draped on left shoulder, right.
Rv: [p]I[etas aug]
exergue: S C
Priestly implements: knife, sprinkler, pitcher, lituus and ladle
Reference: RIC III, 1240a
Findspot: 1973, barrack 1, m 36/6, -0.80 m; phase Ib.
Inv. No: c.c. 99/1973.

ANTONINUS PIUS: M. Aurelius (Caesar)
320. Denomination: as
Axis: 11; D: 26.2 mm; W: 9.2 g.
Mint: Rome
Dating: AD 140-144
Obv: AVRELIVS CAE-SAR AVG PII [f cos]
Head bare, right.
Rv: IVVEN[t]AS; S - C
Juventas, draped, standing left dropping incense onto altar left, and holding patera.
Reference: RIC III, 1238
Findspot: 1966, near barrack 5, near the E wall flanking *via praetoria*.
Inv. No: c.c. 48/1966.
BUCIUMI 1972, no. 179.

ANTONINUS PIUS: M. Aurelius (Caesar)
321. Denomination: as
Axis: 7; D: 27.3 x 25.8 mm; W: 10.7 g.
Mint: Rome
Dating: AD 145
Obv: AVRELIVS CAESAR [aug pii f]
Head bare, right.
Rv: [tr] POT [cos ii]; S - C
Minerva standing right with spear and shield.
Reference: RIC III, 1266
Findspot: 1969, barrack 5, -0.60 m; phase Ib.
Inv. No: c.c. 114/1969.
BUCIUMI 1972, no. 180.

ANTONINUS PIUS: M. Aurelius (Caesar)
322. Denomination: dupondius
Axis: -; D: 23.9 x 22.4 mm; W: 7.9 g.
Mint: Rome
Dating: AD 139-161
Obv: Legend erased.
Silhouette of head radiate, right.
Rv: erased.
Reference: -
Findspot: 1966, barrack 5, near the E wall flanking *via praetoria* (2 m from intersection), -0.30 m; phase II.
Inv. No: c.c. 46/1966.
BUCIUMI 1972, no. 162 (but Antoninus Pius).

ANTONINUS PIUS: Diva Faustina I
323. Denomination: denarius, fragment
Axis: 6; D: 17.4 mm; W: 1.4 g.
Mint: Rome
Dating: AD post 141
Obv: [diva faust]INA
Part of bust, right.
Rv: A[ugusta]
Ceres standing left, holding long scepter.
Reference: RIC III, 356
Findspot: 1967, the path between barracks 1 and 2, 30 m from the *via praetoria*.
Inv. No: c.c. 28/1967.
BUCIUMI 1972, no. 163.

ANTONINUS PIUS: Diva Faustina I (Pl. IV, 5)
324. Denomination: sestertius
Axis: 6; D: 32 x 30.8 mm; W: 24,1 g.
Mint: Rome
Dating: AD post 141
Obv: DIVA FAVSTINA
Bust draped, right.
Rv: AETER-NITAS; S - C
Aeternitas standing left, holding globe and raising mantle above head.
Reference: RIC III, 1106
Findspot: 1970, barrack 5, -0.40 m; phase II.
Inv. No: c.c. 11/1970.
BUCIUMI 1972, no. 168.

ANTONINUS PIUS: Diva Faustina I
325. Denomination: sestertius
Axis: 5; D: 33 mm; W: 25.2 g.
Mint: Rome
Dating: AD post 141

Obv: DIVA FAV-S[tina]
Bust draped, right.
Rv: Legend corroded
Exergue: S C
Faustina, veiled and holding scepter, seated in *carpentum* drawn by two elephants guided by riders.
Reference: RIC III, 1113
Findspot: 1968, barrack 5, -0.40 m; phase II.
Inv. No: c.c. 24/1968.
BUCIUMI 1972, no. 170.

ANTONINUS PIUS: Diva Faustina I
326. Denomination: sestertius
Axis: 11; D: 29.7 x 26.6 mm; W: 19.7 g.
Mint: Rome
Dating: AD post 141
Obv: DIVA FAVS[tina]
Bust draped, right.
Rv: Legend corroded; [s] - C
Vesta standing left, holding torch and palladium.
Reference: RIC III, 1125
Findspot: 1969, barrack 5, excavated ground.
Inv. No: c.c. 112/1969.
BUCIUMI 1972, no. 166.

ANTONINUS PIUS: Diva Faustina I
327. Denomination: as
Axis: 5; D: 26.9 mm; W: 9.5 g.
Mint: Rome
Dating: AD post 141
Obv: DIVA FAVS[tina]
Bust draped, right.
Rv: AVGVS – [ta]; S - C
Vesta standing left, holding torch and palladium.
Reference: RIC III, 1177
Findspot: 1969, barrack 5, -0.60 m; phase Ib.
Inv. No: c.c. 134/1969.
BUCIUMI 1972, no. 167.

ANTONINUS PIUS: Diva Faustina I
328. Denomination: as
Axis: 6; D: 27.1 x 25.9 mm; W: 9.6 g.
Mint: Rome
Dating: AD post 141
Obv: DIVA FAV-STINA
Bust draped, right.
Rv: CONSE-CRATIO; S - C
Vesta standing left, sacrificing from patera over altar to left and holding scepter.
Reference: RIC III, 1187
Findspot: 1970, barrack 4, excavated ground.
Inv. No: c.c. 85/1970.
BUCIUMI 1972, no. 169.

ANTONINUS PIUS: Faustina I/Diva Faustina I
329. Denomination: as
Axis: 6; D: 24.8 mm; W: 7.3 g.
Mint: Rome
Dating: AD 138-post 141

Obv: Legend erased.
Vague silhouette of bust, right.
Rv: Legend erased.
Vague silhouette standing.
Reference: -
Findspot: 1966, the trench (for the water pipeline) SW of the building no. 3.
Inv. No: c.c. 49/1966.
BUCIUMI 1972, no. 171.

ANTONINUS PIUS: Faustina I/Diva Faustina I
330. Denomination: as
Axis: -; D: 25.3 x 24 mm; W: 11.8 g.
Mint: Rome
Dating: AD 138-post 141
Obv: Legend erased.
Vague silhouette of bust, right.
Rv: erased.
Reference: -
Findspot: 1968, barrack 5, excavated ground.
Inv. No: c.c. 30/1968.
BUCIUMI 1972, no. 165.

ANTONINUS PIUS: Faustina I/Diva Faustina I
331. Denomination: as
Axis: 4; D: 23.5 x 21.2 mm; W: 7.6 g.
Mint: Rome
Dating: AD 138-post 141
Obv: Legend erased.
Silhouette of bust, right.
Rv: Legend erased.
Female silhouette standing
Reference: -
Findspot: 1971, barrack 1, -0.50 m; phase Ib.
Inv. No: c.c. 23/1971.

ANTONINUS PIUS: Faustina II (Pl. IV, 6)
332. Denomination: denarius
Axis: 1; D: 17.4 x 15.8 mm; W: 2.6 g.
Mint: Rome
Dating: AD 145-161
Obv: [faustina] – AVGVSTA
Draped bust right, hair arranged in a chignon behind the head.
Rv: AVGVSTI – PII FIL
Venus standing left, holding Victory and leaning on shield set on a helmet.
Reference: RIC III, 495a
Findspot: 1969, barrack 5, excavated ground.
Inv. No: c.c. 143/1969.
BUCIUMI 1972, no. 183.

ANTONINUS PIUS: Faustina II
333. Denomination: sestertius
Axis: 12; D: 31.7 x 29 mm; W: 22 g.
Mint: Rome
Dating: AD 145-161
Obv: FAVSTINAE AVG – PII AVG FIL
Draped bust right, hair arranged in a chignon behind the head.

Rv: V[eneri genetrici]; S – [c].
Venus standing left, holding apple in her raised right hand.
Reference: RIC III, 1386a
Findspot: 1968, barrack 5, -0.40 m; phase II.
Inv. No: c.c. 28/1968.
BUCIUMI 1972, no. 184.

ANTONINUS PIUS: Faustina II
334. Denomination: as
Axis: 5; D: 25.7 x 23.5 mm; W: 10.5 g.
Mint: Rome
Dating: AD 145-161
Obv: FAVSTINA – [augusta]
Draped bust right, hair arranged in a chignon behind the head.
Rv: [aug]VS-TI – PII FIL; S – C.
Venus standing left, holding Victory and leaning on shield set on a helmet.
Reference: RIC III, 1389a
Findspot: 1968, barrack 5, in the red pit with dove bones, -1.25 m; phase Ib.
Inv. No: c.c. 31/1968.
BUCIUMI 1972, no. 185.

MARCUS AURELIUS
335. Denomination: denarius, plated, fragmentary
Axis: 12; D: -; W: 2.3 g.
Mint: -
Dating: cf. AD 163-165 or later
Obv: [antoninus - aug arm]ENIACVS
Head laureate, right.
Rv: [p m]TR P xviii/xix imp ii cos iii]
Emperor standing right with spear, leaning on shield.
Reference: cf. RIC III, 92, 124
Findspot: 1969, barrack 5, -0.60 m; phase Ib.
Inv. No: c.c. 99/1969.
BUCIUMI 1972, no. 174.

MARCUS AURELIUS (Pl. IV, 7)
336. Denomination: denarius
Axis: 6; D: 17.8 mm; W: 3.1 g.
Mint: Rome
Dating: AD 174
Obv: M ANTONINVS - AVG TR P XXVIII
Head laureate, right.
Rv: IMP VII – COS III
Roma standing left, holding Victory and spear.
Reference: RIC III, 305
Findspot: 1966, barrack 5, last layer, -0.80 m; phase Ib.
Inv. No: c.c. 33/1966.
MUZEU 1968, no. 158 (but Commodus); BUCIUMI 1972, no. 175.

MARCUS AURELIUS
337. Denomination: denarius, plated
Axis: 6; D: 18.9 x 16.9 mm; W: 2.5 g.
Mint: Rome
Dating: AD 175-176 or later
Obv: M ANTONINVS [aug] – GERM SARM
Head laureate, right.
Rv: TR P XXX IMP - VIII COS III
Aequitas standing left, holding scales and cornucopiae.
Reference: cf. RIC III, 359
Findspot: 1969, barrack 5, excavated ground.
Inv. No: c.c. 141/1969.
BUCIUMI 1972, no. 176.

MARCUS AURELIUS (Pl. IV, 8)
338. Denomination: denarius, ancient counterfeit
Axis: 6; D: 16.9 mm; W: 2.9 g.
Mint: -
Dating: post AD 176-177
Obv: M ANTD(!)NINVS - AVG TR P XXV
Head laureate, right (not the portrait of M. Aurelius).
Rv: TR P XXXI IMP VIII COS III P P
Salus standing left with sceptre and feeding snake twined round altar.
Reference: cf. RIC III, 373 (for reverse)
Findspot: 1967, barrack 5, last layer, -0.60 m; phase II.
Inv. No: c.c. 73/1967.
BUCIUMI 1972, no. 177.
Remarks: An ancient counterfeit. The obverse does not match the reverse. On both sides appears the tribunician power with different values. The portrait of M. Aurelius is slightly modified while the name ANTONINVS is misspelled as ANTDNINVS.

MARCUS AURELIUS
339. Denomination: denarius, plated, fragmentary
Axis: 6; D: 17.9 mm; W: 1.4 g.
Mint: Rome
Dating: AD 161-176
Obv: M ANTONINVS ...
Head laureate, right.
Rv: Legend erased.
Silhouette standing.
Reference: -
Findspot: 1967, *praetorium*.
Inv. No: c.c. 23/1967.
BUCIUMI 1972, no. 178.

MARCUS AURELIUS
340. Denomination: sestertius
Axis: 11; D: 32.6 x 30.7 mm; W: 24.7 g.
Mint: Rome
Dating: AD 161-176
Obv: M ANTONINVS ...
Head laureate, right.
Rv: Legend erased
Pietas/Salus/ Annona standing left sacrificing/ feeding snake over altar/modius.
Reference: -
Findspot: 1965, barrack 1, -0.80 m; phase Ib.
Inv. No: c.c. 4/1965.
MUZEU 1968, no. 158 (but Commodus); BUCIUMI 1972, no. 193 (but Commodus).

MARCUS AURELIUS
341. Denomination: denarius, plated
Axis: -; D: 17.7 mm; W: 1.9 g.
Mint: -
Dating: AD 161-180
Obv: Legend corroded
 Head laureate, right.
Rv: Corroded.
Reference: -
Findspot: 1968, barrack 5.
Inv. No: c.c. 43/1968.
Remark: The coin has been reused later as the hole made through it suggests.

MARCUS AURELIUS
342. Denomination: sestertius
Axis: -; D: 29.2 mm; W: 17.6 g.
Mint: Rome
Dating: AD 161-180
Obv: [...ant]ONINVS – AVG...
 Head laureate, right.
Rv: Corroded.
Reference: -
Findspot: 1968, barrack 5, -0.40 m; last layer; phase II.
Inv. No: c.c. 14/1968.
BUCIUMI 1972, no. 197 (but Commodus).

MARCUS AURELIUS
343. Denomination: dupondius
Axis: -; D: 24.5 mm; W: 10.6 g.
Mint: Rome
Dating: AD 161-180
Obv: Legend vanished.
 Head radiate, right.
Rv: Corroded.
Reference: -
Findspot: 1973, barrack 1, m 4-5/5, -0.80 m; phase Ib.
Inv. No: c.c. 93/1973.

MARCUS AURELIUS (Pl. IV, 9)
344. Denomination: AE, provincial coin
Axis: 5; D: 24.8 mm; W: 9.3 g.
Mint: Stobi Macedoniae
Dating: AD 161-180
Obv: Legend erased.
 Head bare of Marcus Aurelius, right.
Rv: STOBE-NSIVM
 Female standing left, holding long sceptre.
Reference: cf. RPC IV, temp no. 7840 (but female standing right)
Findspot: 1964, *principia*, C2/97, m 17-18, -0.40 m; phase Ib.
Inv. No: c.c. 66/2001.

MARCUS AURELIUS
345. Denomination: AE, provincial coin
Axis: 12; D: 23.9 mm; W: 9.8 g.
Mint: Nikaea Bithyniae?
Dating: AD 161-180
Obv: Legend erased
 Vague silhouette of head, right.
Rv: Legend erased.
 Nike advancing left.
Reference: cf. RPC IV, temp no. 5953
Findspot: 1964, *principia*, base of pedestal 2, -0.80 m; phase Ib.
Inv. No: c.c. 95/1964.
BUCIUMI 1972, p. 26; no. 182.

LUCIUS VERUS
346. Denomination: sestertius
Axis: 6; D: 30.1 x 28.5 mm; W: 18.2 g.
Mint: Rome
Dating: AD 161
Obv: IMP CAES L AVR[el veru]S AVG
 Head bare, right, right.
Rv: [con]CORD [augu]STOR TR P
 Exergue: COS II
 Aurelius and Verus clasping hands.
Reference: RIC III, 1281
Findspot: 1967, *praetorium*, room A.
Inv. No: c.c. 75/1967.
BUCIUMI 1972, no. 190.

LUCIUS VERUS
347. Denomination: denarius
Axis: 6; D: 17.7 x 15.9 mm; W: 2.2 g.
Mint: Rome
Dating: AD 163-164
Obv: [l] VERVS AV[g] ARMENIACVS
 Bust laureate, head bare, right, right.
Rv: TR P IIII – IMP II COS [ii]
 Mars standing right, holding spear and resting hand on shield.
Reference: RIC III, 514
Findspot: 1967, the path between barracks 5 and 6, near the wall of barrack 5.
Inv. No: c.c. 17/1967.
BUCIUMI 1972, no. 189.

LUCIUS VERUS
348. Denomination: dupondius
Axis: 6; D: 26.8 x 22.6 mm; W: 9.8 g.
Mint: Rome
Dating: AD 163-164
Obv: Legend erased.
 Head radiate, right.
Rv: Legend erased; S - C.
 Victory standing right, fixing/inscribing a shield set on a palm-tree.
Reference: cf. RIC III, 1400
Findspot: 1966, end of *via praetoria* towards *porta praetoria*, -0.60 m; phase Ib.
Inv. No: c.c. 44/1966.
BUCIUMI 1972, no. 196 (but Commodus).

MARCUS AURELIUS: Faustina II
349. Denomination: denarius, fragmentary
Axis: 6; D: 15.9 mm; W: 1.5 g.
Mint: Rome

Dating: AD 161-175
Obv: FAVSTIN ...
   Vague bust draped, right.
Rv: FECVN...
   Left part of Fecunditas with an infant at her legs.
Reference: RIC III, 676.
Findspot: 1968, barrack 5, -0.30 m; phase II.
Inv. No: c.c. 18/1968.
BUCIUMI 1972, no. 164

MARCUS AURELIUS: Faustina II
350.   Denomination: sestertius
Axis: 6; D: 30.9 x 29.8 mm; W: 24.7 g.
Mint: Rome
Dating: AD 161-175
Obv: FAVSTINA - AVGVSTA
   Bust draped, right.
Rv: HIL[ar]ITAS; S - C
   Hilaritas standing left, holding long palm and cornucopiae.
Reference: RIC III, 1642.
Findspot: 1966, NW corner of the fort, stray find.
Inv. No: c.c. -/1966.
MUZEU 1968, 142; BUCIUMI 1972, no. 187

MARCUS AURELIUS: Faustina II
351.   Denomination: sestertius
Axis: 12; D: 29.1 x 27.4 mm; W: 23.7 g.
Mint: Rome
Dating: AD 161-175
Obv: FAVSTINA [augusta]
   Bust draped, right.
Rv: Legend erased.
   Concordia standing left, holding patera and double cornucopiae.
Reference: cf. RIC III, 1625 (but as only).
Findspot: 1968, barrack 5.
Inv. No: c.c. 9/1968.
BUCIUMI 1972, no. 186 (but Faustina I).

MARCUS AURELIUS: Faustina II/Diva Faustina II
352.   Denomination: dupondius
Axis: -; D: 26 x 24 mm; W: 12.51 g.
Mint: Rome
Dating: AD 161-180
Obv: ...[faust]INA...
   Vague silhouette of bust, right.
Rv: erased.
Reference: -
Findspot: 1966, the path between barracks 5 and 6, at the intersection with *via praetoria*.
Inv. No: c.c. 42/1966.
BUCIUMI 1972, no. 188.

MARCUS AURELIUS: Faustina II/Diva Faustina II
353.   Denomination: as
Axis: 6; D: 25.7 mm; W: 10.7 g.
Mint: Rome
Dating: AD 161-180
Obv: Legend corroded.
   Vague silhouette of bust, right.
Rv: V ague silhouette of a female seated left.
Reference: -
Findspot: 1973, barrack 1, m 25-26/1-2, -0.75 m; phase Ib.
Inv. No: c.c. 54/1973.

MARCUS AURELIUS/COMMODUS: Crispina
354.   Denomination: dupondius
Axis: 6; D: 25.1x 22 mm; W: 12.8 g.
Mint: Rome
Dating: AD 177-182
Obv: CRISPINA - AVGVSTA
   Bust draped, right.
Rv: IVNO – LVCINA; S - C
   Juno standing left, holding patera and sceptre.
Reference: RIC III, 680
Findspot: 1965, *principia*, near the E side of the wall 3, at 4.50 m from the S wall of trench XIV, -0.60 m; phase Ib.
Inv. No: c.c. 61/1965.
MUZEU 1968, no. 160; BUCIUMI 1972, p. 27; no. 198.

COMMODUS (Pl. IV, 10)
355.   Denomination: denarius
Axis: 12; D: 17.5 mm; W: 3.5 g.
Mint: Rome
Dating: AD 183-184
Obv: M COMMODVS A-TON AVG PIVS
   Head laureate, right.
Rv: P M TR P VIIII – IMP VI COS IIII P P
   Felicitas standing left, holding caduceus and cornucopiae, modius at foot left.
Reference: RIC III, 74
Findspot: 1964, *praetorium*, room C, -0.90 m; phase Ib.
Inv. No: c.c. 60/1964.
BUCIUMI 1972, no. 192.

COMMODUS
356.   Denomination: denarius, plated, fragmentary
Axis: 6; D: -; W: 1.3 g.
Mint: Rome
Dating: AD 186 or later
Obv: [m comm ant p] FEL AVG BRIT
   Head laureate, right.
Rv: [libert aug p m] T R P XI IMP VII COS [v p p]
Libertas standing left, hold pileus and rod.
Reference: cf. RIC III, 135
Findspot: 1973, barrack 2, *via sagularis*, -0.60 m; phase Ib.
Inv. No: c.c. 124/1973.

COMMODUS
357.   Denomination: sestertius
Axis: 12; D: 30.1 mm; W: 22.2 g.
Mint: Rome
Dating: AD 188-189
Obv: M COMMODVS ANT P FELIX AVG BRIT
   Head laureate, right.
Rv: Legend erased.
   Libertas standing left, holding pileus and rod.
Reference: RIC III, 526

Findspot: 1971, barrack 1, -0.40 m; phase Ib.
Inv. No: c.c. 22/1971.

COMMODUS: Divus Marcus Aurelius
358.   Denomination: sestertius
Axis: 6; D: 28.4 mm; W: 19.7 g.
Mint: Rome
Dating: post AD 180
Obv: DIVVS M ANTONINVS PIVS
         Head bare, right.
Rv: [cons]E[cratio]; S - C
         Funerary pyre.
Reference: RIC III, 662
Findspot: 1965, barrack 1, -0.20 m; phase II.
Inv. No: c.c. 8/1965.
BUCIUMI 1972, no. 181.

SEPTIMIUS SEVERUS (Pl. IV, 11)
359.   Denomination: denarius
Axis: 12; D: 17.1 x 15.7 mm; W: 1.8 g.
Mint: Rome
Dating: AD 194
Obv: L SEP SEV [pe]RT AVG IMP III
         Head laureate, right.
Rv: P M TR P – II – COS II P P
         Jupiter seated left, holding Victory and sceptre.
Reference: RIC IV.1, 34
Findspot: 1968, barrack 5, -0.65 m; phase Ib.
Inv. No: c.c. 27/1968.
BUCIUMI 1972, no. 199.

SEPTIMIUS SEVERUS
360.   Denomination: denarius, plated
Axis: 12; D: 16.4 mm; W: 1.7 g.
Mint: Rome
Dating: AD 195 or later
Obv: L SEP SEV PE[rt aug imp] V
         Head laureate, right.
Rv: [p m tr p iii] - COS II P P
         Minerva standing left with spear and round shield.
Reference: cf. RIC IV.1, 61
Findspot: 1973, barrack 2, -0.70 m; phase Ib.
Inv. No: c.c. 121/1973.

SEPTIMIUS SEVERUS
361.   Denomination: denarius, plated
Axis: ?; D: ?; W: 1.9 g.
Mint: Emesa?
Dating: AD 194-195 or later
Obv: IMP CAE L SEP SEV PERT AVG COS II
         Head laureate, right.
Rv: BONA SPES
         Spes standing holding flower and lifting skirt.
Reference: cf. RIC IV.1, 364
Findspot: fort area
Inv. No: ?
BUCIUMI 1972, no. 200.
Remark: Not seen.

SEPTIMIUS SEVERUS
362.   Denomination: denarius, plated
Axis: 12; D: 17.9 x 16.2 mm; W: 2.5 g.
Mint: Emesa?
Dating: AD 194-195 or later
Obv: [imp cae l] SEP SE-V PERT AVG COS [i]I
         Head laureate, right.
Rv: FORTV-N REDVC
         Fortuna seated left, holding rudder and cornucopia.
Reference: cf. RIC IV.1, 379
Findspot: 1968, barrack 5, -0.30 m; phase II.
Inv. No: c.c. 21/1968.
BUCIUMI 1972, no. 201.

SEPTIMIUS SEVERUS (Pl. IV, 12)
363.   Denomination: denarius
Axis: 6; D: 18.1 mm; W: 3 g.
Mint: Rome
Dating: AD 196-197
Obv: L SEPT SEV PERT - AVG [imp viii]
         Head laureate, right.
Rv: ADVENT[i felicissi]MO
         Severus on horseback right raising hand.
Reference: RIC IV.1, 74
Findspot: 1966, *porta praetoria*, W tower.
Inv. No: c.c. 41/1966.
BUCIUMI 1972, p. 18; no. 202.

SEPTIMIUS SEVERUS (Pl. IV, 13)
364.   Denomination: denarius
Axis: 12; D: 16.5 mm; W: 3.1 g.
Mint: Rome
Dating: AD 196-197
Obv: L SEPT SEV PERT - AVG IMP [viii]
         Head laureate, right.
Rv: [her]CVLI DEFENS
         Hercules standing right, holding club on ground in right hand, bow in left.
Reference: RIC IV.1, 79
Findspot: 1976, fort area, stray find.
Inv. No: c.c. 153/1976.

SEPTIMIUS SEVERUS (Pl. IV, 14)
365.   Denomination: denarius
Axis: 6; D: 15.6 x 14.4 mm; W: 1.6 g.
Mint: Rome
Dating: AD 197
Obv: [l sept sev pert au]G IMP VIIII
         Head laureate, right.
Rv: [p] M TR P V – COS II P P
         Genius, naked, standing half-left, holding patera, sacrificing over altar, and corn ears.
Reference: RIC IV.1, 105
Findspot: 1974, *praetorium*, excavated ground.
Inv. No: c.c. 36/1974.

SEPTIMIUS SEVERUS
366.   Denomination: denarius, plated
Axis: 12; D: 16.9 mm; W: 2.4 g.
Mint: -

Dating: AD 197-198 or later
Obv: [l sept seu per]T - AVG IMP X
  Head laureate, right.
Rv: PACI AETERNAE
  Image corroded.
Reference: cf. RIC IV.1, 118
Findspot: 1969, barrack 5.
Inv. No: c.c. 100/1969.
BUCIUMI 1972, no. 203.

SEPTIMIUS SEVERUS (Pl. IV, 15)
367. Denomination: denarius, plated
Axis: 11; D: 17.4 mm; W: 2.5 g.
Mint: -
Dating: AD 199 or later
Obv: L SEPT SEV AVG IMP XI – PART MAX
  Head laureate, right.
Rv: VICTORIAE AVG-G [fe]L
  Victory flying left, holding wreath with both hands over shield set on rock to left.
Reference: cf. RIC IV.1, 144b
Findspot: 1973, barrack 1, m 31-32/1, -1 m, in the filling layer beneath the adobe layer; phase Ib.
Inv. No: c.c. 79/1973.

SEPTIMIUS SEVERUS
368. Denomination: denarius, plated, fragmentary
Axis: 6; D: 16.9 mm; W: 2 g.
Mint: -
Dating: AD 200-201 or later
Obv: [severus aug] - PART MAX
  Head laureate, right.
Rv: RESTITVTOR - VRBIS
  Septimius standing left, holding patera in right hand over tripod altar and spear in left.
Reference: cf. RIC IV.1, 167a
Findspot: 1973, barrack 1, excavated ground.
Inv. No: c.c. 120/1973.

SEPTIMIUS SEVERUS
369. Denomination: denarius, plated
Axis: 12; D: 18.2 mm; W: 2.3 g.
Mint: -
Dating: AD 200-201 or later
Obv: SEVERVS AVG - PART MAX
  Head laureate, right.
Rv: RESTITV[tor] - VRBIS
  Septimius standing left, holding patera in right hand over tripod altar and spear in left.
Reference: cf. RIC IV.1, 167a
Findspot: 1973, barrack 1, excavated ground.
Inv. No: c.c. 119/1973.

SEPTIMIUS SEVERUS
370. Denomination: denarius, plated
Axis: 12; D: 18.3 x 16.5 mm; W: 2.2 g.
Mint: -
Dating: AD 202 or later
Obv: SEVERVS – PIVS AVG
  Head laureate, right.

Rv: PART MAX – [tr p] X COS [iii p p]
  Trophy of arms and armour with two Parthian captives seated either side at base.
Reference: cf. RIC IV.1, 176
Findspot: 1974, *praetorium*, excavated ground.
Inv. No: c.c. 38/1974.

SEPTIMIUS SEVERUS
371. Denomination: denarius
Axis: 6; D: 18.3 mm; W: 1.5 g.
Mint: Rome
Dating: AD 210
Obv: SEVERVS - PIVS AVG BRIT
  Head laureate, right.
Rv: P M TR P XVIII – COS III P P
  Neptune standing left, holding trident, foot on globe.
Reference: RIC IV.1, 234
Findspot: 1975, building C 1, 4 m from the E wall and 4 m from the N wall, -0.70 m; phase Ib.
Inv. No: c.c. 42/1975.

SEPTIMIUS SEVERUS (Pl. IV, 16)
372. Denomination: denarius, plated
Axis: 6; D: 18.1 mm; W: 2.4 g.
Mint: -
Dating: AD 202-210 or later
Obv: [se]V[e]RVS - PIVS AVG
  Head laureate, right.
Rv: FVNDAT-OR – [p]ACIS
  Septimius, togate and veiled, standing left, holding olive branch.
Reference: cf. RIC IV.1, 265
Findspot: 1970, *praetorium*, near the SW wall on the *via sagularis*.
Inv. No: c.c. 15/1970.
BUCIUMI 1972, no. 205.

SEPTIMIUS SEVERUS: Caracalla (Augustus)
(Pl. IV, 17)
373. Denomination: denarius
Axis: 6; D: 19.3 x 18.5 mm; W: 3.4 g.
Mint: Rome
Dating: AD 199
Obv: ANTONINVS - AVGVSTVS
  Bust laureate, draped and cuirassed, right.
Rv: PONT – TR P II
  Securitas reclining right, holding staff, altar before.
Reference: RIC IV.1, 29
Findspot: 1964, *praetorium*, room C, -0.90 m.
Inv. No: c.c. 61/1964.
BUCIUMI 1972, no. 213.

SEPTIMIUS SEVERUS: Caracalla (Augustus)
374. Denomination: denarius, plated
Axis: 6; D: 17.9 mm; W: 2.4 g.
Mint: Rome
Dating: AD 200 or later
Obv: ANTONINVS – [august]VS

Bust laureate, draped and cuirassed, right (the face is missing due to corrosion).
Rv: PONTIF – TR P III
Sol standing front, radiate, naked, holding orb and spear.
Reference: cf. RIC IV.1, 30a
Findspot: 1969, barrack 5, -0.20 m; phase II.
Inv. No: c.c. 98/1969.
BUCIUMI 1972, no. 215.

SEPTIMIUS SEVERUS: Caracalla (Augustus)
(Pl. IV, 18)
375.   Denomination: denarius, plated
Axis: 12; D: 17.8 mm; W: 2.8 g.
Mint: Rome
Dating: AD 201 or later
Obv: ANTONINVS – PIVS AVG
Bust laureate, draped and cuirassed, right.
Rv: PART MAX PONT TR P IIII
Two captives bound and seated back to back at base of trophy.
Reference: RIC IV.1, 54a
Findspot: 1974, *praetorium*, excavated ground.
Inv. No: c.c. 39/1974.

SEPTIMIUS SEVERUS: Caracalla (Augustus)
(Pl. IV, 19)
376.   Denomination: denarius, fragmentary
Axis: 12; D: 17.8 mm; W: 2.5 g.
Mint: Rome
Dating: AD 201
Obv: ANTONINVS – [pius au]G
Bust laureate, draped and cuirassed, right.
Rv: [part max p]ONT TR P IIII
Two captives bound and seated back to back at base of trophy.
Reference: RIC IV.1, 54a
Findspot: 1973, barrack 1, m 2/4, -0.30 m; phase II.
Inv. No: c.c. 50/1973.

SEPTIMIUS SEVERUS: Caracalla (Augustus)
(Pl. IV, 20)
377.   Denomination: denarius
Axis: 6; D: 19.3 x 16.8 mm; W: 2.8 g.
Mint: Rome
Dating: AD 206-210
Obv: ANTONINVS – PIVS AVG
Head laureate, right.
Rv: LIBERT-AS AVG
Libertas standing left, holding pileus and scepter.
Reference: RIC IV.1, 161
Findspot: 1965, barrack 1, -0.30 m; phase II.
Inv. No: c.c. 1a/1965.
BUCIUMI 1972, no. 217 (but barrack 5).

SEPTIMIUS SEVERUS: Caracalla (Augustus)
(Pl. V, 1)
378.   Denomination: denarius
Axis: 5; D: 18.1 mm; W: 2.2 g.
Mint: Rome

Dating: AD 206-210
Obv: ANTONINVS – PIVS AVG
Head laureate, right.
Rv: VOTA SVS-CEPTA X
Caracalla veiled, standing left, sacrificing out of patera over tripod altar.
Reference: RIC IV.1, 179
Findspot: 1969, barrack 5, -0.40 m; phase II.
Inv. No: c.c. 97/1969.
BUCIUMI 1972, no. 216.

SEPTIMIUS SEVERUS: Caracalla (Augustus) (Pl. V, 2)
379.   Denomination: denarius, plated
Axis: 12; D: 20.5 x 19 mm; W: 3.1 g.
Mint: -
Dating: AD 210 or post
Obv: ANTONINVS PIVS AVG BRIT
Head laureate, right.
Rv: PONTIF TR P – XIII COS III
Concordia seated left, holding patera and cornucopiae.
Reference: cf. RIC IV.1, 116b (but double cornucopiae)
Findspot: 1967, *praetorium*.
Inv. No: c.c. 20/1967.
BUCIUMI 1972, no. 218.

SEPTIMIUS SEVERUS: Caracalla (Augustus)
380.   Denomination: denarius, plated, fragment
Axis: -; D: -; W: 1.4 g.
Mint: -
Dating: AD 203-210 or later
Obv: [antoninus] PIVS AVG
Bust laureate, right.
Rv: corroded.
Reference: cf. RIC IV.1, 116b (but double cornucopiae)
Findspot: 1970, near the fort.
Inv. No: c.c. 86/1970.
BUCIUMI 1972, no. 214.

SEPTIMIUS SEVERUS: Geta (Caesar) (Pl. V, 3)
381.   Denomination: denarius
Axis: 6; D: 19.2 x 16.9 mm; W: 3.1 g.
Mint: Rome
Dating: AD 200-202 or later
Obv: P SEPT GETA – CAES PONT
Bust draped and cuirassed, right.
Rv: FELICITAS - PVBLICA
Felicitas standing left, holding caduceus and cornucopia.
Reference: RIC IV.1, 9b
Findspot: 1968, barrack 5, -0.40 m; phase II.
Inv. No: c.c. 25/1968.
BUCIUMI 1972, no. 222.

SEPTIMIUS SEVERUS: Geta (Caesar)
382.   Denomination: denarius, plated
Axis: 6; D: 18.5 mm; W: 2.5 g.
Mint: -
Dating: AD 200-202 or later

Obv: P SEPT GETA – CAES PONT
Bust draped and cuirassed, right.
Rv: PRI-NC iVEN-TVT
Geta, in military dress, standing left, holding branch and reversed spear, trophy of shields and arms behind.
Reference: cf. RIC IV.1, 17
Findspot: 1970, barrack 5, excavated ground.
Inv. No: c.c. 30/1970.
BUCIUMI 1972, no. 223.

SEPTIMIUS SEVERUS: Geta (Caesar)
383.   Denomination: denarius, plated
Axis: 6; D: 17.8 x 16.5 mm; W: 2.4 g.
Mint: -
Dating: AD 200-202 or later
Obv: P SEPT GETA – CAES PONT
Bust draped and cuirassed, right.
Rv: SECVR[it i]MPERII
Securitas seated left, holding globe.
Reference: cf. RIC IV.1, 20
Findspot: 1967, *praetorium*.
Inv. No: c.c. 24/1967.
BUCIUMI 1972, no. 224.

SEPTIMIUS SEVERUS: Geta (Caesar)
384.   Denomination: denarius, plated
Axis: -; D: 18 x 16.9 mm; W: 2.5 g.
Mint: -
Dating: AD 200-202 or later
Obv: P SEPT GETA – CAES PONT
Bust draped and cuirassed, right.
Rv: corroded.
Reference: -
Findspot: 1966, barrack 5.
Inv. No: c.c. 27/1966.
BUCIUMI 1972, no. 225.

SEPTIMIUS SEVERUS: Geta (Caesar) (Pl. V, 4)
385.   Denomination: denarius, plated
Axis: 12; D: 18.3 mm; W: 2.6 g.
Mint: -
Dating: AD 203 or later
Obv: P SEPTIMIVS GETA CAES
Bust draped and cuirassed, right.
Rv: MARTI VICTORI
Mars advancing right, holding spear and trophy.
Reference: cf. RIC IV.1, 103
Findspot: 1966, barrack 5, -0.30 m; phase II.
Inv. No: c.c. 16/1968.
BUCIUMI 1972, no. 226.

SEPTIMIUS SEVERUS: Caracalla/Geta
386.   Denomination: denarius, plated
Axis: -; D: 15 x 14 mm; W: 2.4 g.
Mint: -
Dating: AD 196-211 or later
Obv: Legend erased.
Vague silhouette of a young bust, right.
Rv: corroded.
Reference: -
Findspot: 1973, barrack 1, m 3.50/5, -0.10 m; phase II.
Inv. No: c.c. 80/1973.

SEPTIMIUS SEVERUS: Caracalla/Geta
387.   Denomination: denarius, plated
Axis: -; D: -; W: 1.6 g.
Mint: -
Dating: AD 200-211 or later
Obv: Legend erased.
Vague silhouette of a young bust, right.
Rv: ...COS...
Vague silhouette standing.
Reference: -
Findspot: 1973, barrack 1, m 4-5/6, -0.80 m; phase Ib.
Inv. No: c.c. 96/1973.

SEPTIMIUS SEVERUS: Iulia Domna
388.   Denomination: denarius, plated
Axis: 6; D: 18.9 mm; W: 2.3 g.
Mint: -
Dating: AD 193-211 or later
Obv: IVLIA - AVGVSTA
Bust draped, right.
Rv: MATER – DEVM
Cybele, towered, enthroned left between two lions, leaning on drum and holding branch and scepter.
Reference: cf. RIC IV.1, 564
Findspot: 1964, *praetorium*, base of pedestal 1, -0.95, m; phase Ib.
Inv. No: c.c. 98/1964.
BUCIUMI 1972, p. 26; no. 210.

SEPTIMIUS SEVERUS: Iulia Domna
389.   Denomination: denarius, plated, fragmentary
Axis: 6; D: 17.7 mm; W: 1.8 g.
Mint: -
Dating: AD 196-211 or later
Obv: [iulia] – AVG[usta]
Bust draped, right.
Rv: [vener]I V[i]C[t?] R?.
Venus standing right, naked to waist, leaning on column to left, holding palm and apple.
Reference: cf. RIC IV.1, 579 (but aureus)
Findspot: 1965, trench XV, wall 1 m 10.15 on the N side of *praetorium*, -0.75 m; phase Ib.
Inv. No: c.c. 84/1965.
BUCIUMI 1972, no. 207.

SEPTIMIUS SEVERUS: Iulia Domna (Pl. V, 5)
390.   Denomination: denarius
Axis: 6; D: 17.1 mm; W: 3.2 g.
Mint: Rome
Dating: AD 196-211
Obv: IVLIA – AVGVSTA
Bust draped, right.
Rv: VENVS - FELIX
Venus standing left, holding apple and drawing out fold of drapery.

Reference: RIC IV.1, 580
Findspot: 1967, the path between barracks 1 and 2.
Inv. No: c.c. 19/1967.
BUCIUMI 1972, no. 211.

SEPTIMIUS SEVERUS: Iulia Domna (Pl. V, 6)
391.   Denomination: denarius
Axis: 1; D: 18.8 x 17.8 mm; W: 2.9 g.
Mint: Laodicea ad Mare
Dating: AD 196-202
Obv: IVLIA – AVGVSTA
            Bust draped, right.
Rv: VENVS - FELIX
            Venus standing left, holding apple and sceptre.
Reference: RIC IV.1, 646
Findspot: 1970, barrack 4, -0.30 m; phase II.
Inv. No: c.c. 36/1970.
BUCIUMI 1972, no. 208.

SEPTIMIUS SEVERUS: Iulia Domna
392.   Denomination: denarius, plated, fragmentary
Axis: -; D: 18.1 mm; W: 1.1 g.
Mint: -
Dating: AD 196-211 or later
Obv: [iu]LIA – AVGVSTA
            Bust draped, right.
Rv: corroded.
Reference: -
Findspot: 1969, barrack 5, -0.80 m; phase Ib.
Inv. No: c.c. 132/1969.

SEPTIMIUS SEVERUS/CARACALLA: Plautilla
393.   Denomination: denarius, plated
Axis: 6; D: 17.9 mm; W: 2.3 g.
Mint: -
Dating: AD 202-204 or later
Obv: PLAVTILLA – AVGVSTA
            Bust draped, right.
Rv: PIETAS - AVGG
            Pietas standing right, holding scepter and child.
Reference: cf. RIC IV.1, 367
Findspot: 1966, barrack 5.
Inv. No: c.c. 26/1966.
BUCIUMI 1972, no. 221.

SEPTIMIUS SEVERUS/CARACALLA: Plautilla
394.   Denomination: denarius, plated
Axis: 6; D: 20.2 mm; W: 2.4 g.
Mint: -
Dating: AD 202-204 or later
Obv: PLAVTILLA – [augus]TA
            Bust draped, right.
Rv: VENVS - VICTRIX
            Venus standing left, holding apple and palm, leaning on shield, Cupid at her feet.
Reference: cf. RIC IV.1, 369
Findspot: 1966, barrack 1, near buttress 2, near *via principalis*, trench SXIII.
Inv. No: c.c. 51/1966.
BUCIUMI 1972, no. 220.

CARACALLA (Pl. V, 7)
395.   Denomination: denarius
Axis: 6; D: 18.8 mm; W: 2.6 g.
Mint: Rome
Dating: AD 215
Obv: ANTONINVS PIVS AVG GERM
            Head laureate, right.
Rv: VENVS VICTRIX
            Venus standing left, holding Victory and scepter, helmet on ground to right.
Reference: RIC IV.1, 311b
Findspot: 1972, barrack 1, -0.80 m; phase Ib.
Inv. No: c.c. 351/1972.

CARACALLA
396.   Denomination: denarius
Axis: 6; D: 18.5 mm; W: 2.4 g.
Mint: Rome
Dating: AD 209-217
Obv: ANTONINVS PIVS …
            Head laureate, right.
Rv: Legend corroded.
            Silhouette standing.
Reference: -
Findspot: 1966, trench 2 (water pipeline) N of late annexes (former C3).
Inv. No: c.c. 50/1966.
BUCIUMI 1972, no. 219.

CARACALLA: Iulia Domna
397.   Denomination: denarius, plated
Axis: 6; D: 18.5 x 17.7 mm; W: 3 g.
Mint: -
Dating: AD 211-217 or later
Obv: IVLIA PIA – FELIX AVG
            Bust draped, right.
Rv: DIANA LVCIFERA
            Diana standing left, holding long torch with both hands.
Reference: cf. RIC IV.1, 373A
Findspot: 1971, barrack 1, -0.40 m; phase Ib.
Inv. No: c.c. 12/1971.

CARACALLA: Iulia Domna (Pl. V, 9)
398.   Denomination: denarius, plated
Axis: 6; D: 18.3 x 16.7 mm; W: 2.2 g.
Mint: -
Dating: AD 211-217 or later
Obv: IVLIA PIA – FELIX AVG
            Bust draped, right.
Rv: MATRI - DEVM
            Cybele standing left, leaning on column, holding drum & scepter, lion at foot.
Reference: cf. RIC IV.1, 382
Findspot: 1997, *principia*, C2/97, m 13-14, -0.40 m; phase Ib.
Inv. No: c.c. 89/2001.
BUCIUMI 2000, p. 346, no. 2 (but as)

ELAGABALUS (Pl. V, 10)
399. Denomination: denarius
Axis: 6; D: 17.8 mm; W: 2.9 g.
Mint: Antioch
Dating: AD 218-219
Obv: IMP ANTO-NINVS AVG
  Bust laureate, seen 2/3 from behind, draped and cuirassed, right.
Rv: CONSVL – II P P
  Aequitas standing left, holding scales and cornucopiae.
Reference: RIC IV.2, 168
Findspot: 1969, barrack 5, -0.30 m; phase Ib.
Inv. No: c.c. 122/1969.
BUCIUMI 1972, no. 228.

ELAGABALUS (Pl. V, 11)
400. Denomination: denarius, plated
Axis: 6; D: 19.8 x 17.9 mm; W: 2.2 g.
Mint: Rome
Dating: AD 221 or later
Obv: IMP ANTONINVS PIVS AVG
  Bust laureate, draped and cuirassed, right.
Rv: [p m t]R P IIII - COS [iii p p]
  Sol, radiate, advancing left, raising right hand and holding whip, star to left.
Reference: cf. RIC IV.2, 40
Findspot: 1966, near the intermediary tower 1.
Inv. No: c.c. 38/1966.
BUCIUMI 1972, no. 231.

ELAGABALUS
401. Denomination: denarius
Axis: 6; D: 18.2 mm; W: 2.2 g.
Mint: Rome
Dating: AD 221
Obv: IMP ANTO[ninus] - PIVS AVG
  Bust laureate, draped and cuirassed, turned 2/3, right.
Rv: [p m tr p] IIII COS III P P
  Providentia standing left, holding rod over globe and cornucopiae; star in field right.
Reference: RIC IV.2, 42
Findspot: 1973, barrack 2, near the *via sagularis*, m 48, -0.90 m; phase Ib.
Inv. No: c.c. 128/1973.

ELAGABALUS
402. Denomination: denarius
Axis: 12; D: 19.4 x 18.2 mm; W: 3 g.
Mint: Rome
Dating: AD 221
Obv: IMP ANTONINVS - PIVS AVG
  Bust laureate, horned, draped and cuirassed, turned facing 2/3, right.
Rv: P M TR P IIII COS III P P
  Elagabalus standing left, sacrificing from patera over lighted altar, holding branch in left hand.
Reference: RIC IV.2, 46
Findspot: 1975, barrack 2, trench 26, m 1, -1.10 m; phase Ia (!).
Inv. No: c.c. 45/1975.

ELAGABALUS
403. Denomination: denarius
Axis: 12; D: 17.1 x 15.9 mm; W: 2.5 g.
Mint: Rome
Dating: AD 221
Obv: [imp anton]INVS - PIVS AVG
  Bust laureate, horned, draped and cuirassed, turned 2/3, right.
Rv: [p m t]R P IIII C[os iii p p]
  Elagabalus standing left, sacrificing from patera over lighted altar, holding branch in left hand.
Reference: RIC IV.2, 46
Findspot: 1967, *praetorium*, room B.
Inv. No: c.c. 15/1967.
BUCIUMI 1972, p. 30; no. 229.

ELAGABALUS (Pl. V, 12)
404. Denomination: denarius
Axis: 12; D: 20.3 x 17.8 mm; W: 2.8 g.
Mint: Rome
Dating: AD 221
Obv: IMP ANTONINVS PIVS AVG
  Bust laureate, horned, draped and cuirassed, turned 2/3, right.
Rv: P M TR P IIII CO-S III P P
  Elagabalus standing left, sacrificing from patera over altar, holding club, spear surmounted by helmet to left, spear with wreath to right, star in left field.
Reference: RIC IV.2, 51
Findspot: 1964, *praetorium*, room C, -0.90 m; phase Ib.
Inv. No: c.c. 62/1964.
BUCIUMI 1972, no. 230.

ELAGABALUS
405. Denomination: denarius
Axis: 11; D: 18.4 x 17.4 mm; W: 2.2 g.
Mint: Rome
Dating: AD 221
Obv: IMP ANTO-NINVS PIVS AVG
  Bust laureate, draped and cuirassed, turned 2/3, right.
Rv: [libert]AS - AVGVSTI
  Libertas seated left, holding cap and scepter.
Reference: RIC IV.2, 115
Findspot: 1975, building C 1, near the W wall, -0.65 m; phase Ib.
Inv. No: c.c. 39/1975.

ELAGABALUS: Iulia Soaemias (Pl. V, 13)
406. Denomination: denarius
Axis: 6; D: 18.3 mm; W: 2.7 g.
Mint: Rome
Dating: AD 218-222
Obv: IVLIA SOAEMIAS AVG
  Bust draped, right.

Rv: VENVS CAELESTIS
   Venus seated left, holding scepter, extending her hand to Cupid standing before her.
Reference: RIC IV.2, 243
Findspot: 1964, *praetorium*, near pedestals, 0.35 m north of the 2nd pedestal, -1.13 m; phase Ia (!).
Inv. No: c.c. 97/1964.
BUCIUMI 1972, no. 232.

ELAGABALUS: Iulia Soaemias
407.   Denomination: denarius
Axis: 6; D: 18.6 x 16.4 mm; W: 2.5 g.
Mint: Rome
Dating: AD 218-222
Obv: [iulia s]OAEMIAS AVG
   Bust draped, right.
Rv: [venu]S CAELESTIS
   Venus seated left, holding scepter, extending her hand to Cupid standing before her.
Reference: RIC IV.2, 243
Findspot: 1973, barrack 1, m 39/7, -0.95 m; phase Ia (!).
Inv. No: c.c. 105/1973.

ELAGABALUS: Iulia Maesa
408.   Denomination: denarius
Axis: 12; D: 19.5 mm; W: 2.5 g.
Mint: Rome
Dating: AD 218-222
Obv: IVLIA MAESA AVG
   Bust draped, right.
Rv: PVDICITIA
   Pudicitia seated left, raising veil and holding scepter.
Reference: RIC IV.2, 268
Findspot: 1970, barrack 5, excavated ground.
Inv. No: c.c. 29/1970.
BUCIUMI 1972, no. 233.

ELAGABALUS: Iulia Maesa
409.   Denomination: denarius
Axis: 12; D: 19.8 x 16.7 mm; W: 1.6 g.
Mint: Rome
Dating: AD 218-222
Obv: [iulia m]AESA AVG
   Bust draped, right.
Rv: PVDI[citia]
   Pudicitia seated left, raising veil and holding scepter.
Reference: RIC IV.2, 268
Findspot: 1967, the path between barracks 2 and 3.
Inv. No: c.c. 26/1967.
BUCIUMI 1972, no. 234.

ELAGABALUS: Iulia Maesa
410.   Denomination: denarius, plated
Axis: 12; D: 19.3 x 17.9 mm; W: 1.9 g.
Mint: -
Dating: AD 218-222 or later
Obv: [iul]IA MA-ESA AVG
   Bust draped, right.

Rv: PVDI[citi]A
   Pudicitia seated left, raising veil and holding scepter.
Reference: cf. RIC IV.2, 268
Findspot: 1973, barrack 1, m 38/6, -0.85 m; phase Ib.
Inv. No: c.c. 102/1973.

SEVERUS ALEXANDER (Pl. V, 14)
411.   Denomination: denarius
Axis: 6; D: 19.9 mm; W: 2.1 g.
Mint: Rome
Dating: AD 223
Obv: IMP C M AVR SEV ALEXAND AVG
   Bust laureate, draped, right.
Rv: P M TR P - II - COS P P
   Mars standing left, holding branch and reversed spear.
Reference: RIC IV.2, 23
Findspot: 1968, barrack 5.
Inv. No: c.c. 19/1968.
BUCIUMI 1972, no. 236.

SEVERUS ALEXANDER
412.   Denomination: denarius, plated, fragmentary
Axis: 11; D: 18.9 mm; W: 2.1 g.
Mint: Rome
Dating: AD 222-224 or later
Obv: IMP C M AVR SEV [alexan]D AVG
   Bust laureate, draped, right.
Rv: P M TR [p ?] COS P P
   Mars standing front, head left, holding branch in extended right hand, spear in left.
Reference: RIC IV.2, 7, 23, 37
Findspot: 1973, barrack 1, m 0/0, -0.60 m; phase Ib.
Inv. No: c.c. 159/1973.

SEVERUS ALEXANDER
413.   Denomination: denarius
Axis: 12; D: 18.9 x 17.5 mm; W: 2.6 g.
Mint: Rome
Dating: AD 222-224
Obv: IMP C M AVR SEV ALEXAND AVG
   Bust laureate, draped, right.
Rv: [p m tr p ?] COS P P
   Salus seated left, holding patera and feeding serpent arising from altar left.
Reference: RIC IV.2, 14, 32, 42
Findspot: 1973, barrack 1, m 9/2, -0.60 m; phase Ib.
Inv. No: c.c. 67/1973.

SEVERUS ALEXANDER
414.   Denomination: denarius
Axis: 12; D: 19.3 mm; W: 1.6 g.
Mint: Rome
Dating: AD 226
Obv: [imp c m aur sev alexa]ND AVG
   Bust laureate, draped, right.
Rv: P M TR P V - COS II P P

Severus Alexander standing left, sacrificing over altar.
Reference: RIC IV.2, 55
Findspot: 1970, barrack 4, -0.30 m; phase II.
Inv. No: c.c. 34/1970.
BUCIUMI 1972, no. 237.

SEVERUS ALEXANDER
415. Denomination: denarius
Axis: 11; D: 17.8 mm; W: 2.2 g.
Mint: Rome
Dating: AD 227
Obv: IMP C M AVR SEV ALEXAND AVG
Bust laureate, draped, right.
Rv: P M TR P VI - COS II P P
Pax running left, holding olive branch and sceptre.
Reference: RIC IV.2, 67
Findspot: 1976, fort area, stray find.
Inv. No: c.c. 154/1976.

SEVERUS ALEXANDER (Pl. V, 15)
416. Denomination: denarius
Axis: 2; D: 20.9 x 18.5 mm; W: 2.8 g.
Mint: Rome
Dating: AD 227
Obv: IMP [c m aur sev ale]XAND AVG
Bust laureate, draped, right.
Rv: P M TR P VI - COS II P P
The emperor standing left, sacrificing out of patera over altar.
Reference: RIC IV.2, 70
Findspot: 1964, *praetorium*, near room G.
Inv. No: c.c. 78/1964.
BUCIUMI 1972, p. 26; no. 239.
Remark: double stroke ? Half of the legend on the reverse is misplaced, and on the corresponding room on the obverse the legend vanished due to the misplacing of the die and striking pressure.

SEVERUS ALEXANDER
417. Denomination: denarius
Axis: 1; D: 18.4 x 16.3 mm; W: 2.1 g.
Mint: Rome
Dating: AD 228
Obv: IMP C M AVR SEV - ALEXAND AVG
Bust laureate, draped, right.
Rv: P M TR P VII - COS II P P
Mars walking right, holding transverse spear and trophy over shoulder.
Reference: RIC IV.2, 82
Findspot: 1970, barrack 5.
Inv. No: c.c. 25/1970.
BUCIUMI 1972, no. 238.

SEVERUS ALEXANDER
418. Denomination: denarius, plated
Axis: 12; D: 18.4 mm; W: 2.6 g.
Mint: Rome
Dating: AD 222-228 or later
Obv: IMP C M A[ur sev a]LEXAND AVG
Bust laureate, draped, right.
Rv: AN[non]A AVG
Annona standing left with corn-ears and cornucopiae, modius at foot.
Reference: cf. RIC IV.2, 133
Findspot: 1973, barrack 1, -0.60 m; phase Ib.
Inv. No: c.c. 125/1973.

SEVERUS ALEXANDER (Pl. V, 16)
419. Denomination: denarius
Axis: 12; D: 17.9 mm; W: 2.2 g.
Mint: Rome
Dating: AD 222-228
Obv: IMP C M AVR SEV ALEXAND AVG
Bust laureate, draped, right.
Rv: LIBERALITAS - AVG
Liberalitas standing left with abacus and cornucopiae.
Reference: RIC IV.2, 148
Findspot: 1970, barrack 5, excavated ground.
Inv. No: c.c. 27/1970.
BUCIUMI 1972, no. 235.

SEVERUS ALEXANDER (Pl. V, 17)
420. Denomination: denarius
Axis: 6; D: 20.2 x 18.9 mm; W: 2.2 g.
Mint: Rome
Dating: AD 222-228
Obv: I MP C M AVR SEV ALEXAND AVG
Bust laureate, draped, right.
Rv: PAX - AVG
Pax advancing left, holding branch and sceptre.
Reference: RIC IV.2, 168
Findspot: 1966, barrack 5.
Inv. No: c.c. 19/1966.
BUCIUMI 1972, no. 240.

SEVERUS ALEXANDER
421. Denomination: denarius, fragmentary
Axis: 6; D: -; W: 1 g.
Mint: Rome
Dating: AD 222-228
Obv: IMP C M AVR SEV [alexand aug]
Bust laureate, draped, right.
Rv: [?] COS II
Salus seated left, feeding snake arising from altar?
Reference: -
Findspot: 1973, barrack 1, excavated ground.
Inv. No: c.c. 48/1973.

SEVERUS ALEXANDER
422. Denomination: denarius, plated, fragmentary
Axis: -; D: 16.1 mm; W: 1.5 g.
Mint: Rome
Dating: AD 222-228
Obv: IMP C M AVR [sev alexand aug]
Silhouette of head laureate, right.
Rv: Corroded.
Reference: -
Findspot: 1973, barrack 1, m 45-46/1, -0.30 m; phase II.

Inv. No: c.c. 53/1973.

SEVERUS ALEXANDER (Pl. V, 18)
423. Denomination: denarius
Axis: 6; D: 18.2 mm; W: 2.7 g.
Mint: Rome
Dating: AD 228-231
Obv: [imp] SEV ALE-XAND AVG
  Bust laureate, draped, right.
Rv: PERPETVI-TATI AVG
  Perpetuitas standing left with globe and sceptre, leaning on column.
Reference: RIC IV.2, 208
Findspot: 1969, barrack 5, -0.40 m; phase Ib.
Inv. No: c.c. 140/1969.
BUCIUMI 1972, no. 241.

SEVERUS ALEXANDER (Pl. V, 19)
424. Denomination: sestertius
Axis: 1; D: 29.9 mm; W: 19.8 g.
Mint: Rome
Dating: AD 230
Obv: IMP SEV ALE-XANDER AVG
  Bust laureate, right.
Rv: P M TR P V-IIII - COS [iii] P P; S - C
Sol standing facing, head left, raising hand and holding whip.
Reference: RIC IV.2, 500
Findspot: 1967, the E corner tower.
Inv. No: c.c. 13/1967.
BUCIUMI 1972, no. 242.

SEVERUS ALEXANDER (Pl. V, 20)
425. Denomination: denarius
Axis: 12; D: 19.4 mm; W: 2.2 g.
Mint: Rome
Dating: AD 232
Obv: IMP ALEXAN-DER PIVS AVG
  Bust laureate, draped and right.
Rv: P M TR P X-I - COS III P P
  Sol standing left with raised hand and whip.
Reference: RIC IV.2, 112
Findspot: 1973, barrack 1, m 11/9, -0.95 m; phase Ia (!).
Inv. No: c.c. 108/1973.

SEVERUS ALEXANDER: Julia Mammaea (Pl. VI, 1)
426. Denomination: denarius
Axis: 5; D: 19 x 16.9 mm; W: 2.5 g.
Mint: Rome
Dating: AD 222-235
Obv: IVLIA MA-MAMEA AVG
  Bust laureate, draped, right.
Rv: VESTA
  Vesta standing left, holding palladium and sceptre.
Reference: RIC IV.2, 360
Findspot: 1966, near the intermediary tower 1, trench I/1963.
Inv. No: c.c. 37/1966.
BUCIUMI 1972, no. 244.

SEVERUS ALEXANDER: Julia Mammaea (Pl. VI, 2)
427. Denomination: denarius, plated
Axis: 12; D: 19.5 x 16.2 mm; W: 2.3 g.
Mint: -
Dating: AD 222-235
Obv: IVLIA MA-MAMEA AVG
  Bust laureate, draped, right.
Rv: VE-S-TA
  Vesta standing left, holding palladium and sceptre.
Reference: cf. RIC IV.2, 360
Findspot: 1970, building (C1?) north of the main wall, -1.25 m; phase Ia (!).
Inv. No: c.c. 16/1970.
BUCIUMI 1972, no. 246.

MAXIMINUS I THRAX
428. Denomination: denarius, plated
Axis: 6; D: 18.5.1 x 17 mm; W: 2.5 g.
Mint: -
Dating: AD 235-236 or later
Obv: IMP MAXIMINVS AVG
  Bust laureate, draped, right.
Rv: PROVIDEN-TIA AVG
  Providence standing left, holding cornucopiae and wand pointed at globe at foot.
Reference: cf. RIC IV.2, 13
Findspot: 1965, barrack 2, -0.30 m; phase II.
Inv. No: c.c. 2/1965.
BUCIUMI 1972, no. 247.

GORDIANUS III (Pl. VI, 3)
429. Denomination: antoninianus
Axis: 6; D: 24.1 x 22.2 mm; W: 3.9 g.
Mint: Rome
Dating: AD 238-239
Obv: IMP CAES M ANT GORDIANVS AVG
  Bust radiate, draped and cuirassed, right.
Rv: VIRTVS AVG
  Virtus standing facing in military dress, head left, with shield and spear.
Reference: RIC IV.3, 6
Findspot: 1967, *praetorium*, room P (the room in the SW corner).
Inv. No: c.c. 16/1967.
BUCIUMI 1972, no. 252.

GORDIANUS III (Pl. VI, 4)
430. Denomination: antoninianus
Axis: 12; D: 22.1 mm; W: 2.1 g.
Mint: Rome
Dating: AD 240
Obv: IMP CAES M ANT GORDIANVS AVG
  Bust radiate, draped and cuirassed, right.
Rv: ROMAE – [ae]TERNAE
  Roma, helmeted and seated left on shield, holding Victory and spear.
Reference: RIC IV.3, 38
Findspot: 1973, barrack 1, m 6/5, -0.60 m; phase Ib.
Inv. No: c.c. 81/1973.

GORDIANUS III (Pl. VI, 5)
431.   Denomination: sestertius
Axis: 12; D: 30.3 x 27.2 mm; W: 17.1 g.
Mint: Rome
Dating: AD 240
Obv: IMP GORDIANVS PIVS FEL A[u]G
        Bust radiate, draped and cuirassed, right.
Rv: LIBERALITAS AVG III; S - C
        Liberalitas standing facing, holding abacus and cornucopiae.
Reference: RIC IV.3, 290a
Findspot: 1967, *praetorium*.
Inv. No: c.c. 22/1967.
BUCIUMI 1972, no. 253.

GORDIANUS III
432.   Denomination: denarius, plated
Axis: 12; D: 20.2 mm; W: 2.6 g.
Mint: Rome
Dating: AD 241 or later
Obv: IMP GORDIANVS PIVS FEL AVG
        Bust laureate, draped and cuirassed, right.
Rv: VENVS VICTRIX
        Venus standing left with helmet and sceptre, leaning on shield.
Reference: RIC IV.3, 131
Findspot: 1973, barrack 2, m 35/2, -1.50 m; phase Ia (!).
Inv. No: c.c. 152/1973.

GORDIANUS III
433.   Denomination: antoninianus, plated
Axis: 1; D: 21.7 x 20.1 mm; W: 3.3 g.
Mint: Rome
Dating: AD 241-243
Obv: IMP GORDIANVS PIV[s fel aug]
        Bust radiate, draped and cuirassed, right.
Rv: IOVI - STATORI
        Jupiter standing right with scepter and thunderbolt.
Reference: RIC IV.3, 84.
Findspot: 1967, *praetorium*.
Inv. No: c.c. 25/1967.
BUCIUMI 1972, no. 250.

GORDIANUS III
434.   Denomination: antoninianus, plated
Axis: 5; D: 20.9 mm; W: 4.7 g.
Mint: Rome
Dating: AD 241-243
Obv: IMP GORDIANVS PIVS FEL AVG
        Bust radiate, draped and cuirassed, right.
Rv: P M TR P V COS II P P
        Apollo, bare to waist, seated left with branch, resting elbow on lyre.
Reference: RIC IV.3, 89.
Findspot: 1968, barrack 5, -0.30 m; phase II.
Inv. No: c.c. 15/1968.
BUCIUMI 1972, no. 251.

GORDIANUS III (Pl. VI, 6)
435.   Denomination: sestertius
Axis: 1; D: 30.2 mm; W: 15.1 g.
Mint: Viminacium
Dating: AD 242-243
Obv: IMP GORDIANVS PIVS FEL AVG
        Bust laureate, draped and cuirassed, right.
Rv: P M S CO-L VIM
        exergue: AN IIII
        Provincia Moesia Superior standing between bull and lion.
Reference: MARTIN, 1.34.1.
Findspot: 1966, on the western wall near the *via praetoria*, 3 m N of the 2nd side road, the road between barracks 2 and 3.
Inv. No: c.c. 45/1966.
BUCIUMI 1972, no. 254.

GORDIANUS III (Pl. VI, 7)
436.   Denomination: antoninianus
Axis: 12; D: 20.7 mm; W: 3.3 g.
Mint: Rome
Dating: AD 243-244
Obv: IMP GORDIANVS PIVS FEL AVG
        Bust radiate, draped and cuirassed, right.
Rv: FELICIT TEMP
        Apollo, bare to waist, seated left with branch, resting elbow on lyre.
Reference: RIC IV.3, 140.
Findspot: 1969, barrack 5, -0.50 m; phase II.
Inv. No: c.c. 130/1969.
BUCIUMI 1972, no. 248.

GORDIANUS III (Pl. VI, 8)
437.   Denomination: antoninianus, plated
Axis: 6; D: 22 mm; W: 3.4 g.
Mint: Rome
Dating: AD 243-244 or later
Obv: IMP GORDIANVS PIVS FEL AVG
        Bust radiate, draped and cuirassed, right.
Rv: FORT REDVX
        Fortuna seated left with rudder and cornucopiae, wheel beneath.
Reference: cf. RIC IV.3, 143.
Findspot: 1970, barrack 5, between the NW walls, -0.50 m; phase II.
Inv. No: c.c. 10/1970.
BUCIUMI 1972, no. 249.

GORDIANUS III
438.   Denomination: denarius, plated
Axis: -; D: 19.4 x 18.3 mm; W: 1.8 g.
Mint: Rome
Dating: AD 238-244 or later
Obv: IMP GORDIANVS ...
        Silhouette of laureate bust, right.
Rv: erased.
Reference: -
Findspot: 1970, stray find.
Inv. No: c.c. 87/1970.

PHILIPPUS I
439. Denomination: sestertius
Axis: 7; D: 27.8 mm; W: 11.8 g.
Mint: Rome
Dating: AD 246-247
Obv: IMP M IVL PHIL[ippus]VG
Bust laureate, draped and cuirassed, seen 2/3 from behind, right.
Rv: PROVINCIA DACIA
exergue: AN•I•
Provincia Dacia standing left between aquila and lion, holding standard.
Reference: MARTIN, 2.51.1
Findspot: 1966, the path between barracks 5 and 6, -0.40 m; phase II.
Inv. No: c.c. 43/1966.
BUCIUMI 1972, no. 258.

PHILIPPUS I
440. Denomination: sestertius
Axis: 8; D: 26.7 mm; W: 12.4 g.
Mint: Apulum
Dating: 247-248
Obv: IMP M IVL PHILIPPVS AVG
Bust laureate, draped, cuirassed, right.
Rv: PROVINCIA DACIA
exergue: AN II
Provincia Dacia seated left between aquila and lion, holding standards.
Reference: MARTIN, 2.57.1
Findspot: 1966, barrack 4, the outer side towards *via praetoria* (2 m from intersection), -0.30 m; phase II.
Inv. No: c.c. 47/1966.
BUCIUMI 1972, no. 259.

PHILIPPUS I
441. Denomination: antoninianus, plated
Axis: 5; D: 22.3 mm; W: 4.2 g.
Mint: Rome
Dating: 248
Obv: IMP PHILIPPVS AVG
Bust radiate, draped, cuirassed, right.
Rv: TRANQVILLITAS [augg]
Tranquillitas standing left with Capricorn and scepter; B left in field.
Reference: RIC IV.3, 9
Findspot: 1968, barrack 5, west end, top soil; phase II.
Inv. No: c.c. 13/1968.
BUCIUMI 1972, no. 256.

PHILIPPUS I (Pl. VI, 9)
442. Denomination: antoninianus
Axis: 2; D: 21.1 x 19.4 mm; W: 3.5 g.
Mint: Rome
Dating: 248
Obv: IMP PHILIPPVS AVG
Bust radiate, draped, cuirassed, right.
Rv: SAECVLARES AVGG
exergue: U
Stag walking right.
Reference: RIC IV.3, 19
Findspot: 1967, *praetorium*, room G.
Inv. No: c.c. 74/1967.
BUCIUMI 1972, p. 29; no. 255.

PHILIPPUS I (Pl. VI, 10)
443. Denomination: antoninianus
Axis: 6; D: 23.2 mm; W: 4.1 g.
Mint: Rome
Dating: 244-247
Obv: IMP M IVL PHILIPPVS AVG
Bust radiate, draped, cuirassed, right.
Rv: VICTORIA AVGG
Victory standing left, holding a wreath and a palm.
Reference: RIC IV.3, 51
Findspot: 1968, barrack 5, upper layer, -0.15-0.20 cm; phase II.
Inv. No: c.c. 23/1968.
BUCIUMI 1972, no. 257.

PHILIPPUS I
444. Denomination: antoninianus, plated, fragmentary
Axis: 2; D: 22.5 mm; W: 2 g.
Mint: Rome
Dating: 244-249 or later
Obv: Legend erased.
Bust radiate, draped, cuirassed, right.
Rv: Legend erased.
Silhouette standing left, holding sceptre.
Reference: -
Findspot: 1971, barrack 1, -0.40 cm; phase II.
Inv. No: c.c. 19/1971.

TREBONIANUS GALLUS (Pl. VI, 11)
445. Denomination: antoninianus
Axis: 5; D: 19.1 mm; W: 2 g.
Mint: Rome
Dating: 251-253
Obv: IMP [ca]E C VI[b treb g]ALLVS AVG
Bust radiate, draped, cuirassed, right.
Rv: LIBERTAS AVGG
Libertas standing left with pileus and sceptre; star, right in field.
Reference: RIC IV.3, 38
Findspot: 1971, barrack 1, -0.30 cm; phase II.
Inv. No: c.c. 27/1971.

Pseudo-autonomous coin: Ankyra, Phrygiae (Pl. VI, 12)
446. Denomination: AE 15, provincial, bronze
Axis: 6; D: 17.8 x 15.8 mm; W: 2.2 g.
Mint: Ankyra, Phrygiae
Dating: 2nd-3rd c. AD
Obv: ΘEA PΩMH
Draped bust of Roma right, wearing *polos*.
Rv: ANK[YPA]NΩN
Dionysus, naked to waist, standing left, holding *kantharos* and *thyrsos*.
Reference: SNG München, 90
Findspot: 1968, the upper inhabited layer, -0.30 m; phase II.

Inv. No: c.c. 22/1968.

Unidentified coin
447. Denomination: denarius, plated
Axis: -; D: 18.1 mm; W: 2.6 g.
Mint: -
Dating: 1st-3rd c. AD
Obv/Rv: corroded
Reference: -
Findspot: 1970, barrack 4, -1.30 m.
Inv. No: c.c. 80/1970.

Unidentified coin
448. Denomination: denarius, plated, fragment
Axis: -; D: -; W: 2 g.
Mint: -
Dating: 1st-3rd c. AD
Obv/Rv: corroded
Reference: -
Findspot: 1973, barrack 1, m 34, -0.80 m.
Inv. No: c.c. 117/1973.

Unidentified coin
449. Denomination: sestertius
Axis: -; D: 27.7 x 25 mm; W: 15.9 g.
Mint: -
Dating: 2nd-3rd c. AD
Obv: Vague silhouette of a head, right
Rv: erased.
Reference: -
Findspot: 1971, barrack 1, m 40/6, -0.90 m.
Inv. No: c.c. 103/1973.

Unidentified coin
450. Denomination: as?
Axis: -; D: 26.8 mm; W: 6.2 g.
Mint: -
Dating: 1st c. AD?
Obv: Vague silhouette of a head, left
Rv: corroded
Reference: -
Findspot: 1973, barrack 1, m 30/8, -1.20 m.
Inv. No: c.c. 111/1973.

Unidentified coin
451. Denomination: bronze
Axis: -; D: 23.7 x 22.9 mm; W: 7.9 g.
Mint: -
Dating: 1st-3rd c. AD
Obv: Vague silhouette of a draped bust, right
Rv: corroded
Reference: -
Findspot: 1971, barrack 1, excavated ground.
Inv. No: c.c. 11/1971.

Unidentified coin
452. Denomination: bronze
Axis: -; D: 22.6 mm; W: 3.8 g.
Mint: -
Dating: 1st-3rd c. AD
Obv/Rv: corroded.
Reference: -
Findspot: 1966, barrack 5.
Inv. No: c.c. 28/1966.

Unidentified coin
453. Denomination: bronze
Axis: -; D: c. 29 mm; W: 11.5 g (with corrosion)
Mint: -
Dating: 1st-3rd c. AD
Obv/Rv: corroded
Reference: -
Findspot: 1967, building 4, room 4.
Inv. No: c.c. 27/1967.

Unidentified coin
454. Denomination: bronze
Axis: -; D: 28.4 mm; W: 9.2 g
Mint: -
Dating: 1st-3rd c. AD
Obv/Rv: corroded
Reference: -
Findspot: 1968, barrack 5, -0.75 m.
Inv. No: c.c. 41/1968.
BUCIUMI 1972, no. 263

Unidentified coin
455. Denomination: bronze
Axis: -; D: 27.7 mm; W: 8 g
Mint: -
Dating: 1st-3rd c. AD
Obv/Rv: corroded
Reference: -
Findspot: 1970, barrack 5, northern corridor, near the NE corner, -0.50 m.
Inv. No: c.c. 7/1970.

Unidentified coin
456. Denomination: bronze
Axis: -; D: 27.7 mm; W: 6.7 g
Mint: -
Dating: 1st-3rd c. AD
Obv/Rv: corroded
Reference: -
Findspot: 1970, barrack 4, -0.80 m.
Inv. No: c.c. 74/1970.

Unidentified coin
457. Denomination: bronze
Axis: -; D: 28.1 mm; W: 10.1 g
Mint: -
Dating: 1st-3rd c. AD
Obv/Rv: corroded
Reference: -
Findspot: 1973, barrack 1, -0.60 m.
Inv. No: c.c. 86/1973.

Unidentified coin
458. Denomination: bronze, fragment
Axis: -; D: -; W: -

Mint: -
Dating: 1st-3rd c. AD
Obv/Rv: corroded
Reference: -
Findspot: 1972, barrack 2, -0.80 m.
Inv. No: c.c. 368/1972.

Unidentified coin
459. Denomination: bronze, fragment
Axis: -; D: -; W: -
Mint: -
Dating: 1st-3rd c. AD
Obv/Rv: corroded
Reference: -
Findspot: 1973, barrack 2, quadrant 41, -1 m.
Inv. No: c.c. 133/1973.

Unidentified coin
460. Denomination: bronze
Axis: -; D: 24 mm; W: 7.3 g
Mint: -
Dating: 1st-3rd c. AD
Obv/Rv: corroded
Reference: -
Findspot: 1973, barrack 1, m 3/6, -0.80 m.
Inv. No: c.c. 88/1973.

Unidentified coin?
461. Denomination: bronze, fragment
Axis: -; D: -; W: 0.4 g
Mint: -
Dating: -
Obv/Rv: corroded
Reference: -
Findspot: 1969, barrack 5, excavated ground.
Inv. No: c.c. 142/1969.

Unidentified coin?
462. Denomination: bronze, fragment
Axis: -; D: -; W: -
Mint: -
Dating: -
Obv/Rv: corroded
Reference: -
Findspot: 1970, barrack 4, -1 m.
Inv. No: c.c. 69/1970.

The Silviu Papiriu-Pop collection

VESPASIANUS
1. Denomination: denarius
Axis: 6; D: 16.4 x 14.9 mm; W: 2.4 g.
Mint: Rome
Dating: AD 70
Obv: [imp] CAESAR VESPA[sianus aug]
　　　Head laureate, right.
Rv: COS I[ter tr p]OT
　　　Pax seated left, holding branch and caduceus.
Reference: RIC II.1, 29
Findspot: 1966, fort area, stray find.
Inv. No: c.c. 430/1966.
BUCIUMI 1972, no. 20

TRAIANUS
2. Denomination: denarius, plated
Axis: 6; D: 17.5 mm; W: 2.4 g.
Mint: -
Dating: AD 101-102 or later
Obv: IMP CAES NERVA TRAIAN AVG GERM
　　　Head laureate, right.
Rv: P M TR P[ot cos iiii p p]
　　　Mars advancing right, carrying spear and trophy.
Reference: MIR 14, 104a
Findspot: 1966, fort area, stray find.
Inv. No: c.c. 497/1966.
BUCIUMI 1972, no. 50

TRAIANUS (Pl. II, 16)
3. Denomination: denarius
Axis: 6; D: 17.7 mm; W: 2.9 g.
Mint: Rome
Dating: AD 108-110
Obv: IMP TRAIANO AVG GER DAC P M TR P
　　　Bust laureate, draped on left shoulder, right.
Rv: COS V P P S P Q R OPTIMO PRINC
　　　Arabia standing left, holding a branch and a bundle of canes, camel at feet.
Reference: MIR 14, 285b
Findspot: 1966, fort area, stray find.
Inv. No: c.c. 438/1966.
BUCIUMI 1972, no. 56

HADRIANUS: Sabina
4. Denomination: as
Axis: 5; D: 27.1 mm; W: 10.8 g.
Mint: Rome
Dating: AD 117-138
Obv: SABINA AVGVSTA - HADRIANI AVG P P
　　　Bust draped right, a triple tiara above the brow behind which the hair is drawn up in elaborate plaiting.
Rv: No legend.
　　　exergue: S C
　　　Vesta seated left, holding palladium and sceptre.
Reference: RIC II, 1020
Findspot: 1962, fort area, stray find.
Inv. No: c.c. 532/1966.
BUCIUMI 1972, no. 144

ANTONINUS PIUS (Pl. III, 13)
5. Denomination: as
Axis: 5; D: 27.8 x 25.9 mm; W: 12.5 g.
Mint: Rome
Dating: AD 140-144
Obv: ANTONINVS AVG PI-VS P P TR P COS III
　　　Head laureate, right.
Rv: CONCORDIA – EXERCITVVM; S - C
　　　Concordia standing left, holding Victory and legionary eagle.
Reference: RIC III, 678
Findspot: 1966, fort area, stray find.
Inv. No: c.c. 502/1966.
BUCIUMI 1972, no. 156.

ANTONINUS PIUS (Pl. III, 15)
6. Denomination: denarius
Axis: 6; D: 18.1 x 15.9 mm; W: 2.5 g.
Mint: Rome
Dating: AD 151-152
Obv: AN[to]NINVS AVG PI-VS P P TR P XV
　　　Head laureate, right.
Rv: CO[s] - IIII
　　　Annona standing left, holding corn ears and placing left hand on modius set on ship, which is half seen.
Reference: RIC III, 204
Findspot: 1966, barrack 5.
Inv. No: c.c. 458/1966.
BUCIUMI 1972, no. 146.

ANTONINUS PIUS (Pl. III, 18)
7. Denomination: denarius
Axis: 6; D: 16.7 x 15.6 mm; W: 2.7 g.
Mint: Rome
Dating: AD 157-158
Obv: ANTONINVS AVG PI-VS P P IM[p ii]
　　　Head laureate, right.
Rv: TR POT – XX-I COS IIII
　　　Annona standing right with rudder and modius with corn ears, foot on prow to right.
Reference: RIC III, 275
Findspot: 1966.
Inv. No: c.c. 459/1966.
BUCIUMI 1972, no. 148.

ANTONINUS PIUS
8. Denomination: as
Axis: 4; D: 27.3 x 25.2 mm; W: 10.1 g.
Mint: Rome
Dating: AD 138-161
Obv: ANTONINVS - AVG […]
　　　Head laureate, right.
Rv: Legend corroded.
　　　Silhouette standing.
Reference: -
Findspot: 1969, 150 m from the fort, -1.20 m, while digging a pit, stray find.
Inv. No: c.c. 406/1970.
BUCIUMI 1972, no. 158.

ANTONINUS PIUS: M. Aurelius (Caesar) (Pl. IV, 4)
9. Denomination: denarius, fragmentary
Axis: 7; D: 18 mm; W: 2.5 g.
Mint: Rome
Dating: AD 148-149
Obv: AVRELIVS CAE-SAR [aug] PII F
　　　Head bare, right.
Rv: TR POT III - [co]S II
　　　Minerva standing right, holding spear and resting hand on shield.
Reference: RIC III, 444
Findspot: 1965, fort area, stray find.
Inv. No: c.c. 466/1966.
BUCIUMI 1972, no. 173.

M. AURELIUS: Lucilla
10. Denomination: sestertius
Axis: 4; D: 29.2 x 27.7 mm; W: 23.8 g.
Mint: Rome
Dating: AD 169-180?
Obv: [luci]LLAE AVG – ANTON[ini aug f]
　　　Bust draped, right.
Rv: [venu]S; S - C
　　　Venus standing left, holding apple and scepter.
Reference: RIC III, 1763
Findspot: 1966, fort area, stray find.
Inv. No: c.c. 506/1966.
BUCIUMI 1972, no. 191.

SEPTIMIUS SEVERUS
11. Denomination: denarius, plated, fragmentary
Axis: 12; D: 17.2 mm; W: 2.4 g.
Mint: -
Dating: AD 203 or later
Obv: SEVERVS – PIVS AVG
　　　Head laureate, right.
Rv: TR P XI COS III P P
　　　Fortuna seated left with rudder and cornucopia, wheel beneath her seat.
Reference: cf. RIC IV.1, 189b
Findspot: 1966, fort area, stray find.
Inv. No: c.c. 513/1966.
BUCIUMI 1972, no. 204.

SEPTIMIUS SEVERUS
12. Denomination: denarius, plated, fragmentary
Axis: 12; D: 18.2 mm; W: 2.7 g.
Mint: -
Dating: AD 202-210 or later
Obv: [se]VERVS – PIVS AVG
　　　Part of the neck and beard, right.
Rv: [fundat]O[r paci]S
　　　Septimius, togate and veiled, standing left, holding olive branch.
Reference: cf. RIC IV.1, 265
Findspot: 1966, fort area, stray find.
Inv. No: c.c. 477/1966.
BUCIUMI 1972, no. 209 (but Julia Domna).

MACRINUS: Diadumenianus (Pl. V, 8)
13. Denomination: denarius, plated, fragmentary
Axis: 12; D: 19.4 mm; W: 1.9 g.
Mint: -
Dating: AD 217-218 or later
Obv: M OPEL ANT DIADVMENIA [caes]
　　　Bust cuirassed, head bare, right.
Rv: [pri]NC IVVENTVTIS
　　　Diadumenian standing front, looking right, holding sceptre and standard, two standards behind.
Reference: cf. RIC IV.2, 102b
Findspot: 1959, fort area, stray find.
Inv. No: c.c. 522/1966.
BUCIUMI 1972, no. 227.

SEVERUS ALEXANDER
14. Denomination: sestertius
Axis: 12; D: 29.9 x 27.9 mm; W: 19 g.
Mint: Rome
Dating: AD 232
Obv: IMP ALEXANDER PIVS AVG
　　　Bust laureate, draped and cuirassed, seen 2/3 frontal, right.
Rv: [tr] P X-I COS III P P; S - C
　　　Sol standing left, raising right hand and holding whip.
Reference: RIC IV.2, 531
Findspot: 1966, fort area, stray find.
Inv. No: c.c. 529/1966.
BUCIUMI 1972, no. 243.

SEVERUS ALEXANDER: Julia Mamaea
15. Denomination: denarius, plated
Axis: 5; D: 17.9 mm; W: 2.1 g.
Mint: -
Dating: AD 222-235 or later
Obv: IVLIA MA-MAEA AVG
　　　Bust draped, right.
Rv: VES[ta]
　　　Vesta standing half-left, holding palladium and scepter.
Reference: cf. RIC IV.2, 360
Findspot: 1966, fort area, stray find.
Inv. No: c.c. 533/1966.
BUCIUMI 1972, no. 245.

Plate I

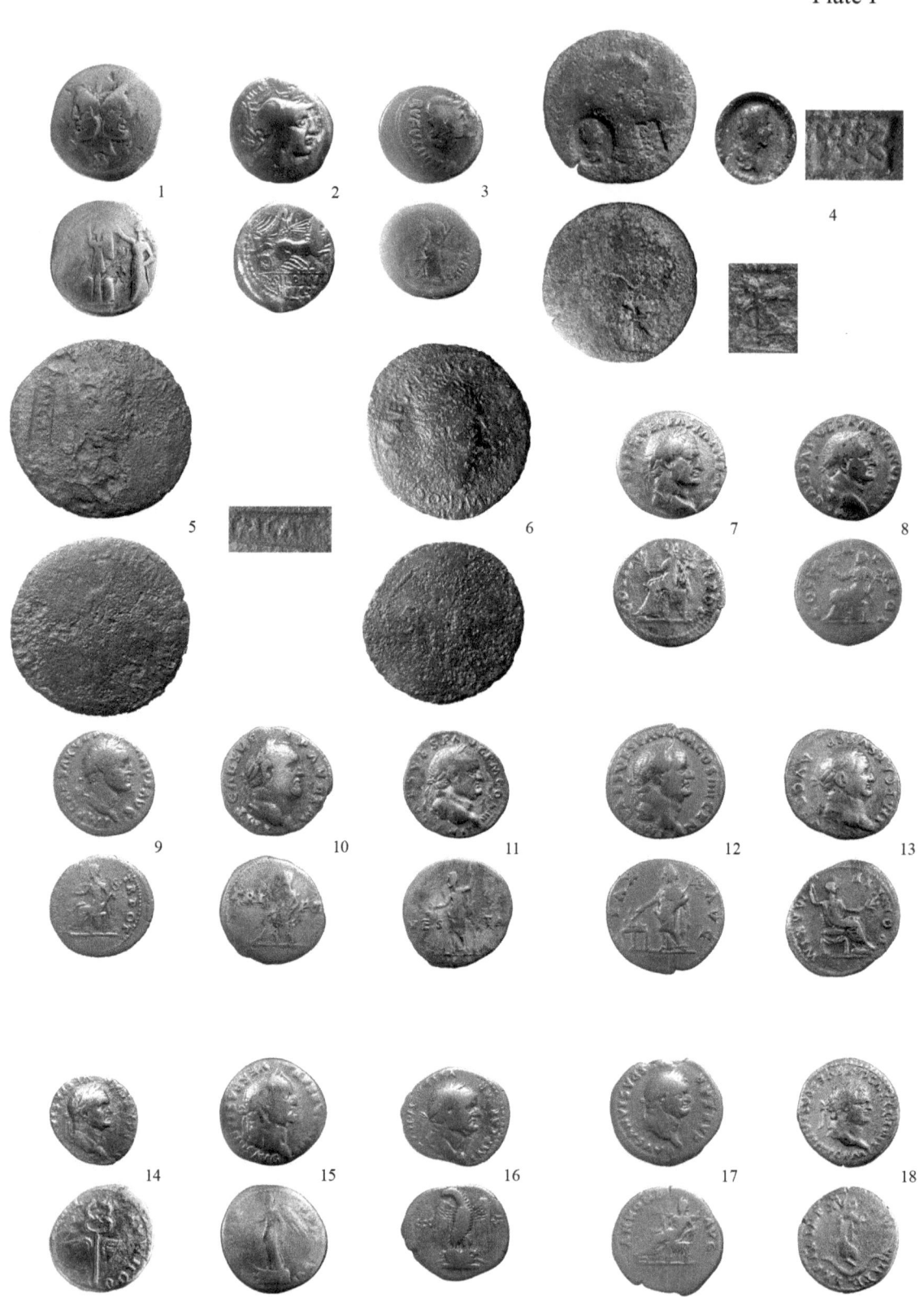

Plate II

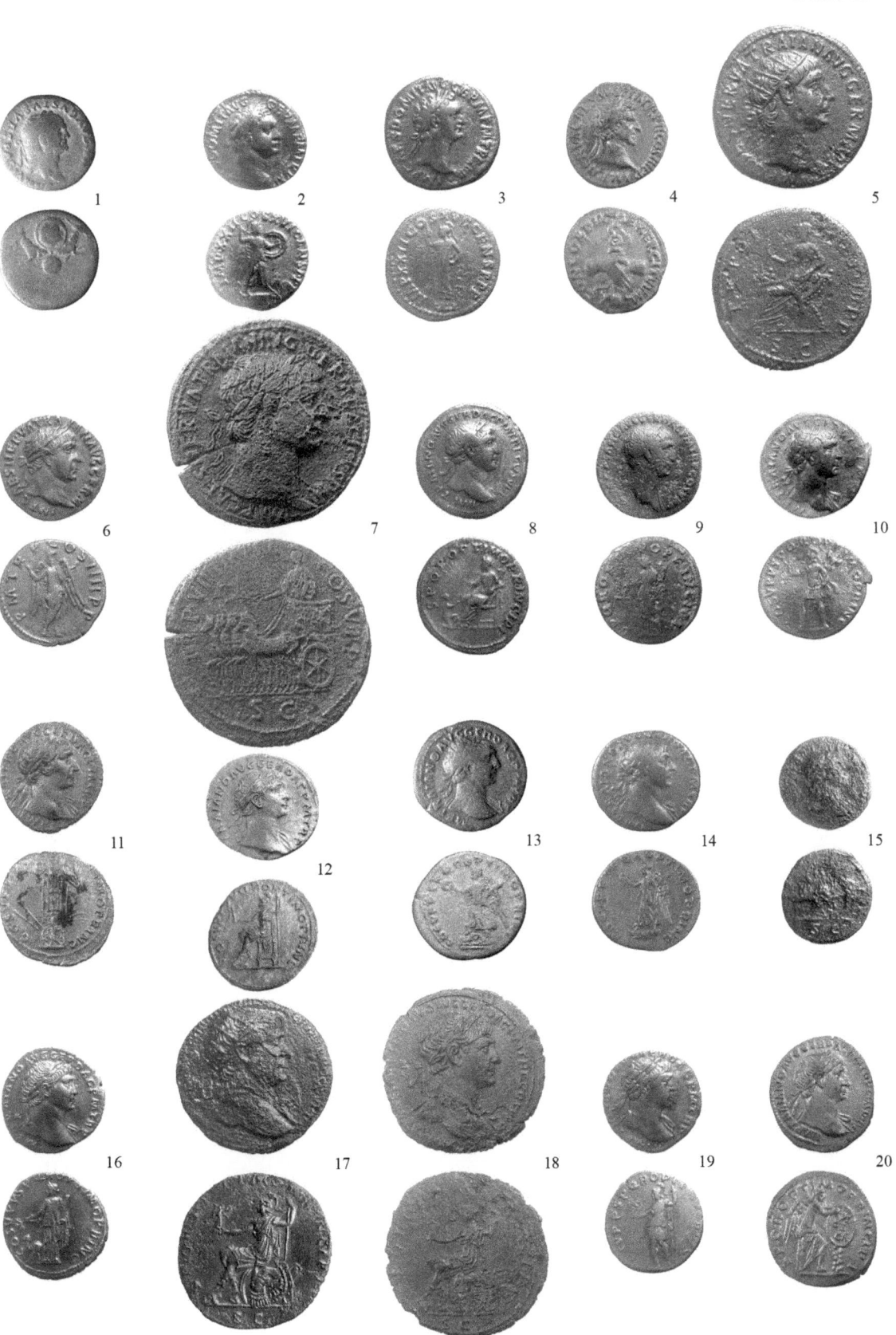

Plate III

Plate IV

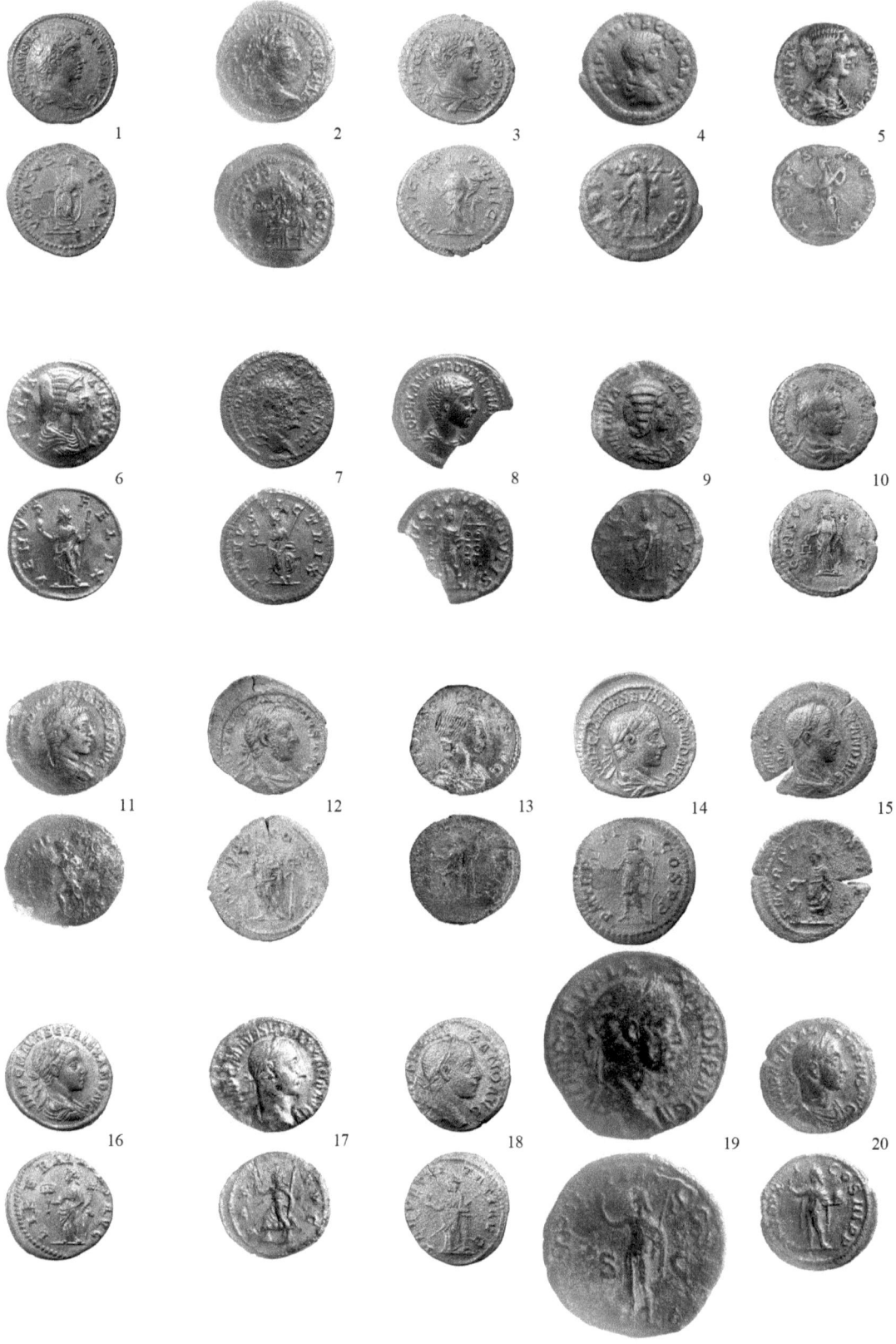

Plate V

The Roman Auxiliary Fort at Buciumi (Roman Dacia, Romania): Coins in archaeological context

Plate VI

Abbreviations and Bibliography

Periodicals

AMN = *Acta Musei Napocensis*, Cluj-Napoca, Romania
AMP = *Acta Musei Porolissensis*, Zalău, Romania
AVSL = *Archiv des Vereines für siebenbürgische Landeskunde*, Hermannstadt/Sibiu, Romania
NZ = *Numismatische Zeitschrift*, Wien, Austria
SFMA = *Studien zu Fundmünzen der Antike*, Berlin, Germany

Catalogues

BMC
Catalogue of the Greek coins in the British Museum (London, 1876-)
HOWGEGO 1985
Howgego, Ch., *Greek Imperial countermarks. Studies in the provincial coinage of the Roman Empire* (London)
MARTIN
Martin, F., *Kolonialprägungen aus Moesia Superior und Dacia* (Budapest, 1992)
MIR 14
Woytek, B., *Die Reichsprägung des Kaisers Traianus (98–117)*. Moneta Imperii Romani 14. (Wien, 2010)
MOUSHMOV
Moushmov, N.A., *Ancient Coins of the Balkan Peninsula and the Coins and the Coins of the Russian Czars* (Sofia, 1912)
RIC
The Roman Imperial Coinage (London, 1923-)
RPC
Roman Provincial Coinage (London, 1992-)
RRC
Crawford, M., *Roman Republican Coinage* (Cambridge 1974)
SNG München
Sylloge Nummorum Graecorum München. (München, 1968-).
SNG von Aulock
Sylloge Nummorum Graecorum von Aulock. (New York, 1987).

BUCIUMI 1972
***, *Castrul roman de la Buciumi. Contribuţii la cercetarea limesului Daciei Porolissensis* (Cluj).
BUCIUMI 2000
Timoc, C., Bejinariu, I., *Cercetări arheologice în principia castrului roman de la Buciumi*. AMP 23/1, 345-357.
GĂZDAC 2008
Găzdac, C., *Aspects of coin circulation in Roman Dacia*. In: Roman Coins outside the Empire. Ways and Phases, Contexts and Functions, Proceedings of the ESF/SCH Exploratory Workshop Radziwill Palace, Nieborow (Poland), 3-6 September 2005 [Moneta 82], 269-294.
GĂZDAC 2009
Găzdac, C., *The distribution of silver counterfeited coins in the forts from Roman Dacia. Fraud or monetary policy?*. In: Limes XX. The XXth International Congress of Roman Frontier Studies (eds. Morillo, Á./ Hanel, N./Martin, E.) [Gladius 13], 1487-1497.
GĂZDAC 2010
Găzdac, C., *Monetary circulation in Dacia and the provinces from the Middle and Lower Danube from Trajan to Constantine I (AD 106-337)* [Coins from Roman Sites and Collections of Roman Coins from Romania 7 (ed. Găzdac, C.)] (Cluj-Napoca).
GĂZDAC/ALFÖLDY-GĂZDAC 2001
Găzdac, C./Alföldy-Găzdac, Á., *The Roman law against counterfeiting between theory and practice: the case of Roman Dacia*. AMN, 38/I, 137-154.
GĂZDAC/ALFÖLDY-GĂZDAC 2008
Găzdac, C./Alföldy-Găzdac, Á., *The management of a monetary crisis? The 'P M S COL VIM' and 'PROVINCIA DACIA' coinages in the Roman monetary policy of the 3rd century AD*. NZ 116/117, 135-171.
GĂZDAC/COCIŞ 2004
Găzdac, C./Cociş, S., *Ulpia Traiana Sarmizegetusa* [Coins from Roman Sites and Collections of Roman Coins from Romania 1 (ed. Găzdac, C.)] (Cluj-Napoca).
GĂZDAC/GAIU 2011
Găzdac, C./Gaiu, C., *Arcobadara (Ilişua)* [Coins from Roman Sites and Collections of Roman Coins from Romania 6 (ed. Găzdac, C.)] (Cluj-Napoca).
GĂZDAC/GUDEA 2006
Găzdac, C./Gudea, N., *Porolissum* [Coins from Roman Sites and Collections of Roman Coins from Romania 2 (ed. Găzdac, C.)] (Cluj-Napoca).

GĂZDAC/ISAC 2007
Găzdac, C./Isac, D., *The auxiliary forts from Samum (Căşeiu) and Gilău* [Coins from Roman Sites and Collections of Roman Coins from Romania 4 (ed. Găzdac, C.)] (Cluj-Napoca).

GĂZDAC/SUCIU/ALFÖLDY-GĂZDAC 2009
Găzdac, C./Suciu, V./Alföldy-Găzdac, Á., *Apulum* [Coins from Roman Sites and Collections of Roman Coins from Romania 5 (ed. Găzdac, C.)] (Cluj-Napoca).

GOOSS 1876
Gooss, C., *Chronik der arch*äologischen *Funde Siebenbürgens. Im Auftrage des Vereins für siebenbürgische Landeskunde*. AVSL 1.2, 203-338.

GUDEA 1997
Gudea, N., *Castrul roman de la Buciumi* [Ghid al monumentelor arheologice din Dacia Porolissensis] (Zalău).

HARL 1996
Harl, K., *Coinage in the Roman economy, 300 B.C. to A.D. 700*. (Baltimore-London).

KING 1996
King, C., *Roman copies*. In: Coin Finds and Coin Use in the Roman World (eds. King, C./Wigg, D.) [SFMA 10] (Berlin), 237-263.

MARCU 2009
Marcu, F., *Organizarea internă castrelor din Dacia* (Cluj-Napoca).

MUZEU 1968
***, *Muzeul Zalău. Catalogul colecţiei de monete antice* (Zalău).

REECE 1986
Reece, R., *The coins*. In: McWhirr, A., Houses in Roman Cirencester. Cirencester Excavations III (London), 98-114.